THE NETS OF MODERNISM

Maud Ellmann synthesizes her work on modernism, psychoanalysis, and Irish literature in this important new book. In sinuous readings of Henry James, James Joyce, and Virginia Woolf, she examines the interconnections between developing technological networks in modernity and the structures of modernist fiction, linking both to Freudian psychoanalysis. *The Nets of Modernism* examines the significance of images of bodily violation and exchange – scar, bite, wound, and their psychic equivalents – showing how these images correspond to "vampirism" and related obsessions in early twentieth-century culture. Subtle, original, and a pleasure to read, this book offers a new perspective on the inter-implications of Freudian psychoanalysis and anglophone modernism that will influence the field for years to come.

MAUD ELLMANN, formerly the Donald and Marilyn Keough Professor of Irish Studies at the University of Notre Dame, is currently the Randy L. and Melvin R. Berlin Professor of the Development of the Novel in English at the University of Chicago. A well-known scholar of modernism and psychoanalysis, she has also written *The Poetics of Impersonality: T. S. Eliot and Ezra Pound* (1987), *The Hunger Artists: Starving, Writing, and Imprisonment* (1993) and *Elizabeth Bowen: The Shadow Across the Page* (winner of the 2004 Crawshay Prize from the British Academy), and has edited a *Longman Critical Reader in Psychoanalytic Literary Criticism* (1994).

D0862724

THE NETS OF MODERNISM

Henry James, Virginia Woolf,
James Joyce, and Sigmund Freud

MAUD ELLMANN

CAMBRIDGE
UNIVERSITY PRESS

CAMBRIDGE UNIVERSITY PRESS
Cambridge, New York, Melbourne, Madrid, Cape Town, Singapore,
São Paulo, Delhi, Dubai, Tokyo, Mexico City

Cambridge University Press
The Edinburgh Building, Cambridge CB2 8RU, UK

Published in the United States of America by Cambridge University Press, New York

www.cambridge.org
Information on this title: www.cambridge.org/9780521681094

© Maud Ellmann 2010

First published 2010

Printed in the United Kingdom at the University Press, Cambridge

A catalogue record for this publication is available from the British Library

Library of Congress Cataloguing in Publication data
Ellmann, Maud, 1954–
The nets of modernism : Henry James, Virginia Woolf, James Joyce, and
Sigmund Freud / Maud Ellmann.
p.   cm.
Includes bibliographical references and index.
ISBN 978-0-521-86256-1 – ISBN 978-0-521-68109-4 (pbk.)
1. English fiction–20th century–History and criticism.   2. Modernism (Literature)–Great
Britain.   3. Psychoanalysis and literature.   4. Joyce, James, 1882–1941–Criticism and
interpretation.   5. Woolf, Virginia, 1882–1941–Criticism and interpretation.   6. James,
Henry, 1843–1916–Criticism and interpretation.   7. Freud, Sigmund, 1856–1939–Influence.
8. American fiction–20th century–History and criticism.   9. Psychological
fiction–History and criticism.   10. Modernism (Literature)   I. Title.
PR888.M63E45 2010
823′.9109112–dc22
2010021895

ISBN 978-0-521-86256-1 Hardback
ISBN 978-0-521-68109-4 Paperback

To John Wilkinson

Contents

Acknowledgements

This book was completed while I was the Donald and Marilyn Keough Professor of Irish Studies at the University of Notre Dame, where I received generous support for my research, especially from Christopher Fox, the Director of the Keough-Naughton Institute for Irish Studies. Many other friends, colleagues, and students have contributed to this book. My greatest debts are to Annie Janowitz and John Wilkinson, who have seen this project develop over several years, and have provided invaluable criticism and encouragement at every stage. Anita Sokolsky, Stephen Tifft, Jessa Leff, and David Hillman were kind enough to read the manuscript, offering shrewd, imaginative criticism. In addition, the book has benefited from conversations with Isobel Armstrong, Derek Attridge, Gillian Beer, Peter de Bolla, Rachel Bowlby, Ronald Bush, Stefan Collini, Margaret Doody, Lucy Ellmann, Stephen Ellmann, Judith Farquhar, Christine Froula, John Limon, Luke Gibbons, Heather Glen, Graham Hammill, Jeri Johnson, Colin MacCabe, Josephine McDonagh, Todd McEwan, Ruth Morse, Ian Patterson, Jean-Michel Rabaté, Neil Reeve, Nicholas Royle, David Trotter, and Robert Young. I have also had the pleasure of collaborating with Marilyn Reizbaum, who is the co-author of the section on Joyce's story "Two Gallants" in Chapter 5. A fellowship from the National Humanities Center gave me the opportunity to pull the project together, and I wish to thank the director Geoffrey Harpham, the co-director Kent Mullikan, the librarians Eliza Robertson, Josiah Drewry, and Jean Houston, and all the staff and fellows, especially Judith Farquhar, Kate Flint, Elizabeth Helsinger, Alison Keith, Nigel Smith, and Alex Wettlaufer, who made my stay in North Carolina so rewarding and enjoyable. At Notre Dame, John Sitter was kind enough to "lend" me his research assistant, Michael Norris, whose painstaking work on my bibliography saved me weeks of labor. Kate Ravin offered astute criticism and editorial advice in the final stages of revising the book. Hilary Fox was kind enough to produce the index and to help with the proofreading. I also wish to thank my editors at Cambridge University Press, Ray Ryan and Maartje Sheltens, and my project manager Emma Wildsmith, for all the time and effort they have invested in my book.

It saddens me that Eve Kosofsky Sedgwick, who contributed so much to my personal and intellectual life, died before I could express my gratitude in these acknowledgements. Eve's fearless, brilliant, deeply principled work has inspired two generations of scholars, poets, and activists, and will continue to reverberate for decades to come. To have been her friend was an incalculable blessing.

Abbreviations

A	James, Henry. *The Ambassadors*. 1903. Ed. S. P. Rosenbaum. 2nd edn. New York: Norton, 1994.
BA	Woolf, Virginia. *Between the Acts*. 1941. Ed. Stella McNichol. Notes and Introduction by Gillian Beer. 1992; London: Penguin, 2000.
D	Joyce, James. *Dubliners*. 1914. Ed. Terence Brown. London: Penguin, 1992.
Diary	Woolf, Virginia. *The Diary of Virginia Woolf*. 5 vols. Harmondsworth: Penguin, 1981.
Deming	Deming, Robert H., ed. *James Joyce: The Critical Heritage*. London: Routledge and Kegan Paul, 1970.
Essays	Woolf, Virginia. *The Essays of Virginia Woolf*. Ed. Andrew McNeillie. 4 vols. London: Hogarth Press, 1986–94.
Flush	Woolf, Virginia. *Flush*. 1933. Ed. Kate Flint. Oxford University Press, 1998.
FW	Joyce, James. *Finnegans Wake*. 1939. London: Faber, 1964.
Gardiner	Gardiner, Muriel, ed. *The Wolf Man and Sigmund Freud*. 1971; London: Hogarth, 1972.
GB	James, Henry. *The Golden Bowl*. 1904. Ed. Virginia Llewellyn Smith. Oxford University Press, 1983.
JJ	Ellmann, Richard. *James Joyce*. 1959. Rev. edn. Oxford University Press, 1982.
Letters	Woolf, Virginia. *The Letters of Virginia Woolf 1888–1941*. Ed. Nigel Nicholson and Joanne Trautmann. 6 vols. London: Hogarth Press, 1975–80.
L	Joyce, James. *Letters*. Ed. Stuart Gilbert and Richard Ellmann. 3 vols. New York: Viking Press, 1957–66.
MB	Woolf, Virginia. *Moments of Being*. Ed. Jeanne Schulkind. 1976. Rev. edn. Ed. Hermione Lee. London: Pimlico, 2000.

O	Homer. *The Odyssey of Homer.* Trans. Richard Lattimore. New York: Harper and Row, 1967.
Obholzer	Obholzer, Karin. *The Wolf-Man: Conversations with Freud's Patient – Sixty Years Later.* 1980. Trans. Michael Shaw. New York: Continuum, 1982.
P	Joyce, James. *A Portrait of the Artist as a Young Man.* 1916. New York: Viking Press, 1964.
SE	Freud, Sigmund. *The Complete Psychological Works of Sigmund Freud.* Trans. James Strachey. 24 vols. London: Hogarth, 1953–74.
SL	Joyce, James. *Selected Letters.* Ed. Richard Ellmann. London: Faber, 1975.
TL	Woolf, Virginia. *To the Lighthouse.* 1927. Ed. David Bradshaw. Oxford University Press, 2008.
U	Joyce, James. *Ulysses.* 1922. Ed. Hans Walter Gabler. London: Bodley Head, 1986. Cited by chapter and line numbers.
Wings	James, Henry. *The Wings of the Dove.* 1902. Ed. Millicent Bell. London: Penguin, 2008.
Waves	Woolf, Virginia. *The Waves.* 1931. Ed. Kate Flint. London: Penguin, 1992.

CHAPTER I

Introduction: what hole?

> When the soul of a man is born in this country there are nets flung
> at it to hold it back from flight. You talk to me of nationality, lan-
> guage, religion. I shall try to fly by those nets …
>
> Joyce, *A Portrait of the Artist as a Young Man*

Stephen Dedalus's statement that he means to fly by the nets of nationality, language, and religion is often regarded as Joyce's modernist manifesto, his declaration of independence from the past (*P* 199). Yet the
Stephen of *A Portrait of the Artist*, who longs to fly by nets, is superseded
in *Ulysses* by a Stephen torn between the dream of flight and the recognition of entanglement. *The Nets of Modernism* investigates how four
modernist writers – Joyce, Woolf, James, and Freud – confront the entangled nature of the self, caught in the nets of intersubjectivity and intertextuality. "Really … relations stop nowhere," Henry James famously
declared: his writings, like those of Woolf, Joyce, and Freud, portray the
human subject as enmeshed in relations of exchange – sexual, linguistic,
financial, pathogenic – that violate the limits of identity.[1]

The chapters of this book have been written over several years, and
each may still be read as a stand-alone essay. I have rewritten them in
response to the kind request from friends and colleagues that my forays
into modernism and psychoanalysis be collected in a single volume. In
the process of revision I have tried to highlight interconnecting themes.
The most conspicuous of these is interconnectivity itself, as exemplified
by Stephen Dedalus's nets, or Mrs. Ramsay's knitting needles, or the networks of association that Freud elicits out of the laconic script of dreams.
My book focuses on a cluster of modernist images arising from these nets
and networks.

One such image is the rat, a creature notorious for its infiltration of
modern networks: the sewers, the transportation system, and the netherworld of pipes and cables that circulate utilities around the city. In

modernist writing, images of rats proliferate as furiously as the animal itself, resurfacing in Eliot's "rats' alley," in the cemetery episode of Joyce's *Ulysses*, and in the elaborate "rat-currency" that Freud investigates in the case history of the Rat Man (SE 10:212). Rats, moreover, bear a family likeness to the vampire, another dominant figure of anxiety at the turn of the century. In Bram Stoker's *Dracula* (1897), the vampire invades Britain by transforming himself into a swarm of rats, which suggests an affinity between these menacing creatures. Both violate boundaries, the vampire by penetrating bodies, the rat by penetrating walls, and both act as parasites on networks, the vampire leeching off the circulation of the blood, the rat off the circulatory systems of the metropolis.

The fin-de-siècle obsession with vampires, epitomized in Stoker's potboiler, also reasserts itself in "highbrow" novels of the period, such as James's *The Sacred Fount* (1901) – whose characters (at least in the mind of the prurient narrator) undergo a vampiric interchange of wit and youthfulness. Likewise a vampire kiss provides the subject of Stephen's only poem in *Ulysses* (1922).[2] The widespread recurrence of this theme indicates that vampirism, which undermines the boundary between self and other, also jeopardizes the distinction between "high" and "low" modernism. Stoker's Van Helsing remarks that the vampire, once he is invited in, can come and go as he pleases, and the same could be said of the literary theme of vampirism, which overrides the "great divide" separating modernism from popular culture.[3]

Vampirism, together with other characteristic obsessions of the fin de siècle, such as telepathy, spiritualism, demonic possession, and invasion, has been interpreted as a phobic reaction to innovations in technology.[4] This was the period in which the world was "networked," particularly in the metropolis where the installation of utilities – gas, water, electricity – rendered private homes dependent on clandestine networks of supply.[5] In the same period the telephone invaded the privacy of the home, offering uncanny powers of communication *in absentia* while subordinating users to a central system of exchange.[6] Such networks insinuate the public in the private sphere, creating mysterious and uncontrollable relations of dependency.[7] This networked world threatens to reduce the human subject to a knot or intersection, rather than an independent agent, in the webs of communication, commodities, and capital. "As telegraphers and physiologists discovered long ago," Michel Foucault writes, "networks both empower and disempower. They offer exciting new relationships and relative knowledge even as they destroy obsolescent fantasies of autonomy."[8]

A particularly suggestive image of networks occurs in the "Proteus" episode of *Ulysses*. Here Stephen Dedalus, strolling along Sandymount Strand, catches sight of two old women descending to the beach, one swinging her "midwife's bag," which sparks off Stephen's associations on the theme of birth.

> One of her sisterhood lugged me squealing into life. Creation from nothing. What has she in the bag? A misbirth with a trailing navelcord, hushed in ruddy wool. The cords of all link back, strandentwining cable of all flesh. That is why mystic monks. Will you be as gods? Gaze in your omphalos. Hello. Kinch here. Put me on to Edenville. Aleph, alpha: nought, nought, one. (*U* 32:33–40)

In this passage Stephen contemplates the umbilical cord, or (as he puts it in a later chapter) the "successive anastomosis of navelcords" that links each newborn back to its original progenitors in the Garden of Eden (*U* 320:300). Since Stephen would prefer to create himself from nothing, he feels imprisoned by this "strandentwining cable of all flesh." But he allows himself to be distracted from his "moody brooding" by a pun: the term "cable" reminds him of a telephone wire, which prompts him to phone up the Garden of Eden, giving the operator the telephone number for the first cause (aleph and alpha being the first letters of the Hebrew and the Greek alphabets, respectively), followed by the formula for creation from nothing: "nought, nought, one." This riff may be understood as a symptom of Stephen's desire to fly by the nets that bind him to his flesh and blood, especially to his dead mother, and his ambition to create himself *ex nihilo*. Yet at the same time, this passage reveals a fascination with the nets – umbilical, linguistic, commercial – that crisscross the body, the text, and the metropolis.

H. G. Wells, in a famous review of *A Portrait of the Artist*, accused Joyce of a "cloacal obsession." "How right Wells was," Joyce later commented (*JJ* 414). Wells was referring to the scatological dimension of the *Portrait*, but Joyce is even more obsessed with the networks of cloacae than with their odorous contents. An instance of this obsession is the passage in the "Ithaca" chapter of *Ulysses* where the Dublin waterworks are mapped out in fanatical detail, the catechistical narrator tracing the odyssey of water from Roundwood reservoir in county Wicklow through all the "subterranean aqueducts" that lead to Leopold Bloom's tap at 7 Eccles Street:

> What did Bloom do at the range?
> He removed the saucepan to the left hob, rose and carried the iron kettle to the sink in order to tap the current by turning the faucet to let it flow.

Did it flow?

Yes. From Roundwood reservoir in county Wicklow of a cubic capacity of 2400 million gallons, percolating through a subterranean aqueduct of filter mains of single and double pipeage constructed at an initial plant cost of £5 per linear yard by way of the Dargle, Rathdown, Glen of the Downs and Callowhill to the 26 acre reservoir at Stillorgan, a distance of 22 statute miles, and thence, through a system of relieving tanks, by a gradient of 250 feet to the city boundary at Eustace bridge, upper Leeson street …(*U* 548:160–70)[9]

Meanwhile Joyce portrays the human body, with its "intestines like pipes" (*U* 147:1048) and telephonic navelcords, as a net within nets, linked through "successive anastomosis" to the pipelines, sewers, cables, wires, traffic arteries, railway tracks, and postal tentacles of urban life.

If the navel marks the point at which the body is plugged into networks of circulation and exchange, this birth-scar also stands for the severance of such connections. The navel signifies the exile of the infant from its first home in the mother's body, which induces the hunger for home – nostalgia – that motivates odysseys ancient and modern. As we shall see, odysseys provide the framework for three of the novels analysed in this book – Joyce's *Ulysses*, Woolf's *To the Lighthouse*, and James's *The Ambassadors* – but these modernist works frustrate the expectation of a nostos or homecoming; instead, the journey is postponed, interrupted, or prolonged indefinitely.

In *Ulysses*, Stephen's odyssey begins in the Martello tower that Buck Mulligan wryly dubs the "*omphalos*" – the Greek word for the navel of the world at Delphi, shrine of the Delphic oracle (*U* 15:544) – an omphalos to which Stephen will never return. In Greek legend Zeus sent two eagles to fly across the world, and the point at which they met was thought to be the navel of the earth. To mark this spot, a drumlin-shaped stone called an omphalos was erected in several would-be navels of the Mediterranean. The most famous of these is the omphalos-stone at Delphi, which is hollow in the middle and covered with a carving of a knotted net. It was at this shrine that the Delphic priestess, seated on a tripod over a chasm and inspired by mephitic vapors rising from the depths, chanted her enigmatic prophecies.

Scholars have argued that the omphalos marks the victory of Apollo over a previous matriarchal earth-goddess, a conquest memorialized by the erection of a phallic stone in the place of the mephitic cleft. Apollo slew the snake Python, guardian of the omphalos and child of Gaia the earth-goddess, and buried the serpent under the omphalic stone, the new god thereby setting up his temple on the grave of his defeated rival.

Elizabeth Bronfen has made the ingenious suggestion that the Python, shown coiling around the omphalos-stone in one Pompeian fresco, represents the umbilical cord, while its burial by Apollo signifies the suppression of the matrilineal order.[10]

For Stephen Dedalus, the omphalos or navel signifies interconnectedness, the "strandentwining cable of all flesh," but also marks the primal wound of separation from the mother's body. This association of the navel with bodily rupture emerges in one of Joyce's early epiphanies, recording a dramatic scene in which the author's mother bursts into the room where Joyce is playing the piano to announce that his dying brother Georgie is hemorrhaging from the navel.

MRS. JOYCE – (crimson, trembling, appears at the parlour door) – Jim!
JOYCE – (at the piano) … Yes?
MRS. JOYCE – Do you know anything about the body? … What ought I to do? … There's some matter coming away from the hole in Georgie's stomach … Did you ever hear of that happening?
JOYCE – (surprised) … I don't know …
MRS. JOYCE – Ought I send for the doctor, do you think?
JOYCE – I don't know … what hole?
MRS. JOYCE – (impatient) … The hole we all have … here (points)
JOYCE – (stands up)[11]

"What hole?" The mother's pointing finger scarcely resolves this question, since "the hole we all have – here" could be anywhere or everywhere. Because the deictic "here" is unlocateable, it opens up a puncture in the text itself, a hole through which its meanings hemorrhage. In Joyce's writing, the navel – "the hole we all have" – signifies the hole or absent center of the nets in which the subject is enmeshed. Like the Delphic omphalos, hollow in the middle and encased in knotted nets, the navel is both seam and fissure, knot and not. (This pun, incidentally, is also used in Beckett's *Watt* [1953], where Mr. Knott [not] is the absent master of the house tenanted by Watt [what]; Knott therefore functions as the not that knots the nets of power, much as the navel is the not that knots the body in its skin.)

The navel, in its dual role as separation and connection, could be compared to Derrida's conception of the "brisure," a term from carpentry denoting both a break and a junction; the term "cleavage" is a sexy if inexact equivalent in English.[12] The double-sided concept of the navel – both gap and knot, both break and hinge – offers a model for the structure of several of the works of fiction discussed in the following chapters of this book. In these fictions, it is absence that gives rise to ramifying networks in which language, money, and libido circulate. Mrs. Newsome, in James's *The Ambassadors* (1903), functions as the absence or "central reserve" that instigates the circulation of letters and desire. In Joyce's *Dubliners* (1914), the relation between absence and the nets of circulation is encapsulated in the terms "gnomon" and "simony" which, together with the term "paralysis," cast a strange enchantment over the boy-narrator of "The Sisters." The "gnomon" in geometry means a parallelogram with a missing corner, while "simony" means the traffic in sacred things.[13] In *Dubliners*, the absent father functions as the gnomon or the missing corner that instigates the simoniac traffic in paternal substitutes.

GAZE IN YOUR OMPHALOS

Despite its Delphic ancestry, the navel is rarely taken seriously. Known to children as the belly button, either an "innie" or an "outie," the navel forms a hollow or hillock on the belly, signifying nothing, "gathering fluff." In popular usage, as Fred Botting has pointed out, the navel is associated with the time-wasting, self-indulgent activity of "navelgazing," a term denoting "idle cogitation upon unanswerable questions, useless speculation or circular self-reflection."[14] "Gaze in your *omphalos*," Stephen counsels himself in "Proteus" as he wanders aimlessly around Sandymount Strand (*U* 32:38).

Purposeless though it seems, the navel has always troubled believers in creation from nothing. Did Adam and Eve have navels? If our first parents were begotten not made, there was no reason for their bellies to be dimpled by these natal scars. Hence Stephen ponders "naked Eve" in "Proteus": "She had no navel. Belly without blemish, bulging big, a buckler of taut vellum …" (*U* 32:41–42). Yet Michelangelo, in the Sistine fresco depicting the creation of Adam, daubs the first man's belly with a navel. In 1646 Thomas Browne objected to such paintings for besmirching our first parents with "that tortuosity or complicated nodosity we usually call the Navel." Browne insists that navels are mere "superfluities." Why would God ordain "parts without use or office"? Having no anatomical navel, Adam retained "an umbilicality even with God himself," an unbroken connection to his maker.[15]

Two centuries later Philip Henry Gosse (father of the more famous Edmund) takes issue with Browne's contemptuous dismissal of the navel. In a bizarre defence of creationism, *Omphalos: An Attempt to Untie the Geological Knot* (1857), the elder Gosse insists: "The Man would not have been a Man without a Navel."[16] Much ridiculed by its Victorian audience, *Omphalos* argues that the world was created instantaneously, but in the deceptive form of a planet on which life had existed for aeons. God gave Adam a navel for the same reason that he buried fossils in the earth, to test our faith by providing false proofs of a non-existent past. In his memoir *Father and Son* (1907), Edmund Gosse remembers that "even Charles Kingsley, from whom my father had expected the most instant appreciation, wrote that he could not … 'believe that God has written on the rocks one enormous and superfluous lie' … a gloom, cold and dismal, descended upon our morning teacups."[17] Borges, on the other hand, admires the "monstrous elegance" of Gosse's *Omphalos*, and Baudrillard likewise relishes the implication that God is "an evil genius of simulation." Gosse's hypothesis is coming true, Baudrillard declares, given that "the whole of our past is indeed sliding into a fossilized simulacrum …"[18]

The navel troubles Stephen Dedalus because it proves he was "made not begotten," unlike Christ who was begotten not made (*U* 32:45). His "neverstop navelcord" links him back to his first home in his mother's all-too-blemished belly (*FW* 475:14). Yet if Stephen feels trapped by the nets of home and homeland, he also feels homeless in the English language. In *A Portrait of the Artist* Stephen realizes that every word he speaks or writes in English entails an exile from the home-grown tongue of Ireland, compelling him to fret in the shadow of the language of imperialism (*P* 189). To vary a quip of Oscar Wilde's, the English have condemned Stephen to write in the language of Shakespeare.

Joyce's writing in the English language could be seen as the elastic navelcord that ties him to the past while also ostracizing him from Ireland. "Where there is a reconciliation," Stephen intones, "there must have been first a sundering" (*U* 159:334). In Joyce, the navel signifies this primal sundering (the not), yet also represents the artist's strandentwining cable of indebtedness (the net). The game Joyce plays with navelcords could be compared to the game Freud's grandson plays with a spool of thread in the famous fort/da game of *Beyond the Pleasure Principle* (1920). In an attempt to exercise remote control over his mother's comings and goings, the child flings a spool into his curtained cot, uttering "oooo," and then retracts this umbilical thread with a triumphant "da" [here]. Freud interprets the first vowel as a childish pronunciation of the German word *fort*, meaning gone, and argues that the child is staging his mother's departures and returns to gain symbolic mastery over her intermittency. According to Freud, this game performs a psychic function similar to the catharsis of Greek tragedy, which inflicts upon the audience the painful experience of loss while wresting pleasure out of the aesthetic mastery of that experience (SE 18:14–17).[19]

In the fort/da game, the child reenacts the primal separation from the mother while creating a symbolic substitute for the umbilical cord. Like Walt Whitman's noiseless patient spider, the little boy launches forth "filament, filament, filament" "to explore the vacant vast surrounding," "measureless oceans of space."[20] Yet the cord the child casts into the dark hollows out the very absence that he strives to overcome. This filament links the child to the mother, but also usurps the mother's place, substituting the auto-erotic pleasures of the sign – the toy, the alternating phonemes – for the plenitude of the lost object. Each time the child throws the spool away, he murders his mother in effigy, yet what he really kills is presence and immediacy. Henceforth all his encounters with the real will be mediated by symbolic substitutes. The loops he outlines with his spool constitute the nets that bind him in a world of signs.

It is worth noting that the fort/da game stages an odyssey in miniature, in which the bobbin is cast away to bring about a future homecoming. As little Ernst expels his toy, so James expels ambassadors to Paris, Woolf sends the Ramsays to the lighthouse, and Joyce dispatches Bloom and Stephen on their odysseys through Dublin. But the toy that Ernst ejects is not the same as that which he retrieves, for it is death that he lassoes out of the void (by a poignant coincidence, the little boy's mother died shortly after Freud witnessed the fort/da game) (SE 18:14–16). Like the child's bobbin, Bloom goes forth in exile and circles back to 7 Eccles Street, but it is unclear whether the Ithaca that he returns to is the same place that he left in "Lotus-Eaters." In the meantime his wife Molly has rearranged the furniture, and her lover Blazes Boylan has left his imprint on the bed, along with telltale flakes of Plumtree's potted meat. As for Lambert Strether, the hero of James's *The Ambassadors*, who returns to Massachusetts after his odyssey to Paris, "he goes back other, and to other things," as James records (*A* 403). To go back other, and to other things, epitomizes the fate of the modernist Odysseus.

In the "Ithaca" episode of *Ulysses*, we are told that Leopold Bloom once marked a florin with three notches and launched it "for circulation on the waters of civic finance, for possible, circuitous or direct, return." "Had Bloom's coin returned?" the narrator demands, to which the implacable riposte is "Never" (*U* 571:979–88). Never is a long time. Modernist writing confronts the possibility that what is forfeited to circulation never returns, or else returns too fast and furiously, as in the compulsive repetition of primordial traumas. "Returns" in the economic sense refer to the profits or losses that result from launching money, like persons, into circulation. But the fate of Bloom's florin implies that the modernist wanderer is destined for dissemination rather than return.

The three notches with which Bloom marks his florin could be compared to the scar by which Odysseus is recognized on his return to Ithaca. These notches also correspond to the navel-scar with which the neonate is launched into the world, since the severance of the umbilical cord represents the first notch that culture inflicts upon the human body. The fantasy of castration, understood in post-Freudian psychoanalysis as the infant's violent initiation into culture, could be interpreted as a symbolic reenactment of the primal scarification of the navel. While Lacan regards the castration fantasy as the open sesame to the symbolic order, and identifies the symbolic phallus with the name-of-the-father, the present study proposes that the navel memorializes a pre-symbolic order under the aegis of the nameless mother.

Freud's most famous reference to the navel occurs in a footnote to *The Interpretation of Dreams*. "There is at least one spot in every dream at which it is unplumbable – a navel, as it were, that is its point of contact with the unknown" (SE 4:111n). It is appropriate that the navel of the dream makes its first appearance as a footnote, since the anatomical navel also functions as a footnote in the flesh, marking an indelible debt to the lost mother. Later Freud incorporates this umbilical footnote into the body of his text, when he redefines the navel as a "tangle of the dream-thoughts which cannot be unraveled and which moreover adds nothing to our knowledge of the content of the dream." A knot that adds nothing, this navel opens up the void from which "the dream-thoughts branch out in every direction into the intricate network of our world of thought." It is where this "meshwork is particularly close" that the dream-wish rises "like a mushroom out of its mycelium" (SE 5:525).

The navel of the dream marks the point at which the nets of meaning dissolve in their own density, leaving a black hole in the center of the dreamwork. For this reason the Freudian dream-navel encompasses the contradictory ideas of not and net, absence and entanglement, embodied in the hollow netted omphalos-stone at Delphi. Furthermore Freud's image of the mushroom rising out of its mycelium evokes the "rhizomatic" structure that Deleuze and Guattari have opposed to the "arboreal" structure of conventional thought. The authors argue that rhizomatic thought, like the associative property of language, "grows between" other things, like weeds or grass; it has "neither beginning nor end, but always a middle [*milieu*] from which it grows and which it overspills."[21] Rhizomatic thought, characterized by Vicki Mahaffey as an "associative, omnidirectional, ever-changing process of exploration without a set goal," corresponds to Freud's conception of the dream-navel as a mycelium, a shallow creeping fungus.[22] Stephen's vision of the matrilineal nets of navelcords could also be described as rhizomatic, as opposed to the arboreal structure of the family tree, governed by the name of the father.

The Nets of Modernism uses the concept of the navel, in its dual aspect as hole and net, to investigate the structure of modernist fiction, including Freudian psychoanalysis, which could be seen as a serial fiction – part autobiography, part epistolary novel, part Viennese soap opera. As many commentators have pointed out, Freud's work bears a strong resemblance to Proust's *À la recherche du temps perdu*, another serial fiction delving into dreams, erotic obsessions, and the psychopathology of everyday life; Proust also ventures into quasi-scientific speculations on sexology, enlivened by case histories at least as spectacular as Freud's. Similar resemblances to Freud may be found in Joyce's *Ulysses*, where streams-of-consciousness unfurl as rhizomatically as the associative networks of the Freudian dream. Meanwhile Joyce's characters dramatize what Freud calls the psychopathology of everyday life, exhibiting such symptoms as the first Freudian slip in English literature, when Bloom substitutes "the wife's admirers" for her "advisors" (*U* 257:767). As for sexology, the "Circe" episode offers a psychedelic encyclopedia of sexual perversions, largely based on Krafft-Ebing's *Psychopathia Sexualis* (1886), a source also exploited by Freud. Finally *Finnegans Wake* could be seen as a monstrously extended Freudian slip, where puns break down the barrier between the conscious and the unconscious mind, facilitating the return of the repressed.

It is well documented that Freudian ideas were "in the air" at the time that Joyce, Woolf, and James were composing their novels, yet none of these novelists set out to write psychoanalytic fictions. Woolf, on the contrary, avoided reading Freud, even though she published the Strachey translation of his works, for fear of being outmaneuvered by Freudian insights.[23] Henry James, during his 1904 visit to the United States, consulted a doctor influenced by Freud, a treatment that the novelist experienced as beneficial; his brother William James, meanwhile, believed that Freud held the future of psychology in his hands.[24] Beyond these circumstances, however, there is little reason to suppose that Henry James was directly influenced by Freud. Joyce, on the other hand, speaks of being "yung and easily freudened" in *Finnegans Wake*, possibly ridiculing his own susceptibility to psychoanalysis (*FW* 115.22–23). Elsewhere Joyce declares: "As for psychoanalysis it's neither more nor less than blackmail" – an enigmatic dismissal, to say the least (*JJ* 524). Yet despite his professed distrust of psychoanalysis, Joyce consigned his psychotic daughter Lucia to an abortive analysis with Jung, collected works by Freud, Jung, and Ernest Jones in his Trieste Library, and made extensive use of Freud's case history of the Wolf Man in the composition of *Finnegans Wake*, as Daniel Ferrer's genetic analysis has demonstrated.[25] Evidently Joyce recognized much of his own phantasmagoria in psychoanalysis, yet his works anticipate the insights that he found in Freud, and transform those insights into Joycean fireworks.

Shoshana Felman, in her now classic essay on James's *The Turn of the Screw*, argues for the "implication" rather than the "application" of psychoanalysis in literary studies.[26] In other words, the psychoanalytic critic should attend to the ways in which the literary text invites, resists, preempts, and transforms the theories brought to bear upon it. Just as psychoanalysis incorporates elements of fiction – notably the detective story often compared to Freud's case histories – so literary fictions harbor elements of theory that anticipate their own interpreters. For this reason I have tried to draw my critical vocabulary from the literary texts, such as the notion of the navel from *Ulysses*, rather than imposing psychoanalytic terms upon these works. The aim is not to seize the psychoanalytic truth disguised within the literary work, for such an enterprise can only prove reductive, but to set up a frictional interplay between these discourses. To enhance this interplay, and to make this study as accessible as possible, I have striven to avoid the over-use of technical vocabulary, allowing the novels to generate the terms of their analysis.

This means that each chapter of this study develops along independent lines, adapting its terms to the respective literary works. While the notion of the navel, in the double sense of breakage and connection, provides an overarching structural metaphor, each chapter addresses specific themes arising from the texts discussed. Among these themes is animality; in different ways, both psychoanalysis and modernism call into question the boundary between the human and the animal. Freud, for instance, becomes a kind of Circe who transforms his patients into animals, nominally if not corporeally, in the case histories of the Wolf Man and the Rat Man, as well as in the case of Little Hans, who is entitled to be called the

Horse Boy. The next chapter of my book argues that the rat is the animal that dominates the modernist imagination, largely because rats are associated with the networks characteristic of modernity – the sewers, subways, pipes, and railway lines, as well as the mazes of the scientific laboratory. In this sense the rat could be seen as the modernist minotaur – half-beast, half-human – entrammeled in the Daedalean labyrinths of urban life.

The third chapter turns to James's *The Ambassadors*, tracing the rat-like networks of representation that extend from the absent mother, Mrs. Newsome, who could be seen as the navel of the novel, its broken yet all-embracing umbilical cord. This chapter also introduces the theme of the primal scene, in this case the foreclosed scene of Chad Newsome's love affair, which functions as the blind spot at the core of Strether's vision, the gap from which his speculations radiate. Chapter 4 examines the resurgence of the primal scene in Woolf's *To the Lighthouse* and Freud's case history of the Wolf Man. In *To the Lighthouse*, this resurgence culminates in Lily's painting; in the Wolf Man's case, both his paintings and his dreams strive to restage the primal scene. Forgotten, blotted out or "scotomized," and reconstructed only from its scattered traces, the primal scene may never have occurred. Yet it leaves a gap that generates the impulse to make further scenes, whose frozen images disrupt the continuity of narrative.

The notion of scotomization, or symptomatic blindness, is taken up again in the fifth chapter of this book, originally written for a special issue on *The Blind Short Story* for the *Oxford Literary Review*.[27] Chapter 5 examines the recurrent theme of blindness in short stories and considers possible affinities between the symptom and the genre, analyzing short fictions ranging from Gide and Conrad to Nella Larsen. The central portion of the chapter focuses on Joyce's *Dubliners*, a work that opens with the image of a darkened blind and closes with a blinding snowstorm. A close reading of Joyce's story "Two Gallants," jointly written with Marilyn Reizbaum, connects the Joycean theme of blindness to Freud's account of fetishism, in which the "scotomized" perception of the mother's missing penis instigates the process of symbolic substitution.

The last two chapters of my book, which are the most explicitly omphalocentric, trace the image of the navel and the navelcord through Joyce's works. Chapter 6 juxtaposes Homer's account of Odysseus's scar to the umbilical imagery of *A Portrait of the Artist*, particularly to the scene in Cork where Stephen, searching for his father's initials in the anatomy theatre, discovers the word "foetus" carved into a desk. This inscription, which is presented as a wound or scar, and provokes a crisis of masculinity in Stephen, could be seen as a navel, the mark of a denied maternal order irrupting in the place of the name of the father. My final chapter, "Skinscapes in Modernism," makes use of the psychoanalyst Didier Anzieu's concept of the "skin ego" to examine the adventures of skin in *Ulysses*, and the role of the navel as both hole and "button" (Molly Bloom's term) of the bodily envelope.

It will be clear from this prospectus that *The Nets of Modernism* consists of several interwoven arguments, rather than a single go-ahead polemic. In the widest terms, this book strives to sharpen our sense of what has been called the "dissolution of the self" in modernist fiction, particularly by exploring the significance of images of bodily violation and exchange – scar, bite, wound, and their psychic equivalents – to the modernist imagination. Among these scars, the navel, which combines the contradictory ideas of breaking and connecting, provides a means of rethinking the structure of the modernist fictions under discussion. Yet these fictions in turn elicit further themes, such as vision, blindness, corporeality, and animality, which beckon the analysis in different directions. What the argument lacks in singlemindedness it strives to make up for in variety. My focus on canonical literary texts may seem old-fashioned, at a time when modernist studies has become much more inclusive – a development I welcome and have tried to foster, particularly in my recent monograph on Elizabeth Bowen. The present book, without making any claims to exhaustiveness, justifies its choice of literary texts by their fertile correspondences to psychoanalysis; other literary works, many of them less canonical, might have stimulated similar investigations. The most a critic can hope for is to invigorate debate, including debate about well-known works, and it is my hope that at least some of my analyses fulfill that purpose.

CHAPTER 2

The modernist rat

There is a legend that intertwined rats' tails can fuse together, producing a many-headed monster known as a rat-king. The largest mummified specimen of this phenomenon, whose tails were probably tied together after death, is displayed in the science museum in Altenburg, Germany. As a collective fantasy, the rat-king provides an apt analogy for the tangle of cultural anxieties represented by the rat in modernism. This chapter attempts to unravel these strands while stressing their knotted interdependence. Foremost among them is the notion of excess, whether negatively figured in the form of waste, or positively in the form of plenty. Other strands connect the atavistic to the futuristic, the savage to the citified, the bestial to the human, the mechanical to the organic, the polluted to the sterilized, the superstitious to the scientific, the foreign to the inbred, the heterogeneous to the homogenized, the chaotic to the systematic.

The modernist rat provokes such oppositions only to confound them. Popping up irrepressibly in modernist texts, the rat signals the breakdown of boundaries, at once calamitous and liberating. Traditionally feared as a parasite on literature, a bibliophagous menace to the authority of the book, the rat represents the forces of decomposition endemic to the work of composition. As we shall see, the recurrence of the rat in modernist texts intimates that writing is riddled with erasure, and that literature is a self-gnawing artefact.

"I think we are in rats' alley / Where the dead men lost their bones," Eliot writes in *The Waste Land*. "Rats' alley," which is reminiscent of the trenches of World War I, could also refer to *The Waste Land* itself, strewn with the bones of former texts, the vandalized remains of the dead poets. Yet although rats invade this poem, along with many other literary alleyways of modernism, their ubiquity is often overlooked. Steve Baker, for example, insists that there is "no 'modernist' animal," and that the animal is "the first thing to be ruled out of modernism's bounds." Drawing his evidence primarily from visual rather than literary culture, Baker argues that animals in modernism represent only the "human imagining-itself-other." Brancusi's bird, turtle, and fish, for instance, embody "the dream of unimpeded movement through air or water: a non-human, *non-pedestrian* movement."[1] Instead of tackling the pelt and weight of animality, Brancusi purifies his creatures into principles of engineering.

Margot Norris, on the other hand, identifies a "zoocentric" strand in modernism, exemplified in writers such as Lawrence, Nietzsche, and Jack London, who reject the Enlightenment project of mastering nature in order to extol the untamed majesty of wild animals – innocent, masculine, implacable.[2] Neither Norris nor Baker, however, acknowledges the prominence of rats and other vermin in the modernist imagination, perhaps because these creatures' animality is compromised by their parasitical dependency on human life. Too close to civilization to be romanticized as other, and yet too far to be admitted as akin, rats are "abject," in Julia Kristeva's definition of the term: they represent "the in-between, the ambiguous, the composite."[3] The abject is that which a culture casts away (ab-jects) in order to determine what is not itself, through rituals such as burning, burial, and exorcism.

The resilience of rats reveals the failure of these rituals, proving that the abject always springs back up again, adapting itself to each new persecution. Georges Bataille defines abjection as "the inability to assume with sufficient strength the imperative act of excluding abject things," an act that "establishes the foundations of collective existence."[4] The rat is a gnawing reminder of this inability. Like Derrida's "dangerous supplement," the rat implies that civilization is founded on that which it excludes: on excess, excrement, exteriority.[5] The legend of the Pied Piper, who lured the rats of Hamlin to a watery grave, but proceeded to entomb the children in a mountainside, suggests that the future of the human species may depend on the survival of its oldest and most intimate antagonist.

If the animal is the first thing to be ruled out of modernism's bounds, as Baker claims, the rat is the first outcast to creep back in again. In fact, what bothers modernism about rats is their defiance of such bounds; they multiply too fast, and spread too far. Migrants and globetrotters, rats evade immigration controls, sweeping across borders with the rapacity of a multinational company. In Isaac Rosenberg's famous war poem "Break of Day in the Trenches" (1916), the "queer sardonic rat" holds "cosmopolitan sympathies," scavenging off both sides of the battlefield.[6] But the rat shares these sympathies with modernists and Jews, those exiles and émigrés attracted to the cosmopolitanism of the capital, with its confusions of ethnicity, morality, and language. Streetwise denizens of the multicultural city, rats also invade the heart of domesticity, dismantling the opposition between inside and outside, tame and wild, *heimlich* and *unheimlich*.

Hans Zinsser, in his classic work *Rats, Lice, and History* (1935), points out that rats and human beings have gradually "spread across the earth, keeping pace with each other and unable to destroy each other, though continually hostile."[7] Rats congregate wherever there is garbage; that is, wherever there are people. Hitchhikers, stowaways, and squatters, rats travel on the backs of war, religion, commerce, and imperialism, free-loading off armies, missionaries, merchants, and colonists to extend their empire over the planet. Like human beings, rats take over wherever they invade, ousting the indigenous species; where garbage is scarce, they even develop a caste system, so that the upper rats get more to eat, forcing the lower rats to make do with the leftovers. Thus the rat participates in the human rampage of the planet, uninhibited by moral or environmental qualms. Greed and overpopulation, common to both rats and people, have opened up the terrifying prospect of a future deprived of all biodiversity, a world reduced to two invasive species, endlessly warring on each other – or even worse, a world controlled by rats alone: "We, indestructible!" these rodents cry in Günter Grass's apocalyptic novel *The Rat*.

At once inhuman and all too human, rats have always been our doubles, our semblables – "the serried footnotes to man, his proliferating company," as Grass describes them.[8] For this reason prejudice against the species – rattism – goes back to the origins of Western civilization. But the vilification of the rat has varied between times and climes. The Romans disregarded the difference between rat and mouse, categorizing the former as a bigger version of the latter, and the King James version of the Bible never mentions rats, reserving most of its verminophobia for dogs. A possible exception may be found in 1 Samuel 6, in which the Philistines seize the ark of the covenant, thereby bringing down the wrath of God, who unleashes a plague of tumors and rats (translated as "mice" in the King James version). The priests advise the Philistines to return the ark to the Israelites, accompanied with a guilt-offering of "five gold tumours and five gold rats" (I Samuel 6.4). Here the exchange of golden rats for ruinous rats implies a metaphorical reversibility, whereby rats may stand for riches as well as devastation.

This biblical transaction anticipates Freud's Rat Man, for whom rats become synonymous with money: "so many florins, so many rats," the patient ruminates when Freud names his hourly fee (SE 10:213). A similar association may be found in Japanese mythology, in which Daikoku, the god of prosperity, is usually portrayed with his rat-assistant poking its nose out of his bag of hidden treasure. A possible explanation is that the rat is a freeloader whose depredations imply a superfluity of wealth. In Bataille's terms, Daikoku's rat could signify the movement from a "restricted economy" of thrift to a "general economy" of waste. According to Bataille, a restricted economy is one in which excess is put to use and reincorporated in the system, whereas a general economy is one in which this excess can no longer be absorbed: "it must necessarily be lost without profit; it must be spent, willingly or not, gloriously or catastrophically."⁹

RATOPHOBIA AND RATOPHILIA

The glorious is usually overshadowed by the catastrophic in modern Western images of rats, which associate the rodent with contagion and disaster. A deadly outbreak of the bubonic plague in Canton in 1894 led to the discovery that the disease was carried by the fleas that piggyback on rats.¹⁰ The plague spread to Bombay in 1896, transported by flea-infested rats through shipping and railway lines, and killing an estimated ten million people in the next twenty years (the rat fatalities remain unrecorded). In Western Europe, as Peter Stallybrass and Allon White have argued, the transition from a rural to an urban industrial economy meant that the "rat was no longer primarily an economic liability (as the spoiler of grain, for instance): it was an object of fear and loathing, a threat to civilized life."¹¹ In big cities like Paris and London, improvements to municipal sewage systems in the later nineteenth century removed excreta from the public eye, but the rats that traveled between the sewers and the streets endangered the dividing line between the filth below and the purity above. Because of this inbetweenness, as Christopher Herbert has pointed out, the Victorian rat came to embody "uncleanness in its fully animate form."¹²

Given these associations, it is not surprising that the rat rarely features in Victorian visual art. In modernism, similarly, no Brancusi attempts to idealize the locomotion of the rat, despite its nimbleness, contractibility, and speed. An exception is Calder, who produced his aerodynamic black "Rat" in 1948, with its perky ears, tapered body, curvaceous tail, and baubles dangling from its streamlined snout, the whole lightsome assemblage suspended on a bright red curling tripod. This sculpture defies the conventional uglification of the rat, but also corroborates Baker's view that animals in modernism embody human dreams of defying gravity. Among fin-de-siècle artists only Vincent Van Gogh portrays rats with sympathetic realism: in his painting "Two Rats" (1884), these animals huddle close together in the dark, nibbling a crust of bread, and watch the viewer with as much suspicion as the viewer watches them, their stealthy feast a mockery of greedy eyes.

In Van Gogh's day, ratophobia was escalating in response to the explosion of rodent and human populations in the metropolis. This explosion meant big business for rat-catchers, who discovered a lucrative sideline in selling rats for fights, in which dogs would be set loose on packs of rats for the entertainment of London pub-goers and New York barflies. A London publican called Jimmy Shaw claimed to buy 26,000 rats a year at threepence each to be torn to pieces in these bloodbaths.[13] In New York, Kit Burns, an Irish immigrant from Donegal, also known as the "rodentary magnate," opened up a bar in 1840 called the Sportsman's Hall, which was said to hold "250 decent people and 400 indecent ones." They gathered to drink Burns's homemade liquor and watch dogs killing rats by the hundreds. Despite their popularity, these rat-fights were eventually outlawed, thanks to crusaders such as Richard Martin in Britain, also known as "Humanity Dick," and Henry Bergh in the United States, "the ubiquitous and humane biped," who founded the American Society for the Prevention of Cruelty to Animals in 1866.[14]

Nonetheless a new affection for the rat emerged at the nadir of its reputation in the late nineteenth century. This reversal was instigated by the same rat-catchers who profited from the mass destruction of the species. Since these rat-catchers were paid per rat, they soon discovered that breeding rats was easier than catching new ones to increase their earnings. Further profits could be gained by reserving attractive specimens to breed as pets, a practice that gave rise to a fad for "fancy rats" – named for their fanciers rather than their fanciness. The most famous of the rat-tycoons was Jack Black, official Rat Catcher and Mole Destroyer by appointment to Queen Victoria, who was immortalized by Henry Mayhew in his monumental *London Labour and the London Poor*. Jack Black cut a striking figure in his self-designed uniform of white leather breeches, scarlet waistcoat, green topcoat, and black leather sash inset with cast-iron rats, "in the same pose one might expect from a pride of lions."[15] When Jack Black caught rats of unusual colors, he would breed them for elegant "young ladies to keep in squirrel cages."[16] Even Queen Victoria is reputed to have kept a rat or two. Beatrix Potter, born in 1866, is thought to have been one of Jack Black's customers, and in 1908 she dedicated her book *The Roly-Poly Pudding* – a terrifying fable, incidentally – to the memory of her pet rat Samuel Whiskers.[17] This was the same year that Kenneth Grahame published *The Wind in the Willows*, starring Ratty the endearing water-rat.

These positive role models reflected the success of rats as pets, a capacity in which they proved intelligent, affectionate, trainable, clean, and (best of all) short-lived. The National Mouse Club, founded in 1895, expanded to include classes for rats at their pet shows in 1901, reflecting a growing interest in the creation of rat breeds for aesthetic purposes. Pet-breeding of cats and dogs, which had been fashionable since the second half of the nineteenth century, involved the classification of breeds and pedigrees, regulated by societies with strict rules and procedures. As Harriet Ritvo has shown, pet-breeding was steeped in ideologies of class and race, and borrowed much of its momentum from the eugenic movement, which was committed to improving human "stock."[18] Later, laboratory rats would be manipulated for eugenic purposes in the United States, where strains of rats were bred to prove the intellectual inferiority of African Americans. In these experiments, as one commentator puts it, "even the rat was white."[19]

During the period when rats were transformed into pets and sentimentalized in children's literature, they also infiltrated the burgeoning subgenre of vampire fiction. Bram Stoker's *Dracula*, published in 1897, unleashed the vampire-epidemic that still stalks the cinema today, the revival of the dead having found its niche in an art form based on the reanimation of the still. In Stoker's novel, Count Dracula, landing in his ship of death at Whitby Harbour, sneaks through British customs by disguising himself as a swarm of rats.[20] This image probably derives from the contemporary gutter press, in which refugees from Eastern Europe, particularly Jews in flight from the pogroms, were routinely vilified as swarming parasites.

Rats and vampires have much in common, notably the bite, as well as the capacity to reproduce at epidemic rates. Both, moreover, are associated with disease, rats with bubonic plague and vampires with syphilis, an infection that spreads through seduction and exchange of bodily fluids. Furthermore, both rats and vampires are toothy throwbacks signifying the resurgence of the primitive: rats are associated with medieval plague, vampires with medieval feudalism.[21] Stoker's Count Dracula is a feudal tyrant who creates relations of vassalage through blood. Yet he also yearns for the liquidity of modern capital: like the modern-day counts and princes in Henry James's fiction, Dracula needs to supplement his real estate with fluid assets, such as the "stream of gold" that pours out of his coat when he is stabbed. Franco Moretti, revisiting a famous metaphor from Marx, has argued that vampirism represents monopoly capitalism, with its destruction of all forms of economic independence. Yet vampirism also harks back to feudalism, thus confounding atavistic with contemporary forms of economic exploitation.[22]

The most recent fin de siècle, from the 1980s onwards, has witnessed a revival of the vampire in literary and cultural studies, proving – if nothing else – that vampires breed metaphors as rampantly as Dracula breeds bloodsuckers. In these studies, vampirism has been connected to perversion, menstruation, venereal disease, female sexuality, male homosexuality, feudal aristocracy, monopoly capitalism, the proletariat, the Jew, the primal father, the Antichrist, and the typewriter. More intriguing than this metaphorical fecundity, however, is the reversal of such tropes into their opposites, particularly with regard to the archaic and the modern. Like rats, vampires signal the incursion of the past into the present, affirming Horkheimer and Adorno's paradox that the "curse of irresistible progress is irresistible regression."[23] Thus Stoker's Dracula exercises his primeval power with all the know-how of a modern rat, by infiltrating the networks of the postal and transportation systems. He even ships himself to Britain, packaged in his coffin, although venturing "outside the box" to vamp the sailors. Meanwhile his mysterious access to British real estate agents, all the way from Transylvania, anticipates the worldwide web. Rats and vampires therefore share an appetite for the networks of travel and communication, networks in which bodies, energies, and voices cross and interpenetrate.

A further form of networking is the transference of thought – telepathy – by which Count Dracula ventriloquizes Mina Harker by remote control.[24] Telepathy, a word invented in 1882 by the Society for Psychical Research, represents the spooky fringe of newly developed communication technologies, such as the telephone and phonograph – technologies in which the "undead" voice acquires a mechanical afterlife.[25] Such technologies are vampiric in the sense that they drain the voice out of the human speaker, much as the typewriter – another innovation that looms large in *Dracula* – detaches writing from the human body, so that the uniqueness of handwriting – still fetishized today in the cult of the signature – is depersonalized into a common type, and absorbed into vast networks of information storage and retrieval.[26] These networks threaten to usurp the self, much as the telepathic Count takes over the body and the mind, sucking blood and thoughts out of his victims.

Rats, like vampires, are associated with the bite, as well as with the infections resulting from this rupture of the bodily envelope. By gnawing through the boundaries of nations and bodies, rats attack the very grounds of "definition," as Eliot glosses this term in his epigraph to *Notes Towards a Definition of Culture*: "DEFINITION: I. The setting of bounds; limitation (rare)." As previously stated, one of the definitions thus eroded are the bounds between the ancient and the modern, since rats, redolent of the Dark Ages, also thrive on state-of-the-art technology. Leopold Bloom, spotting a rat in the cemetery episode of *Ulysses*, describes the creature as an "obese … greatgrandfather," chewing corpses much as Joyce's writings gorge on the remains of the literary tradition (*U* 94:973–74).[27] Yet this old-timer, rodentia dentata, has also proved remarkably adaptable to modern life. "He knows the ropes," Bloom says, a theatrical expression that harks back to the ghost of Hamlet's father, whose son addresses him as "old mole," the burrowing rodent of the underworld beneath the stage.[28]

This obese grey rat of "Hades," by tunneling passageways between the graves, links the dead to the networks of the living, to the capillary netherworld of sewers, pipes, and wires connecting human warrens to municipal supplies. "Underground communication," Bloom comments; "we learned that from them" – a phrase in which the pronoun "them" could refer either to rats or to the dead, suggesting that both are experts in clandestine networking (*U* 94:991). In the modern city, the installation of public utilities creates "underground communication" between dwelling-places, thereby engendering a kind of universal vampirism, with private households leeching off a common source of water, gas, and electricity, while also being drained of their autonomy by municipal control.

THE RAT IN THE MAZE

The navigational skills of rats, which equip them to negotiate these urban networks, have also proved invaluable to behaviorist psychology, which launched its now-proverbial experiments on rats in mazes in the early twentieth century. From this period onwards the rat, which had been neglected by modernist art, discovered its Brancusi in the laboratory.[29] Here the animal was admired for its speed and "kinaesthesis," a mysterious ability to orientate itself by means of "muscle-and-joint sense," reinforced by "thigmophilia," or love of touch, which helps the rat remember routes by means of sensations on its hide and whiskers. As Robert Sullivan observes, "Deep in their rat tendons, rats know history."[30] These rat-feats lent support to early behaviorist theories that emphasized the automatism of actions, a psychology that both reflected and informed the increasing mechanization of work practices.

Behaviorists conceived of the rat mind as a modernized and stream-lined version of its human counterpart. The influential behaviorist John Broadus Watson argued that the rudiments of complex mental processes present themselves in purest form in underdeveloped subjects, such as children, "defective human beings," or "blind, deaf and anosmic animals" – indeed, he acknowledged little difference between these groups.[31] Stripped of baggage such as language, intellection, will, and feeling, rats performed their tasks with greater alacrity than human beings. In Watson's experiments, rats had to find their way to rewards placed in the center of the maze. Their success was measured by speed, which reduced behavior to a matter of mechanical efficiency. A rat that paused, reviewed its options, or meditated on the road not taken was understood to be "maze-dumb," as opposed to the unreflective "maze-bright" rat that hurried to the prize, without wondering why the scientist was starving it: "What have I done? Why has he stopped liking me?"[32] Such emotions held no place in Watson's conception of rational intelligence.

Another well-known behaviorist, Edward Chase Tolman, admits that he used to think "lookings back and forth" were signs of "conscious awareness" in the rat, but later realized this was "a silly idea." He now takes the view that "VTEing," or "vicarious trial and error" – a term invented by K. F. Muenziger to describe the hesitation of the rat at a choice-point of the maze – is merely a sign of imbecility. "The more stupid rats do more VTEing," Tolman declares. Where human cognition is concerned, however, Tolman submits his speculations "simply in the nature of a *rat* psychologist's *rat*iocinations offered free."[33] Watson, by contrast, shows no such modesty or wit, although there is something exhilarating about his iconoclasm towards the much-vaunted superiority of the human mind. Where rats are concerned, Watson argues that their mastery of the maze depends not on sight, smell, or hearing, but on an inbuilt kinaesthetic sense that choreographs their tracks through space. To prove this point, he removed one rat's eyes, olfactory bulb, and vibrissae before sending the poor creature through the maze. At first the rat languished, making little progress towards the reward; it was only with the added motivation of starvation that the animal found the food and thus became – in Watson's words – "the usual automaton."[34] Like Watson, Tolman also takes the view that:

everything important in psychology (except such matters as the building of a super-ego, that is everything save such matters as involve society and words) can be investigated in essence through the continued experimental and theoretical analysis of the determiners of rat behavior at a choice point in the maze.[35]

That's a big "except."

In J. M. Coetzee's novel *Elizabeth Costello*, the eponymous heroine, a novelist-cum-animal-rights-activist, argues that the maze experiments are based on anthropocentric prejudice:

the programme of scientific experimentation that leads you to conclude that animals are imbeciles is profoundly anthropocentric. It values being able to find your way out of a sterile maze, ignoring the fact that if the researcher who designed the maze were to be parachuted into the jungles of Borneo, he or she would be dead of starvation within a week.[36]

Yet it is these anthropocentric standards of intelligence that have ensured the rat's popularity in the laboratory. Not only is the animal adept at navigating manmade networks, but its glandular and neurological systems closely resemble the internal networks of the human body. According to Tolman, "the rat's central nervous system … may be likened to a complicated telephone switchboard."[37] In rats, however, this switchboard develops at a vastly accelerated pace: "the nervous system of the rat grows in the same manner as that of man – only some 30 times as fast."[38] The fact that rats breed even faster than they grow has made them indispensable to scientific research. Scientists under pressure to produce quick results with copious evidence have appreciated the ability of rats, under optimum conditions, to produce offspring every twenty-six days.[39]

When Günter Grass accepted the Nobel Prize in 1999, he remembered the passage in his novel *The Rat* in which the Nobel Prize is awarded to this lowly creature:

The white-haired, red-eyed laboratory rat is finally getting her due. For she more than anyone – or so claims the narrator of my novel – has made possible all the Nobelified research and discoveries in the field of medicine and, as far as Nobel Laureates Watson and Crick are concerned, on the virtually boundless turf of gene manipulation.[40]

In Grass's novel, the human race survives nuclear war by means of a genetic "infusion of rattiness," which is necessary to "liberate man from the I and open him to the we" (here Grass overestimates the rat's collective spirit).[41] The result is a hybrid race of rat-men known as the Watsoncricks, in homage to that famous pair of rat-scientists who paved the way for genetic engineering. Similarly Hugh Sykes Davies's Cold War novel *The*

Papers of Andrew Melmoth imagines a post-nuclear world inhabited by rats alone, a genetic mutation having enabled them to map their underground networks.[42] Such apocalyptic fictions indicate that rats are held in awe, as well as in abomination. While we project onto the rat the loathsome aspects of our species – our greed, promiscuity, and filth – we also see this pest as a hardier, more cunning version of ourselves. So hardy that if Noah had kept rats off the Ark, as Grass proposes, the dove would have returned not only with an olive branch but with tidings of "rat droppings, fresh rat droppings."[43]

THE RAT ON THE COUCH

Behaviorist psychology, by treating rat-behavior as a model of the human mind, challenges the boundary between these species. Freud, on the other hand, challenges this boundary by transforming his patients into animals – nominally if not corporeally – and specifically by turning Dr. Ernst Lanzer into the Rat Man. This patient, who was born in 1878 and killed in World War I, had suffered from obsessive ideas since early childhood. At the time of his analysis, Lanzer was performing his military service, and the obsession that drove him to Freud's couch was precipitated by the Captain of his regiment. This Captain mentioned that a package containing pince-nez had arrived for Lanzer, and that the postal charges had been paid by Lieutenant A. However, Lanzer already knew that it was not Lieutenant A, but an obliging young woman working in the post office, who had remitted these nugatory charges. Nevertheless, instead of reimbursing his benefactress, the Rat Man resolved to enlist Lieutenant B into a labyrinthine railway journey to repay Lieutenant A, thus devising a homosocial circuit of exchange that bypassed the original female creditor. This itinerary grew so complex in the Rat Man's imagination that Freud had to ask the patient to explain his obsessive reasoning three times.

But the Rat Man never carries out this project in reality; this elaborate maze remains within his mind. His inability to act, Freud argues, lies in his unconscious confusion of the debt with rats. The same Captain who misdirected Lanzer to repay Lieutenant A had also told a gruesome story in which a prisoner was tied up with a bucketful of rats placed upside-down on his buttocks, so that the animals tried to escape by boring through his anus. As several commentators have pointed out, this story was not invented by the so-called "cruel Captain," but derives from Octave Mirbeau's pornographic bestseller *The Torture Garden* (1899).[44]

Hence it is worth noting that the Rat Man's rats, like the Wolf Man's wolves, originate in literature rather than reality.

According to Freud, the Rat Man's symbolic equation of rats with money stems from an unconscious pun on *Raten*, the German term for payments or instalments, which closely resembles *Ratten*, the plural for rats. Rats also connote children, by way of Ibsen's play *Little Eyolf* (1894), which is based on the Pied Piper legend. In the unconscious, according to Freud, children are regarded as the symbolic equivalent of faeces, which are the infant's "first gift" to its caretakers.[45] This logic implies that children = faeces = gifts = payments = rats. A further link in this chain of equivalents is worms; during his childhood Lanzer was afflicted with roundworms in his anus. Worms resemble penises, Freud argues, and penises resemble rats as vectors of infection, specifically syphilis, a disease the Rat Man phobically dreads. Furthermore, the Rat Man's father was a sometime gambler or *Spielratte*, which literally means a game-rat. During his military service, Lanzer's father once lost money at cards and was forced to borrow money from a fellow soldier in order to repay the debt. Later he tried to locate his benefactor in an attempt to reimburse him, but failed to track him down. This blocked three-way transaction is re-enacted in Lanzer's obsession with enlisting Lieutenant B into the scheme to repay Lieutenant A, an obsession interpreted by Freud as a belated effort to discharge the paternal debt.

Caught in this network of associations, in which rats embody babies, faeces, penises, gifts, disease, and money, Lanzer identifies himself with the "rat-currency" itself. Instead of sending money through the postal system, he devises an elaborate plan to dispatch his own person through the mazes of the railway system, thus transforming himself into a circulating rat. His identification with his phobic animal stems in part from his fantasy about applying the rat-torture to his loved ones.

Lanzer tells Freud that the "cruel Captain" had no sooner delivered his gruesome punchline than "the idea flashed though my mind *that this was happening to a person who was very dear to me*," namely his fiancée (SE 10:167). Under Freud's cross-examination, Lanzer also confesses to entertaining the idea of his father undergoing the rat-punishment. Soon afterwards Freud is shocked to discover that this father, who plays such a lively part in the Rat Man's fantasy-life, has already been dead for many years. During a visit to his father's grave, the Rat Man had once spotted a rat, and had imagined the creature feasting on the paternal corpse – like the obese gray rat that catches Bloom's beady eye in Glasnevin cemetery.[46] Imagining that rats eat human corpses, Lanzer himself admits to having bitten people as a little boy, thus revealing a ratty tendency to cannibalism.[47]

Rattiest of all are his obsessive thoughts. His associative mazes resemble the "rat-runs" of the kinaesthetic rat, driven by muscle-memory through the same passageways. However, the rat-punishment involves penetration from below, whereas Lanzer's idée fixe originates in penetration from above: the Captain's cruel words bored into his ear, as opposed to Mirbeau's rats, which bore into the anus. Lanzer's obsession therefore involves a reversal of the upper and the lower body, in which the rats that rush into his rectum symbolize the cruel ideas that swarm into his mind.[48] Raped by words, poisoned through the ear like Hamlet's father, the Rat Man prolongs this aural punishment by submitting to analysis with Freud, whom he symptomatically addresses as "Captain." If the original "cruel" Captain drove the rats into the patient's mind, Freud assumes the task of the Pied Piper who must drive them out again. Yet both these "captains" invade the patient's ear, rather than his rectum, alternately filling and emptying his mind of rats.

THE RAT IN THE TEXT

As the previous summary has indicated, Lanzer's rat-phobia originates in a piece of fiction, as opposed to a real encounter with the animal. Two works of literature, *The Torture Garden* and *Little Eyolf*, feature prominently in the case. Meanwhile Freud, who notes the "positively epic character" of the Rat Man's deliria, interweaves his text with literary allusions – to Goethe's *Faust*, Shakespeare's *Julius Caesar*, and Dumas's *The Count of Monte-Cristo*.[49] It is striking that these references to literary rats are often relegated to the footnotes – those underground passageways connecting Freud's writing to the rat-infested catacombs of intertextuality.

These allusions suggest that the Rat Man's fixation originates in literature, and his release depends on the same source, for Freud uses literature to unbind his patient's associative knots. In some of these literary texts, rats themselves perform the service of unbinding: for instance, Freud footnotes a passage in Goethe's *Faust* in which Mephistopheles conjures up a rat to break through a door fastened by a magic pentagram.[50] A similar service is accomplished by rats in Poe's story "The Pit and the Pendulum," where the rats in the dungeon gnaw through the ropes in which the prisoner is bound. Both these works invest the rat with the power to break through barriers, a power suggested by the etymology of the verb "to rat," an archaic meaning of which is "to break up" or "to drive apart."

This association with breaking and unbinding has caused the rat to be demonized as the enemy of literature.[51] As Jacques Berchtold points out in his pioneering study of the literary rat, *Des rats et des ratières* ["Rats and Rat-traps"], rats literally devour books, bindings and all. Among Berchtold's examples is *Gargantua and Pantagruel*, where Rabelais complains that rats have eaten the beginning of his book.[52] Racine, on the other hand, instructs his wife to put a little water in the bookcase to prevent the rats and mice from devouring his library.[53] Later Gerard de Nerval expresses pity for the rats that have gobbled up his uncle's books, since the poet has also overeaten "cette nourriture indigeste ou malsaine pour l'âme." The rat, with its insatiable appetite for print, threatens to destroy the entire heritage of book-learning, reducing literature to an ephemeral, comestible materiality. Worse than the destruction of the library of Alexandria by fire is the prospect of human knowledge slowly disappearing into the belly of a rat.[54]

"Rat" is an anagram of "art," a coincidence exploited by Hugh Sykes Davies in *The Papers of Andrew Melmoth*, where the eponymous scientist, committed to explaining rat behavior to human beings, ultimately rats on his own species, and ends up in the sewers explaining human behavior to an audience of rats.[55] Before joining forces with the rats, however, Melmoth enjoys a brief flirtation with a human female, enlivened by the fact that he talks only about rats, whereas she talks only about art. "He knew about rats: she did not. She knew about art: he did not. Nothing could have been fairer, or more useful to the hastening of their better acquaintance."[56] The word "art," as Berchtold points out, derives from the Latin verb "to fit," while the word "text" derives from the Latin word for web. These etymologies suggest that art and texts are webs or networks, composed by joining, weaving, knotting, fitting. The rat is the force that decomposes these connections, unweaving webs, untying texts, unraveling networks; the rat stands for the tendency to deconstruction endemic to the labor of construction. In this sense the rat represents the other of art, the other of writing, endlessly unbinding that which art and writing bind together. In much the same way, Freudian psychoanalysis weaves and unweaves the "intricate network of our world of thought" (SE 5:525); indeed, "analysis" literally means loosening, unbinding – a ratty enterprise indeed.[57]

In the library episode of *Ulysses* Stephen Dedalus, in an unacknowledged borrowing from Pater, proposes that the artist is forever weaving
and unweaving his own image.[58] The implication is that the renewal of the
artist's image depends on its serial disintegration: "Molecules all change. I
am other I now" (*U* 159–60:376–78, 156:205), Stephen thinks. As weaving
depends on unweaving, so artworks could be said to depend on ratworks,
on the counterforces of unbinding, undermining, deconstruction built
into the creative process. For this reason rats and ratworks are treated
with mixed feelings in modernist texts, the conventional disgust for the
animal competing with reluctant recognitions of affinity. In Kafka's "The
Burrow," for example, written in 1923, the writer assumes the voice of a
paranoid rodent – rat, mole, or groundhog – digging himself into a subterranean network of tunnels (comparable to Stephen Dedalus's network
of navelcords), which he struggles to protect against the probing "muzzle"
of an unknown animal. This rhizomatic burrow has been interpreted as
an image of the mind, the womb, and earthly life, but it also represents
the mazes of the literary work itself, always threatened with invasion by
the muzzle of the reader.

If Kafka associates writing with burrowing, Beckett associates it with
the rattish art of boring holes in language:

As we cannot eliminate language all at once, we should at least leave nothing
undone that might contribute to its falling into disrepute. To bore one hole after
another in it, until what lurks behind it – be it something or nothing – begins to
seep through; I cannot imagine a higher goal for a writer today.[59]

To bore holes in language is to write like a rat, mining words with portals
to a wordless hinterland. Beckett's Watt (whose name sounds like a lisp-
ing form of "rat") totters on the brink of such a hinterland when he finds
that names refuse to stick to things: "And Watt's need of semantic succour
was at times so great that he would set to trying names on things, and on
himself, almost as a woman hats." Deserted by words, Watt anticipates a
final silence when the last rats will abandon the sinking ship of language:

For after these there would be no more rats, not a rat left, and there were times
when Watt almost welcomed this prospect, of being rid of his last rats, at last. It
would be lonely, to be sure, at first, and silent, after the gnawing, the scurrying,
the little cries. (79–81)

In this passage, the "last rats" seem to represent the noise of language, the
sounds left over when the sense is gone: "the gnawing, the scurrying, the
little cries."

Jean-Michel Rabaté has pointed out that Watt's state of linguistic dereliction harks back to Hofmannsthal's famous "Letter of Lord Chandos."[60] In 1902 the Viennese writer Hugo von Hofmannsthal composes a letter in German, supposedly written in 1603 by Philip Chandos, a young English gentleman of letters to his patron, Francis Bacon, in which the letter-writer confesses with dazzling eloquence to his inability to write.[61] Usually interpreted as Hofmannsthal's renunciation of lyric poetry, the Chandos letter begins by evoking the linguistic plenitude the writer feels that he has lost: "To me there was no difference between drinking warm foaming milk which a tousled rustic at my hunting lodge had squeezed into a wooden bucket from the udder of a fine, mild-eyed cow, and drinking in sweet and frothy spiritual nourishment from an old book as I sat in the window seat of my study." This world without separation, permeated with maternal imagery, resembles the Lacanian imaginary. But this Edenic world has fallen, and the milk of language soured into poison: "the abstract words which the tongue must enlist as a matter of course in order to bring out an opinion disintegrated in my mouth like rotten mushrooms." With the collapse of abstractions comes a swarm of disconnected objects (perhaps an allusion to Baconian empiricism), in which things can no longer be contained by thought: "Everything came to pieces, the pieces broke into more pieces, and nothing could be encompassed by one idea." Language falls apart, leaving only "isolated words"; these "swam about me; they turned into eyes that stared at me and into which I had to stare back, dizzying whirlpools which spun around and around and led into the void."

At the end of the letter, these swarming words are replaced by a vision of the dying rats that Chandos has ordered to be poisoned in the milk cellar:

suddenly this cellar unrolled inside me, filled with the death throes of the pack of rats. It was all there. The cool and musty cellar air, full of the sharp, sweetish smell of the poison, and the shrilling of the death cries echoing against mildewed walls. Those convulsed clumps of powerlessness, those desperations colliding with one another in confusion … A mother was there, whose dying young thrashed about her. But she was not looking at those in their death agonies … but off into space, or through space into the infinite, and gnashing her teeth …[62]

Since Chandos associates milk with language before the fall, these rats could be seen as the destroyers of the word, raiders of the milk cellars of language. Chandos's vision of the rats in their death throes echoes his earlier vision of the whirling words that turn into eyes and stare into the void. In a similar way, the mother rat gazes into the void, heedless of the writhing torments of her young. In Kleinian terms, this mother rat might be seen as the bad breast, the monstrous double of the frothy breast of mother language.

Lord Chandos professes his sense of a "vast empathy, a streaming across into those creatures."[63] Yet his letter's rhetorical exuberance betrays an unacknowledged pleasure in the bloodbath. One could imagine the writer making this confession with the same mixed feelings expressed by the Rat Man when he tells Freud about the rat-punishment: "At all the important moments while [the patient] was telling his story," Freud reports, "his face took on a very strange, composite expression. I could only interpret it as one of *horror at pleasure of his own of which he himself was unaware*" (SE 10:166–67). Lord Chandos's empathy is also belied by the fact that it was he who commanded the rat-massacre, yet he identifies himself with his own victims as he contemplates their monstrous fate: "I tell you, my friend, this was in me, and Carthage in flames too …"[64]

Like Chandos, Beckett alternates between empathy and sadism in his treatment of both living and literary rats. On one occasion, according to his biographer James Knowlson, Beckett was staying on a farm whose owners discovered a rat and were about to kill it. "Beckett rushed to intervene, picking the rat up and running across a field to let it run free into a ditch."[65] Beckett leads his readers to expect the same tenderness from Watt and his chum Sam, whose favorite pastime is feeding the water-rats, as if they shared Chandos's "vast empathy" for this abominated species. Defying such expectations, however, Watt and Sam conclude their ritual by feeding the plump young rats to their own parents.[66] According to Mary Bryden, Beckett's ambivalence towards rats also manifests itself in his alternation between English and French, the latter language being less "rattist" than the former. In her essay "Rats in and around Beckett," Bryden revisits the vexed theological question, raised at the beginning of *Watt*, as to what should be done with a rat that eats the consecrated host. As Bryden points out, the manuscript of *Watt* contains a much longer and funnier riff on this dilemma, which becomes the subject of a dissertation by a young seminarian, Matthew McGilligan. In his oral examination McGilligan urges that the offending rat should be "pursued with all the vigour of the Canon Laws and pontifical decrees." When caught, however, the rat should not be buried, because the Real Body would be buried with him. However, if the host is removed from the rat's body, should it be consumed at once or restored to the ciborium? The answer depends on whether the rat has already "done its doolies," and McGilligan is on the point of proposing that the rat's faeces should be eaten when his disquisition is cut short by his superiors, who dispatch him on a holiday to Rome.

This satire of theological dispute reveals Beckett's allegiance to the impious rat, since the satirist also reduces the Blessed Sacrament to doolies. If Beckett takes sides with the hypothetical rat, however, Joyce fears this creature as a menace to his writing. Regarding rats as "bad luck," Joyce was so superstitious in the days preceding the publication of *Ulysses* that he fainted when a friend drew his attention to a rat (*JJ* 517). Thus Joyce, like Beckett, conceives of rats as saboteurs of writing, but Joyce abhors them whereas Beckett sympathizes with them, which is symptomatic of these writers' differences as modernists. For Joyce aims to fatten the library of Western culture, whereas Beckett aims to thin it, gnaw it down.

THE RAT IN THE WASTE LAND

The "last rats" in *Watt* represent the remnants of a dying language, their "little cries" the sonic trash left over when the world, in Watt's words, has "become unspeakable."[67] Similarly, the collapse of language in the *Letter of Lord Chandos* culminates in the dying cries of poisoned rats, where human speech is extinguished in the gnashing of teeth. In Eliot's *The Waste Land*, rats are also associated with an asemantic, pre- or postlinguistic noise, a form of acoustic refuse comparable to the whistling of Kafka's burrow, or to the scuffling of the "last rats" in *Watt*. In *The Waste Land*, this noise is described as a "rattle" – a pun that seems to generate or to be generated by the rats themselves.[68]

The first reference to rats occurs in "A Game of Chess," with the allusion to "rats' alley" where "the dead men lost their bones" (lines 115–16). When the rats reappear in "The Fire Sermon," it is as if they had been summoned by the "rattle" of the dead men's bones:

> But at my back in a cold blast I hear
> The rattle of the bones, and chuckle spread from ear to ear.
>
> A rat crept softly through the vegetation
> Dragging its slimy belly on the bank
> While I was fishing in the dull canal
> On a winter evening round behind the gashouse
> Musing upon the king my brother's wreck
> And on the king my father's death before him.
> White bodies naked on the low damp ground

> And bones cast in a little low dry garret,
> Rattled by the rat's foot only, year to year.[69]

Here it is assonance, rather than meaning, that links the rattle to the rat; semantic connections are subordinated to contagion between sounds. It is appropriate that rats, in view of their long-standing association with disease, should carry this acoustic contagion.

Curiously this rat-borne plague of rattling spreads beyond *The Waste Land*, resurfacing in other works of modernism. A rattle, for example, announces the aged corpse-chewing rat of the "Hades" episode of *Ulysses* – "Rtststr! A rattle of pebbles. Wait. Stop! … An obese grey rat toddled along the side of the crypt … " (*U* 94.970–73). In Wyndham Lewis's novel *The Apes of God* (1930), a decadent Jew called Ratner, who describes his split self as "a rat caught in a rat trap," produces a "rattle" on the rare occasions that he rises out of bed. Ratner's typewriter rattles too, which suggests that Lewis conceives of writing as ratting or becoming-rat, a means of rat-ification.[70]

In the lines from *The Waste Land* quoted above, the rattle of the rats frames the lines from *The Tempest* musing on the death of kings, fathers, and brothers. This juxtaposition aligns the rat with the death-rattle of the patriarchal order. In these lines Shakespeare himself, the father of English literature, is reduced to "the rattle of the bones," the hollow echo of exhumed quotations. Meanwhile the rat that drags its slimy belly on the bank evokes the belated modernist poet, raiding the bank of the already-written. Yet instead of coming back to life, like sons and fathers in *The Tempest*, the bones of tradition are merely pestered by the raiding parasites of modernism: "rattled by the rat's foot only, year by year." The rats of *The Waste Land* connote the waste of inspiration, the garbage of signification, the "rattle" left over when the sense is gone – "the gnawing, the scurrying, the little cries."

Eliot's poem "Burbank with a Beidecker, Bleistein with a Cigar" (1920) offers a preview of the rat-infested waste land:

> The rat is underneath the piles.
> The Jew is underneath the lot.

In this couplet there is neither a logical nor a grammatical link between the rat of the first line and the Jew of the second; all that yokes them is adjacency, along with the syntactical echo between the lines. This technique of piling image upon image, omitting discursive connections, is the trademark of Imagist poetry: the most famous example, Pound's "In a Station of the Metro," juxtaposes faces with petals much as "Burbank" juxtaposes rats with Jews. In Pound's poem, however, the journey underneath the surface of the city transforms the ordinary into something rich and strange, but the reverse occurs in "Burbank," where the lofty "piles" of civilization mask the vermin hidden "underneath the lot." This preposition "underneath" suggests the furtive as well as the foundational, while "the lot" means either everything (the whole) or almost nothing (a vacant lot or urban wasteland). "Piles" is an equally elastic term, referring either to majestic buildings or to wooden stakes; it could also refer to piles of garbage, dear to rats, and reminiscent of the "heap of broken images" of which *The Waste Land* is composed.[71] Nor could a further meaning have escaped a poet who suffered agonies from hemorrhoids: "Whatever you do ... avoid piles," Eliot advised a friend, after a painful operation to remove his own.[72] With this usage in mind, the word "underneath" – used twice in "Burbank," along with two uses of the preposition "under" – suggests a preoccupation with the body's underparts, as well as with the city's underside, and the notion that the rat is underneath the piles harks back to the anal punishment imagined in *The Torture Garden*.

The Nazi propaganda movie *Der Ewige Jude* ("The Eternal Jew") (1940) also employs juxtaposition or montage to insinuate a likeness between rats and Jews. By juxtaposing shots of crowded Jews with those of rats swarming out of sewers, the movie intimates that Jews, like rats, are "underneath the lot," both teeming from an excremental underworld. As the voice-over declares, "rats are cunning, cowardly, and cruel, and are found mostly in large packs. Among the animals, they represent the rudiment of an insidious and underground destruction, just like the Jews among human beings."[73] This fantasy of "an insidious and underground destruction" resurfaces in the image of the modernist rat, as well as in its human avatars – the Jew, the migrant, and the overcrowded poor.

This chapter has attempted to map the modernist anxieties evoked by the figure of the rat. There are the rats that tunnel underneath the city, infesting the charnel alleys of modernity; the rats that bore into the anus like avenging faeces in *The Torture Garden*; the rats that carry vampirism from the atavistic East into the arteries of modern capitalism; the rats that feed on books, sabotaging the dominion of the word, and reducing meaning to "concatenated words from which the sense seemed gone," to the rattle of exhausted signifiers. Revenants from the dark ages, rats assume the role of foreign bodies in the mazes of modernity, both alien and ineradicable. Eroding oppositions between tame and wild, old and new, strange and contemptibly familiar, rats augur the breakdown of barriers, whether semantic, geographical, corporeal, or architectural. Identified with networks, rats are associated with rhizomatic ramification, as opposed to arboreal development. The next chapter of this book examines how such networks operate in Henry James's novel *The Ambassadors*.

CHAPTER 3

Strandentwining cables: Henry James's
The Ambassadors

A rich American businessman falls into conversation in a New York bar with a distant acquaintance of his prodigal son, who has fled to Italy to become a painter. The father, knowing his son is talentless, wants him to come home and embark on a sensible career. On a sudden whim, the father asks the young man in the bar to retrieve his son, little suspecting that his envoy is a conman in the making. This envoy, delighted at the opportunity to escape his current entanglements, sails to Italy, where he falls in love with the businessman's handsome son and soon abandons any effort to restore him to his family. At first the son welcomes this new companion, inviting him to share his home, but his manner cools after catching his guest trying on his own expensive clothes. The conman, humiliated by the son's rejection, murders him. He then takes over the son's identity, wearing his clothes, cashing his cheques, and talking his Italian, even to the point of mutilating the subjunctives.

Just before the businessman dispatches his son's murderer-to-be to Italy, he asks the young man whether he has read Henry James's novel *The Ambassadors*. Patricia Highsmith scarcely needed to call attention to the similarity between James's novel and *The Talented Mr. Ripley* (1955), the plot of which is summarized above. Like Highsmith's Tom Ripley, Lambert Strether goes to Europe to retrieve a wayward New England son, but becomes so entranced with the young man's Bohemian existence that he is sorely tempted to take his place. Highsmith's novel offers a counterfactual version of *The Ambassadors*. What if Strether had identified with Chad Newsome to such an extreme that the ambassador resorted to murder in order to usurp the young man's life? *The Ambassadors* explores the interpsychic battleground between identities, in which the self is constantly at risk of being taken over by the thoughts and desires of the other.

In a Notebook entry of 17 February 1894, James considers the possibility of writing about "a *liaison*, suspected, but of which there is no proof but [the] transfusion of some idiosyncrasy of one party to the being of another …" This notion of "transfusion," producing an "exchange or conversion" between lovers, provides the germ of James's most explicitly vampiric novel, *The Sacred Fount* (1901).[1] In this work, the unnamed narrator suspects two couples of undergoing a clandestine interchange of wit and youthfulness respectively; a dull man grows brighter as his suspected lover grows duller; a wife grows younger as her husband grows older or "doriangrayer" – to borrow Joyce's neologism for a comparable transference (*FW* 186:8). In *The Sacred Fount*, it is impossible to judge the validity of the narrator's increasingly baroque imaginings, since these are unrelieved by any alternative perspective. Finally his hostess, having listened to his lucubrations to the end, simply dismisses him as crazy.[2]

This baffling novel received harsh reviews, including a withering swipe from Rebecca West, and James excluded it from the New York edition of his works.[3] But the notion of transfusion, the surreptitious "transfer" of physical or psychic qualities, recurs in much of James's major fiction.[4] As many readers have observed, the narrator of *The Sacred Fount* resembles the unnamed narrators of *The Turn of the Screw* (1898) and *In the Cage* (1898), in their obsession with covert transferences between others. In *The Ambassadors* (1903), Lambert Strether assumes the role of the obsessive onlooker, investigating the "conversion or exchange" between Chad Newsome and his older mistress Madame de Vionnet. Strether observes that Chad has aged, the young man's hair having turned a distinguished gray, whereas his mistress's "air of youth" is "almost disconcerting" (*A* 127). Chad has also benefited from a transfusion of metropolitan sophistication, so potent as to render him in Strether's eyes "a case of transformation unsurpassed" (*A* 90). By the end of the novel, Chad and Strether have virtually changed places, intimating that Strether himself has partaken of the interpsychic transference that he imputed to the lovers. Indeed it is Strether who undergoes a permanent "conversion" of identity, whereas Chad reverts to his stout-calved provinciality.

James's notion of interpersonal "conversion or exchange" bears an intriguing resemblance to the Freudian concept of transference. The difference is that Freudian transference usually denotes the self's projections onto others, whereas Jamesian "transfusion" refers to the other's invasion of the self. One symptom of this transfusion is the coalescence of voices in James's later novels, where there is little to distinguish one speaker from another, in terms of intonation, diction, or other vocal peculiarities. It is only when intimacies weaken that the parties reassert their verbal tics: in *The Golden Bowl*, for instance, Adam Verver talks "American" on the verge of separation from his daughter Maggie, when his decision to return to American City is heralded by a volley of "I-guesses."

Yet this decision is an idea that Maggie has put into her father's head, while persuading him to take the credit for it. As Sharon Cameron has observed, thinking in James occurs between subjects, not within their minds, which are possessed by, rather than possessed of, consciousness.[5] Strether describes consciousness as a "helpless jelly" poured into the mould of life, and held there "more or less compactly" (*A* 132). But James breaks this mould, allowing the jelly to ooze between the characters. In the first half of *The Golden Bowl*, consciousness circulates between Charlotte, Fanny, and the Prince, but in the second half invests itself entirely in Maggie, leaving its former anchors in the lurch. In Maggie's case, thinking takes form of telepathy and vampirism; not only does she suck up every consciousness into her own, but she uses other characters to "speak her mind," putting words into their mouths like a ventriloquist.

In James's world you "never know whose thoughts you're chewing," as Leopold Bloom ruminates in *Ulysses* (*U* 140.707–08). This is because James presents his characters as vehicles of transference, animated by an interpersonal, nomadic consciousness. In *The Turn of the Screw*, for instance, Miles dies when "his little heart, dispossessed, had stopped," which implies that his life depends on the ghost's possession of his soul.[6] Yet even in James's ostensibly ghost-free novels, characters find themselves possessed by the living rather than the dead, haunted by the consciousness of others. "It is a question of 'coming over to where they are,'" James writes of the children coming over to the ghosts in *The Turn of the Screw*.[7] Desire is a question of coming over to the other's place; erotic relations are determined by geometry, specifically by changing places with a double or rival.

The poet Mallarmé once described himself as a "*syntaxier*," which implies that relations between words matter more than words themselves.[8] Similarly James could be described as a syntaxer of love, whose sexual combinations are determined by a grammar of relations, rather than by any personal endowments of the characters. This grammar has a certain "give" to it; characters may rearrange themselves like parts of speech, altering the syntax of the sentence, but they accrue identity from their positions, from "whereness" rather than from "whoness," to borrow Joyce's coinages (*U* 323:400). The crazed intricacy of James's sentence structure, with clause piled upon dependent clause, repeats at the level of syntax the networks of dependency delineated in the plots, in which desire is a matter of identifying with another desirer.

What is striking about these networks is the frequent absence of their central element. In *The Awkward Age* (1899), the heroine Nanda Brookenham rarely appears, yet she becomes "the most discussed animal in the universe" – to borrow Virginia Woolf's assessment of the species "Woman."[9] Largely excluded from the action, all of which consists of talk, Nanda performs a function comparable to the navel of the Freudian dream, in that she provides the central gap that draws the other filaments into entanglement. Magnetized by her absence, her friends and relations endlessly exchange their views about exchanging Nanda on the marriage market. Similarly, the unnamed Master in *The Turn of the Screw* vacates the chain of command, delegating his authority to the unnamed governess, and his absence instigates the transference of power and desire between the governess, the children, and the ghosts. In *The Wings of the Dove*, it is Milly Theale who gradually absents herself from the intrigues she inspires, disappearing from the novel long before her death. Yet her power waxes as her presence wanes; her posthumous letter to Densher, never opened and hurled by Kate into the flames, drives a wedge between the scheming lovers. Henceforth the loss of this unread letter, as opposed to its possession, becomes the object of Densher's anguished fetishism, superseding every human love.

Adam Verver in *The Golden Bowl* occupies a similar position to the Master in *The Turn of the Screw*, in that Verver bankrolls the traffic of desire while supposedly remaining ignorant of its transgressions. As the characters conspire to preserve his blindness, a virtual taboo descends over his name: "no other name was to be spoken," Maggie wordlessly cautions Fanny Assingham when the latter's questions spiral in on Adam Verver (*GB* 521). Earlier the Prince refrains from naming Verver in the interest of protecting his lover Charlotte (or so Maggie intuits): "To name her father … would be to do the impossible thing, to do neither more nor less than give Charlotte away" (*GB* 440).[10] Here the expression "give … away" punningly gives away the outcome of the novel, when Charlotte is forced to assume her position as a bride rather than a mistress, "given away" to her legal spouse. Yet this "high transaction" (*GB* 478), as James ironically describes it, depends on the presumed unconsciousness of Adam Verver. It is as if the seat of power has to be vacated in order to kick-start this nefarious game of musical chairs.

In *The Awkward Age*, Nanda's absence gives rise to the formation of a network, an improvised community sustained by gossip, and particularly by the drive to know what Nanda knows.[11] Does she know that Vanderbank, the man she loves, has been offered a fortune by Mr.

Longdon to marry her? And does she know that Vanderbank cannot propose because he knows she knows too much, not just about this sordid
bribery but everything that eligible maidens should not know, or show
they know, if their minders are to capitalize on their innocence in the
marriage market? This obsession with knowing what other people know,
as Peter Brooks has pointed out, resembles the phenomenon that Freud
describes as "epistemophilia," which could be defined as the sexualized
search for knowledge.[12] Freud introduces this term in the case history of
the Rat Man, which argues that "the thought-process itself becomes sexualized, for the sexual pleasure which is normally attached to the content
of thought becomes shifted on to the act of thinking itself …" (SE 10:245).
In James's late fiction, sexual excitement is displaced not only onto thinking, but onto thinking other people's thoughts. For this reason critics
who arraign James for excluding sexuality from his "cathedrals of frosted
glass" are looking for sex in the wrong place. If "darkest James" is "a land
where the vices have no bodies and the passions no blood, where nobody
sins because nobody has anything to sin with," this is because sexuality has shifted from the body to the gropings of the mind, pervading
the tender passions of attention and curiosity.[13] Usually there is "nothing"
to know, despite the frenzied conjectures of the characters, or else the
enigma turns out to be banal, a predictable affair of sex and money, much
as the intricacies of the Freudian dream boil down to Oedipal desire, or
the Marxian superstructure boils down to economics. In James, knowledge owes its whole allure to the fantasy that it belongs to someone else.
Jamesian knowledge, like Jamesian desire, is necessarily vicarious and
secondhand, a matter of identifying with another knower or desirer.[14] The
object of knowledge, like the object of desire, circulates between the characters, forming conspiracies between those "in the know."

In this transferential world, it is impossible to mind one's own business, or even to possess a mind or business of one's own. The processes of
transference override the boundaries of personal identity, implicating all
the characters in interpsychic networks of exchange. Within these networks, knowledge, money, and desire come to function as interchangeable currencies, through a process of metaphorical contagion epitomized
in James's puns. Foremost among these puns is the word "knowledge"
itself, freighted as it is with biblical innuendoes.[15] Another crucial pun is
"interest," a term embracing the economic, sexual, and epistemological
dimensions of these works. Interest, which means attraction, concern, or
curiosity, may also denote a business, a stake in a financial enterprise,
or the gains accrued from an investment. The insistent repetition of the

term "interest" in James's later prose, together with such terms as "saving," "value," and "appreciation," which waver between moral, sexual, aesthetic, and financial meanings, hints at the sinister complicity between these spheres of action.[16]

It is "interest" that induces "speculation," another multivalent term that encompasses the principal activities of James's world – looking, wondering, and gambling.[17] Speculation, in the financial sense, produces American millionaires, but the sources of their fortunes tend to be occluded: Christopher Newman admits to having manufactured washtubs in the early novel *The American* (1877), but the "nameless article" responsible for the Newsomes' wealth is never identified in *The Ambassadors*, nor are the origins of the Theale fortune in *The Wings of the Dove* (1902), or the Verver fortune in *The Golden Bowl* (1904). In these late novels, set in Europe, the economic side of speculation remains invisible, relegated to the western side of the Atlantic, but the speculations of the gossips stand in for the speculations that produced their wealth, the risks of guesswork mirroring the risks of finance. Meanwhile the enigmas of the narratives pique the "interest" of James's readers, instigating the speculative gossip that goes by the name of literary criticism.

In late James, it is the absence of the source of money, knowledge, and desire that sustains the speculative interchange between the characters. The most conspicuous absence in these late novels is that of Mrs. Newsome in *The Ambassadors*. The remainder of the present chapter examines how her occlusion from the scene of action gives rise to representation, in both the political and the aesthetic senses of the term. As we shall see, Mrs. Newsome's withdrawal from the novel corresponds to Foucault's conception of the decline of sovereignty, while her networks of representation, including her functionaries, telegrams, and paper-trails, suggest the proliferation of bureaucracies.[18] According to Foucault, the sovereign is "a fantastic personage, both archaic and monstrous," a preposterous fetish left over from a former age. In today's world, power no longer descends from such a lofty center of authority, but branches out in every direction into the rhizomatic networks of modernity. In Paris, still echoing with references to the Terror, Strether bloodlessly beheads his sovereign, asserting the independence of the representative from the original. Yet his own representations also go astray, insofar as Strether misinterprets what he sees, clinging to a deceptive picture of reality. In *The Ambassadors*, it is Strether, rather than his author, who excludes the "literal, vulgar" fact of sex from his cathedrals of frosted glass, and yet this blind spot transforms sex itself into something much more "various and multifold."[19]

"I felt a good deal of despair after "The Ambassadors" were launched, & said to myself "what <can> be expected for a novel with a hero of 55, & properly no heroine at all?" – Letter from James to Mrs. Humphrey Ward, 16 December 1903[20]

It is true that there is "properly no heroine at all" in *The Ambassadors*. But Mrs. Newsome's absence looms over the narrative, growing more oppressive than the presence of other contenders for the role of heroine. The *deus absconditus* of the novel, Mrs. Newsome never enters the narrative directly, yet it is from her empty place that messengers and messages proliferate.[21] In a famous passage from the "Project" for *The Ambassadors*, James writes:

lively element as [Mrs. Newsome] is in the action, we deal with her presence and personality only as an affirmed influence, only in their deputed, represented form; and nothing, of course, can be more artistically interesting than such a little problem as to make her always out of it, yet always *of* it, always absent, yet always felt. (*A* 380)

Mrs. Newsome's absence instigates the transatlantic commerce of the novel, the network of representatives that branches out of Woollett, Massachusetts. The fact that Mrs. Newsome is a writer as well as a tyrant, who sends forth both letters and ambassadors, implies an analogy between these forms of representation. In the political domain, representation involves the delegation of authority, in this case to ambassadors enjoined to represent the moral and financial interests of their native land, where American Puritanism bolsters American rapacity. In the aesthetic domain, representation implies that the work of art reflects a prior, exterior reality, just as the linguistic signifier supposedly reflects the signified.[22] *The Ambassadors* contrasts the harsh light of Woollett, Massachusetts, where the myth of faithful representation reigns unchallenged, to the ambiguous light of Paris, where such fidelity surrenders to the play of "difference" – a word that echoes through the novel and its multiple addenda, including the project, the preface, and the postscripts scattered through James's correspondence. The novel questions the possibility of "faithful" representation, whether in politics or in art, by showing how the representative necessarily betrays the represented and embarks on dangerous liaisons of its own.

In his correspondence James draws attention to his own resemblance to his hero, Lambert Strether, the unfaithful representative of Mrs.

Newsome, and most readers have accepted this affinity. But the fact that Mrs. Newsome, the "moral swell" of Woollett, appears only through her writing, the letters and telegrams with which she bombards her ambassadors, identifies her with her own creator (*A* 52). "Always out of it, yet always felt," she resembles Flaubert's conception of the ideal artist, "présent partout, et visible nulle part."[23] In this sense James's authorship corresponds to Mrs. Newsome's devolved authority: both rely on representation to implement their will, yet both find their power compromised by the waywardness of their "deputed, represented" surrogates. As Mrs. Newsome loses control of her ambassadors, so James's characters stray from his initial plans, particularly Maria Gostrey, who refuses to remain a sounding board for Strether's confidences and asserts her independent claim to "something of the dignity of a prime idea" (*A* 13). James remarks that representation entails an "inevitable deviation," the "exquisite treachery even of the straightest execution" or "the most mature plan" (*A* 14). *The Ambassadors* traces this "exquisite treachery," demonstrating how the representative inevitably strays from the original.

Mrs. Newsome sends forth two delegations to Paris, a doubling typical of the "strange logic" of this text, whose episodes tend to repeat or re-present themselves (*A* 60). First Strether is dispatched to disentangle Chad from the toils of a French adulteress. Chad has ignored his mother's orders to return to Woollett, Massachusetts, where he is expected to take over the family business, "the manufacture of some small, convenient, homely" article of domestic use, too vulgar to be named (*A* 380). Frequently invoked but never identified, this nameless article becomes the funniest of the lacunae scattered through the text to taunt the reader with the promise of an ultimate unveiling.[24] On his way to Paris, Strether pauses in Chester to meet up with his old friend Waymarsh, a self-appointed ambassador for plainspoken America, who opposes a swamp-like resistance to Strether's imaginative flights. In Chester Strether also meets Maria Gostrey, a different kind of American ambassador who describes herself as an "agent for repatriation" (*A* 35), fated to save Americans for America. "I'm a general guide – to 'Europe,' don't you know?" she says. "I wait for people – I put them through. I pick them up – I set them down. I'm a sort of superior 'courier-maid'" (*A* 26). Miss Gostrey questions Strether about his mission, puzzled as to what he stands to gain, and he divulges that his pay-off, should he succeed in "saving" Chad, would be marriage to Mrs. Newsome, with all the perks.

The Ambassadors could therefore be seen as a middle-aged fairy-tale, an autumnal version of *The American*, the early novel in which the youthful

Christopher Newman set forth to Paris to find himself a bride. In *The Ambassadors*, Strether is the aging knight-errant sent by the princess on a dangerous quest to win her hand in marriage. But the trouble with this questor is that he takes so much pleasure in the journey that he gradually forgets about the prize. Like a Lotus-Eater, Strether temporarily forgets his homeland; the lure of "life," experienced by proxy in the form of Chad, eclipses the lure of profit.

Once in Paris, Strether meets the representatives of Chad some time before he catches up with the original. On his first attempt to confront the wayward son, he encounters an ambassador instead, the enigmatic little Bilham, who is keeping Chad's house "warm" for its absent master (*A* 72). An interloper in James's novel as well as in Chad's house, little Bilham hails from George du Maurier's bestseller *Trilby* (1894), where little Billee, an English artist in Paris, falls in love with the eponymous gamine.[25] It is significant that James's little Bilham makes his first appearance on Chad's balcony, blocking the window into Chad's domain. This liminal position suggests that the representative bars the represented (like the guardian of the law in Kafka's fable "Before the Law"), foreclosing Strether's access to the original. The two ambassadors eye one another, little Bilham "amused at an elderly watcher" and "curious even to see what the elderly watcher would do on finding himself watched" (*A* 69). The spies' eventual encounter is elided in the narrative, because the second book draws abruptly to a close as soon as Strether has crossed the porte-cochère. After a hiatus the rendezvous is represented in the tranquillity of Strether's chronically belated consciousness (*A* 70).

When he finally catches up with Chad, Strether is astonished by the transformation. All the crassness of the Woollett youth, memorable mainly for his "tremendously stout legs" in knickerbockers, has been refined into Parisian suavity (*A* 94). The artist responsible for this transformation turns out to be Madame de Vionnet, whose relationship with Chad is described by little Bilham as a "virtuous attachment" (*A* 112) – an expression whose ambiguity enables Strether to maintain his blindness to the scandalous character of the affair. In general Strether's fondness for ambiguity makes him a poor ambassador for Woollett, with its cut-and-dried morality. "Look here, Strether, quit this," the "massive" Waymarsh urges him. "You're being used for a thing you ain't fit for. People don't take a fine-tooth comb to groom a horse" (*A* 74). (Critics have made similar objections to the fine-toothed subtleties with which James grooms the horse of melodrama, the horse in this case being the "dreadful little old tradition, one of the platitudes of the human comedy, that people's moral scheme *does* break down in Paris," as James writes in the Preface to *The Ambassadors* [*A* 7].) Strether, too fine-toothed to execute his coarse commission, embroiders and procrastinates, unwilling to tear Chad away from the improving influences of the left bank.

Exasperated by Strether's dithering, Mrs. Newsome launches a second delegation, consisting of her daughter Sarah, the spitting image of her mother's absolutism, and Sarah's husband Jim Pocock. In *The American Scene* (1907), based on James's visit to the United States soon after the publication of *The Ambassadors*, the author observes that American women are in "peerless possession" of the social world, commanding the domain of manners and morals, whereas their menfolk are relegated to the business world, out of the question as far as matters of feeling are concerned (*AS* 255).[26] Hence Jim Pocock, representative of the managerial American male, understands neither Sarah's stringency nor Strether's subtlety, but thinks Paris is a great place to spend a weekend: "small and fat and constantly facetious," he "gurgled his joy as they rolled through the happy streets" (*A* 215–16). His wife Sarah, by contrast, is not deceived by any talk of virtuous attachments; to her mind, Chad has been debauched, and Strether has also been corrupted by the enemy. As Miss Barrace, a minor luminary, tells little Bilham at a Paris party: "you come over to convert the savages … and the savages simply convert you!" (Little Bilham remonstrates that the savages have eaten him alive; if he has been converted, it is only into food [*A* 125].)

The double deputation in the novel exemplifies two conflicting styles of interpretation. Sarah champions the principle of single meaning: as Strether tells her, she shuts her eyes to each side of the matter, "in order, whichever side comes up, to get rid of the other" (*A* 281). But Strether falls in love with "difference": what Chad is, or what Chad was, matters less to Strether than Chad's capacity for change and transformation. James insisted that "difference" was both the theme and the purpose of the text: "Difference – difference from what he expected, difference in Chad, difference in everything; and the Difference, I also again say, is what I give" (*A* 390). Difference, for Strether, is the lotus-flower that diverts him from his course and tempts him to forget the way home. As soon as he arrives in Paris, he marvels at "the plenitude of his consciousness of difference" (*A* 60), and difference also has the last word in the novel, when Strether takes leave of Miss Gostrey to return to "a great difference" – and nothing more (*A* 346).

Sarah Pocock, on the other hand, interprets Chad's difference as treachery: in her eyes, her brother has betrayed the values he should represent, and the economy of representation therefore demands his realignment with his mother as urgently as the economy of Woollett does. "To 'save' Chad" (*A* 9) would save the family finances and reputation, but would also reunite the signifier with the signified, saving the principle of faithful representation. Strether, on the other hand, conceives of Chad as a text admitting many possibilities of meaning, and revised by the subtlest of editors: "the new edition of an old book that one has been fond of – revised and amended, brought up to date," in little Bilham's words (*A* 111). From the Woollett perspective, Strether's mission is to read between the lines that Madame de Vionnet has superscribed in order to restore the single meaning of Chad's character. But instead of saving meaning, Strether saves the principle of endless reading, demonstrated by the fact that the only booty he takes home from his adventure is "seventy blazing volumes" of Victor Hugo (*A* 176).

Thus Strether's "only logic" is the logic of loss: "Not, out of the whole affair, to have got anything for myself" (*A* 346). He sacrifices all the women offering themselves to him – Mrs. Newsome, Maria Gostrey, and Marie de Vionnet – for the sake of "little super-sensual hour, a kind of vicarious joy, in that *freedom of another*" (*A* 386). What Strether wants is not a woman, nor even perhaps a man, although the mystery surrounding Chad's sexuality, in the wake of the Wilde trial of 1895, whispers of the love that dare not speak its name.[27] What Strether desires is Chad's desire; he wishes to re-experience the "difference" or polymorphous perversity of youth, but "only in deputed, represented form."[28] He opts for the borrowed rather than the brand-new passion, preferring the vicarious to the direct experience of love. To put it another way, he chooses reading over being, skimming the book of Chad instead of surrendering to the young man's nameless pleasures. In view of Highsmith's rewriting of *The Ambassadors* in *The Talented Mr. Ripley*, it is possible that Strether's preference for reading saves Chad from being murdered; Strether's tolerance for mediation, his enjoyment of experience at one remove, prevents him from supplanting Chad.

Since Strether is identified with reading, it is fitting that he bears a literary name. His given names Lewis Lambert come from Balzac's novel *Louis Lambert*, a relatively flawed example of the master's work, as Miss Gostrey slyly observes (*A* 24). Shorn of the Americanized Lewis, the name Lambert Strether is emblazoned on Mrs. Newsome's Woollett magazine, endowing its editor with his meagre claim to recognition:

His name on the green cover, where he had put it for Mrs. Newsome, expressed him doubtless just enough to make the world – the world as distinguished, both for more and for less, from Woollett – ask who he was … He was Lambert Strether because he was on the cover, whereas it should have been, for anything like glory, that he was on the cover because he was Lambert Strether. (*A* 62)[29]

Thus Strether's identity depends upon the text that literally makes his name. His "one presentable little scrap of an identity" (*A* 51), Strether's editorship of Woollett's magazine aligns him with Madame de Vionnet, who is described by little Bilham as the editor of Chad. Both Strether and Madame de Vionnet are reconstructive editors who revise the Chad they read, enlisting "memory and fancy" to their aid (*A* 320). In a letter to Mrs. Humphrey Ward, James admits that he cannot read a novel without rewriting it: "The novel I can *only* read, I can't read at all!"[30] Similarly Strether cannot help rewriting what he reads in Chad. The irony is that Chad eventually reverts to his previous edition, as if to reaffirm James's conception of his own revisions as the clarification of his original intention. "The act of revision," James writes in the Preface to *The Golden Bowl*, "the act of seeing it again, caused whatever I looked at on any page to flower before me as into the only terms that honourably expressed it … " (*GB* lii). As Jerome McGann has pointed out, this notion of revision corresponds to Chad and Strether and other Jamesian characters, who "change under the pressure of events, but the changes are not essential alterations; they are revelations – clarifications – of what was always and originally true."[31]

Ironically it is Sarah Pocock who endorses James's essentialist conception of revision as the revelation of a latent truth. Indeed she fails to notice or acknowledge that Chad has been revised, dismissing any emendations as insubstantial editorial embroidery. Sarah stands for semantic, as well as moral, fixity. In her conception of the world, there is one law, one meaning, and one truth, dictated by one monarch, Mrs. Newsome, whose invisible gaze can skewer an ambassador across an ocean; Strether suspects that Sarah feels the "fixed eyes of [her] admirable absent mother fairly screw into the flat of her back" (*A* 257). But *The Ambassadors* pursues another form of truth, heterodox and volatile, to which James gives the name of "Paris."

What is Paris? Not so much a geographical location as an energy unbinding identities and definitions. Although Paris designates a place, it is inwardly displaced by its globetrotting inhabitants; note that none of the leading characters in *The Ambassadors* is wholly French. A site of transformation, Paris is most itself when it is least itself and passing into other modes of being:

It hung before [Strether] this morning, the vast bright Babylon, like some huge iridescent object, a jewel brilliant and hard, in which parts were not to be discriminated nor differences comfortably marked. It twinkled and trembled and melted together, and what seemed all surface one moment seemed all depth the next. (*A* 64)[32]

This passage quivers like the city it describes, with "signs and tokens … too thick for prompt discrimination" (*A* 120). Paris, among many connotations, stands for the shimmering surface of the prose itself, and the capacity of signs and tokens to transform appearances.[33] "In the light of Paris," little Bilham says, "one sees what things resemble. That's what the light of Paris always seems to show" (*A* 126). Not what things are – leave that to the Pococks – but the metaphoric possibilities of things. Madame de Vionnet, in her role as ambassador for Paris, embodies this alterity; under her influence the binary oppositions of Woollett twinkle and tremble and melt together. While she also represents the dangerous "*femme du monde*," she scrambles Strether's preconceptions of this "type," reminding him of "Cleopatra in the play, indeed various and multifold. She had aspects, characters, days, nights … She was an obscure person, a muffled person one day, and a showy person, an uncovered person the next" (*A* 160). All surface one moment and all depth the next, her power lies in her ability to differ from herself, and to alter everyone who falls under her spell. She even manages to bring out the Mark Antony in Chad, the epicurean hidden in the "brute" (*A* 381).

Mrs. Newsome, on the other hand, "doesn't admit surprises" (*A* 299). James polarizes the rigid Mrs. Newsome to the morally flexible Miss Gostrey by means of their respective neckwear. Mrs. Newsome's "ruff," which Strether associates with Queen Elizabeth, evokes the strangulating certainties of Woollett, whereas the red ribbon encircling Miss Gostrey's throat exemplifies the principle of difference by transforming "the value of every other item" of her dress (*A* 42–43). Given that French aristocrats after the Terror wore red ribbons round their necks to commemorate the guillotine, Miss Gostrey's choker may also anticipate her doom, the severance of her romance with Strether, yet this very ambiguity enhances the ornament's transvaluation of values.

Mrs. Newsome's "fixed intensity," by contrast, leaves nothing open to interpretation (*A* 250). As Strether tells Miss Gostrey:

"there's no room left; no margin, as it were, for any alteration. She's filled as full, packed as tight, as she'll hold, and if you wish to get anything more or different either out or in – "

   "You've got to make over altogether the woman herself?"

   "What it comes to," said Strether, "is that you've got morally and intellectually to get rid of her." (*A* 300)

Packed with positivities, the text of Mrs. Newsome prohibits all revision, emendation, marginalia: "She's the same," says Strether. "She's more than ever the same" (*A* 345). No prefaces or afterwords for her – they take too long. Woollett wants its meanings fast – as fast as it produces nameless articles. But Strether learns that difference demands the "perpetual postponement" deplored by the avatars of Woollett (*A* 391). To read a text like Paris one must be prepared to wait for the charm of difference to emerge. The first paragraph of *The Ambassadors*, made famous by Ian Watt's meticulous close reading, alludes to a "secret principle" that enables Strether to "wait without disappointment" (*A* 17).[34] The secret principle, in this case, refers to Strether's impulse to prolong the grace of freedom before submitting to the gravity of Waymarsh. From the moment he sets foot in Liverpool, Strether makes a habit of waiting without disappointment, later hinting to Miss Gostrey that waiting is a strategy of reading. Chad's "obscure," Strether says, "and that's why I'm waiting" (*A* 194). The novel grows as dilatory as the hero, practicing what Roland Barthes describes as "the infinite deferment of the signified."[35] James himself advised a friend to read the novel in the same way that Strether reads Paris, taking it "very easily and gently":

read five pages a day – be even as deliberate as that … keep along with it step by step – and then the full charm will come out … I find that the very most difficult thing in the art of the novelist is to give the impression of the real lapse of time, the quantity of time, represented by our few poor phrases and pages, and all the drawing-out the reader can contribute helps a little perhaps the production of that spell. (408)[36]

   The Pococks and the Newsomes could never cope with late James. It is easy to imagine them muttering with F. R. Leavis that "the energy of the 'doing' (and the energy demanded for the reading)" are "disproportionate to the issues" of the text; no doubt they would agree with Arnold Bennett that "the book was not quite worth the great trouble of reading it" (438).[37] It is striking that attacks on *The Ambassadors* tend to be framed in mercenary terms, with critics complaining that the novel is not "worth" the words expended on it. James's prose rejects this "restricted economy," refusing to "save" time or space, or to budget the supply of words to the demands of meaning. Rather than delivering his message wholesale, like an assembly line producing nameless articles, James prolongs the process whereby meanings twinkle, tremble, and melt together in the incessant play of difference upon difference. By identifying Woollett with industrial capitalism, James hints that bourgeois readings collude with bourgeois economics in extorting surplus value from the text without acknowledging the labor of signification. Mrs. Newsome's "interest" lies in meaning, and she concerns herself only with the most efficient way to manufacture and recuperate it. Strether, on the other hand, resists the avarice of meaning: he squanders time and sense away to lose himself in someone else's jouissance. Difference is "only repeatable as difference"; and Strether finds that to interpret the difference in Chad is to relive each lingering moment of his transformation.[38]

The Pococks must have answers. But *The Ambassadors* begins with a question, and the narrative runs on questions as an engine runs on fuel. In the course of his adventure Strether relinquishes his "resolve to simplify," a Woollettian obsession, learning instead to draw a warm circle in which every question "would live ... as nowhere else" (*A* 162, 80). The "most difficult of the questions" has to do with the nature of the virtuous attachment, and this is the only question that cannot be asked (*A* 102). The obvious answer is sex, the open secret that disseminates itself throughout the text in gaps and blanks, such as Miss Barrace's "Oh, oh, oh!" or little Bilham's "Ah, ah, ah!" (*A* 124, 127, 157, 160, 165, 166); these vowels are uttered whenever Strether gets too close to guessing the scandalous truth. It is "tact" that deflects Strether from the facts; tact sustains his questions, postponing the knowledge that would terminate his "trial of curiosity."[39]

"Tact" is James's term for a style of discourse that avoids the vulgar truth, but also circumvents the vulgar falsehood. The Vionnet apartments are the architectural embodiment of tact: "large and open, full of revelations ... of the habit of privacy, the peace of intervals, the dignity of distances and approaches ..." (*A* 145). Private and open, distant and revealed, veiled and unveiled at the same time, this architecture confounds the distinction between depth and surface, secrecy and candor. Its discretion marks the generic distance James has traveled since *The American* of 1877, where the Bellegardes' mansion in St. Germain harbors a melodramatic secret, presenting "to the outer world a face as impassive and as suggestive of the concentration of privacy within as the blank walls of Eastern seraglios." Entered via a "dark, dusty, painted portal," which leads to a graveled court "surrounded on three sides with closed windows," the house of Bellegarde, "all in the shade," reminds Newman of a convent.[40] In Madame de Vionnet's house, by contrast, the orientalist overtones have vanished, along with the allusions to imprisonment of women in convents and seraglios. Chad might be speaking for his lover's house when he declares: "I have no secret – though I may have secrets!" (*A* 142).

The expression "virtuous attachment" epitomizes tact, since this apparent falsehood conceals a deeper truth – the virtue of the education of the senses. Strether shudders at the "want of tact" in Mrs. Newsome's letters, which he charitably imputes to the transatlantic time-lag, her tact having to "reckon with the Atlantic Ocean, the General Post office, and the extravagant curve of the globe" (*A* 109–10). Yet Mrs. Newsome's tactlessness exemplifies the Woollett ethic of interpretation, which demands that words should represent their meanings unequivocally, just as ambassadors should represent their leader. In opposition to this ethic, *The Ambassadors* reverses the traditional relation between the representation and its source, in which the former is regarded as the parasite, the latter as the host. Instead Mrs. Newsome, supposedly the host, is described as a neurasthenic invalid, whose decrepitude entails her parasitical dependence on her delegates. The implication is that the source is powerless without the supplement, the dictator without the deputy, the referent without the sign.

Representation both enforces and diminishes the power of its source, in that the representative extends the presence of the represented but also undermines the latter's self-sufficiency. As soon as there is representation there is betrayal, "exquisite treachery," because it is impossible to overcome the "residuum of difference" between the origin and its derivatives (*A* 21). In *The Ambassadors*, this treacherous residuum takes the gigantic form of the Atlantic Ocean. Once across this ocean, an epistemological as well as an aqueous divide, Mrs. Newsome's suitor and her son betray the cause they are supposed to represent, and their waywardness implies that the tyrant can no longer delimit the effects of a decentralized and transferential form of power. Set loose from Mrs. Newsome, the characters become ambassadors to one another, and power ricochets between them, centerless and aleatory. They think, act, speak, desire on behalf of one another, relaying messages, instructions, and requests, and information buzzes round this network of exchange, disconnected from its fading origin.

NETWORKS OF LOSS

The preceding synopsis traces some of the ways in which the theme of representation, in both the political and the aesthetic sense, weaves through *The Ambassadors*. Turning to the process of composition, it is notable that James represented *The Ambassadors* itself in a series of prolegomena and afterwords: the germ recorded in his notebook, the Project presented to his publishers, and the Preface added to the New York edition of his works. This Preface, which is actually a postscript written several years after the novel proper, has become one of James's most anthologized critical works. Prior to the completion of the novel, James had sent his publishers a 20,000-word Project, the size of a novella in itself, detailing Lambert Strether's earlier New England life: "a good many earnest and anxious experiments – professional, practical, intellectual, moral, personal," yet deprived of "any very proportionate sense of acknowledged or achieved success" (*A* 378). In a conventional sense, this Project is more novelistic than the novel, for it contains more story than the finished work, more moral and explanatory intervention by the novelist. The finished work seems to have evolved out of a process of elimination, discarding both events and characters, while reducing the intrusive author of the Project into a "deputed, represented" ghost.

James's Notebook attributes the germ of *The Ambassadors* to his friend Jonathan Sturges, who told James a moving anecdote about their mutual friend, the novelist William Dean Howells. Apparently Howells, having spent some days in Paris with his "domiciled and initiated son," found himself overwhelmed with regret for his lost youth. Howells had therefore entreated Sturges: "Live all you can: it's a mistake not to … I haven't done so – and now I'm old. It's too late. It has gone past me – I've lost it. You have time. You are young. Live!" (*A* 374)[41] In his Preface, James describes *The Ambassadors* as a "*supplement* of situation" (*A* 3) added to this passionate defence of life, which Strether re-delivers – with improvements – at a Paris garden party. If *The Ambassadors* constitutes a "supplement" to Howells's belated recognition of his loss, the Preface, Notebook, and Project supplement this supplement. All these addenda revolve around an emptiness described as "life" and yet defined by its unliveability. In *The Ambassadors*, "life" can be experienced only by proxy, and youth enjoyed only in deputed, represented form. For Strether, "everything represented the substance of his loss" (*A* 283).

This "loss" harks back to Mrs. Newsome's absence from the narrative, a loss which is "represented" by her ambassadors. From a Foucaultian point of view, the withdrawal of Mrs. Newsome corresponds to the decline of sovereignty in the modern world, this centripetal power having been superseded by centrifugal networks of power and resistance. According to Foucault, power no longer oppresses from above but surges from below, implemented by the very forces that resist its "capillary" infiltration. In place of "the unique form of a great power," modern power operates as mutual surveillance, in which all subjects are compelled to monitor each other, without a final point of view to which their prying gazes are referred.[42]

Although debateable as political theory, Foucault's conception of panoptical surveillance provides a valuable insight into the workings of power in *The Ambassadors*. Here Mrs. Newsome's sovereignty grows "thin and vague," her omniscience weakening with each of her representations (*A* 250). Meanwhile her emissaries scrutinize each other constantly: Chad's ambassadors spy on Strether at the same time that he spies on them, while the Pococks spy on the spies. Furthermore, the roles of watched and watcher oscillate throughout the text. Strether first meets Chad in the theatre, the locus of spectatorship par excellence, where "the figures and the faces in the stalls [are] interchangeable with those on the stage" (*A* 43) – the phrase implying that everyone is watched as well as watching. Henceforth Strether tries to penetrate Chad's "private stage" (*A* 64) with the aim of discovering his melodramatic "secret," but is borne along instead by the compulsion to repeat his "secrets" – "various and manifold." Similarly the reader witnesses Chad's love affair only by proxy, through the medium of Strether's re-enactment, his "little super-sensual hour, a kind of vicarious joy, in that *freedom of another*." At the end of the novel, when Strether transfers his allegiance to Madame de Vionnet, while Chad is deserting her for Woollett, it is as if the latecomer had usurped the forerunner, and representation had unseated presence.

In this world, the only person who sees nothing is Mrs. Newsome, the sovereign supposed to see it all. Although her absence instigates the circulation of the gaze, she never comes into the picture, as either the seer or the seen. Paradoxically the seat of power functions as the place of blindness rather than omniscience. Deprived of an ultimate spectator, gazes cross and interweave, enmeshing every subject in their intersecting eyebeams. Caught up in this network, Strether becomes so fond of watching that he forgets what he has been assigned to see. It is only at the end of the novel, when he finally discovers that Chad and Madame de Vionnet are lovers after all, that his representation of their "virtuous attachment" collapses in the face of the "loss" it was constructed to conceal, the loss of innocence.

This rude awakening occurs in the famous scene in Book Eleventh, when Strether takes a trip into the countryside, following an impulse – "artless enough, no doubt" – to refresh his memory of art, specifically of "a certain small Lambinet that had charmed him, long years before, at a Boston dealer's and that he had quite absurdly never forgotten" (*A* 303). In a reversal of the usual order of mimesis, whereby reality precedes representation, Strether construes the real French landscape as a representation of its own representation; that is, of the little Lambinet that he could never own, since it was priced "beyond a dream of possibility" (*A* 303).[43] In his "belated vision," the present scene is marked by absence, mourning, repetition, since the real landscape stands for the represented landscape that "he *would* have bought," but now relinquishes to nature (*A* 313, 303). The illusion that nature is innocent of art, however, is belied by the picture-frame that Strether's gaze imposes on the scene: "The oblong gilt frame disposed its enclosing lines; the poplars and willows, the reeds and river … fell into a composition, full of felicity …" (*A* 304).[44] The irony is that Strether, by keeping sex out of the picture, has been framed by his own frame, caught out by his own representations.

In this violated pastoral, "nature imitates art" (to borrow Wilde's epigram), for images of art pervade the description of the landscape, intensifying the impression that nature is always already represented. References to painting, writing, drama, and even to the art of cooking suggest a mise-en-scène "cooked up" for Strether's benefit. When Strether meets the landlady of his hotel, "the picture and the play seemed supremely to melt together in the good woman's broad sketch of what she could do for her visitor's appetite" (*A* 308). The countryside is described as "the nursery of letters," rather than a nursery of trees, and terms such as "fiction," "romance," "fable," and "performance" insinuate a sense of artfulness in nature's artistry: "not a breath of the evening that wasn't somehow a syllable of the text" (*A* 303, 311, 313, 308).

As he wanders through this picture, drama, text, or feast, Strether begins to think about his growing intimacy with Madame de Vionnet, and by doing so he opens up a gap within the picture, since this object of desire is absent from its frame. He is also meditating on the gap between them – that is, on the uncertainty of his relationship with her – and he reflects that "it was amazing what could still come up without reference to what was going on between them" (*A* 306). An algebra of pronouns and prepositions, this sentence quivers with innuendo: what *is* going on between them, and what, for that matter, is "coming up"? Does "them" refer to Strether and Madame de Vionnet, or to Madame de Vionnet and Chad? The pronoun "them" implicates the former pairing in the latter, creating a hallucinatory subtext in which Strether's fantasy of changing places is fulfilled. Strether has already admitted that he wishes to be "like" Chad (*A* 133); evidently Strether likes to *be like* considerably more than he likes to like, for his desire is mimetic rather than accusative.

In late James, these spirals of vicarious liking are reflected in multivalent pronouns, such as "them" in Strether's thoughts discussed above. To take another example, Maggie's struggle to preserve her marriage in *The Golden Bowl* is subverted by the pronouns, which prefigure every permutation of the two quadrangulated couples. In this novel, where Maggie and her father are excessively devoted to each other, while Charlotte is secretly embroiled with the Prince, the incest that never takes place, and the adultery that does, are constantly enacted at the level of the pronouns. Charlotte, in an outburst virtually ventriloquized by Maggie, ultimately disentangles her own marriage from the toxic foursome. But the pronouns tell another story, swapping wives and husbands with promiscuous abandon. "Our real life isn't here," Charlotte declares.

Maggie held her breath. "'Our's?' – "

"My husband's and mine. I'm not speaking for you … I'm speaking for ourselves. I'm speaking," Charlotte brought out, "for *him*."

"I see. For my father."

"For your father. For whom else?" (*GB* 528)

By leaving pronouns unspecified, James invites the reader to supply the missing names, and thereby to participate in the circulation of desire. In the dialogue above, the negated and the not-said make themselves felt as strongly as Charlotte's stated affirmations, whose vehemence, moreover, indicates that she protests too much. The pronouns "our's" and "him" (as Maggie's interventions intimate) raise the very spectres that Charlotte is trying to exorcize: "our's" could encompass any number of the "cornered six" (the Prince and Princess, the Ververs, and the Assinghams [*GB* 336]), while Charlotte's exasperated "whom else?" indicates that "him" could refer to Maggie's husband as well as to her own.

Similarly, the strategic vagueness of the pronouns in *The Ambassadors* makes the characters conspirators to one another's passions, conscripting the players into the transference of power and desire. The phrase "what [is] going on between them," in the Lambinet scene quoted above, epitomises this process of transference, whereby thinking, liking, and empowering take place *between* subjects, rather than within their independent minds. Indeed one could argue that the import of *The Ambassadors* is encapsulated in the phrase "what-is-going-on-between-them," where "them" may encompass any number of desirers.

Although distracted by his thoughts about Madame de Vionnet, Strether nonetheless "continue[s] in the picture," until he reaches the country inn where he is informed that two unexpected guests have just arrived "in a boat of their own" (*A* 307, 308). Shortly afterwards he encounters this couple who, floating down the river as if to ornament the scene, recall the tiny human figures in French eighteenth-century landscape painting, known as *staffage*, which Kant regarded as redundant to the composition as a whole. But Strether realizes that "these figures, or something like them, had been wanted in the picture" all along (*A* 307).[45] Here the pun on "wanted," meaning either bereft of or hankered after, identifies what is wanted in the picture as the locus of desire. Out of this want emerge the "figures" in the boat: a conjuration reminiscent of the Lacanian conception of desire as the primordial lack that brings forth figuration and symbolic substitution. In Strether's case, the figures that break into his vision also break through his illusions, and even the chapter breaks to mark the fracture of the picture-frame:

while he leaned against a post and continued to look out he saw something that gave him a sharper arrest.

IV [XXXI]

What he saw was exactly the right thing – a boat advancing round the bend and containing a man who held the paddles and a lady, at the stern, with a pink parasol. It was suddenly as if these figures, or something like them, had been wanted in the picture, had been wanted more or less all day, and had now drifted into sight, with the slow current, on purpose to fill up the measure. (*A* 309)

Shortly afterwards, this lady recognizes Strether with a start, before he can identify her as Madame de Vionnet, and before he recognizes her companion, "the coatless hero of the idyll," as the "expert" and initiated Chad (*A* 310, 309).

In this episode, as Kaja Silverman has pointed out, Strether's traumatic enlightenment corresponds to other "primal scenes" in James's fiction, such as the scene in *The Portrait of a Lady* where Isabel catches Madame Merle with Gilbert Osmond, not quite *in flagrante* but "unconsciously and familiarly associated"; or the scene where Maggie confronts Charlotte and Amerigo greeting her from the balcony of her own house.[46] In these wordless scenes, with their Medusa-like effect of petrifying both the viewer and the viewed, the Jamesian protagonist confronts the truth that desire is always anterior and other to the self. The petrifaction inflicted on the watcher and the watched also implies that desire is inextricable from death, the outcome foreshadowed in the lone voyeur's exclusion from the scene of pre-established intimacy.[47]

"Intimacy, at such a point, was *like* that," Strether realizes after an awkward dinner with the lovers in the country inn (*A* 315). Up to this point he has been seeing what he "wants," rather than what is, but this encounter forces him to recognize the gap in his previous representations. Yet what does Strether want? On one level, he wants a euphemism, like the "virtuous attachment," to fling to the prudes of Woollett, but this is because he wants to be like Chad, and to prolong his own "little super-sensual hour, a kind of vicarious joy, in that *freedom of another.*" He also wants to be like Gloriani, little Bilham, Maria Gostrey, and Madame de Vionnet, as opposed to being like the Pococks. In the light of Paris where one sees what things resemble, Strether can indulge in "the imitative" and "the emulative" without congealing in a single identification, thus avoiding the fixity embodied in the Pococks.[48]

It is to prolong this imitative holiday that Strether, up to now, has turned a blind eye to what was "wanted" in his picture of the lovers. Seizing on little Bilham's equivocal expression, the "virtuous attachment," and insistently replacing "virtuous" with "innocent," Strether has "scotomized" or blotted out his own perception of the scandal, much as the Freudian fetishist scotomizes his traumatic glimpse of the absence of the mother's penis. Once Strether has recognized the guilty couple, however, he can no longer deny what he has been trying not to see: "It was a sharp fantastic crisis that had popped up as if in a dream …" (*A* 310). The term "as if in a dream" hints that Strether has already dreamed what he has disavowed, and that the "figures" in the boat have "popped up" – like an erection – from the depths of his unconscious.

Ross Posnock, in a fascinating discussion of this scene, argues that Strether shares James's own "traumatophilia," a term coined by Walter Benjamin to describe Baudelaire's genius at parrying shocks. "Traumatophilia involves the subject deliberately seeking out encounters of difference rather than sameness," Posnock contends.[49] Yet I would argue that Freud's conception of trauma, which includes the crucial element of *déjà vu*, corresponds more closely to Strether's "sharp fantastic crisis." The Freudian child, too young to understand the spectacle of sex, experiences trauma only by deferred effect, when archaic traces of the primal scene are unexpectedly reactivated in the present. Freud's notion of *Nachträglichkeit* or deferred action therefore captures the temporal ambiguity of Strether's trauma, which is unexpected yet implicitly foreseen, fore-dreamed. Rather than confronting the irreducibly other, as Posnock proposes, Strether confronts the "uncanny," the unknown known, or that which James calls the "intimate difference" (*A* 395).[50]

Adeline Tintner, in *Henry James and the Lust of the Eyes*, argues that James, when casting about for a title for his novel in 1900, was influenced by Mary Hervey's book *Holbein's The Ambassadors: The Picture and the Men*, published during the same year. In this celebrated piece of pictorial detective work, Hervey reveals that the two figures in Holbein's painting are not the poets John Leland and Thomas Wyatt, as previously thought, but two French ambassadors to the court of Henry VIII, the politician Jean de Dinteville and the bishop Georges de Selve.[51] On either side of Holbein's canvas, these two rigid ambassadors gaze out symmetrically, mirroring the gaze of the spectator, and surrounded by Renaissance images of vanity, which seem to emphasize the narcissism of this headlong form of vision. Tintner points out that the objects on the table, including navigational instruments and a terrestrial globe, correspond to James's themes of travel, exploration, and culture in *The Ambassadors*. Meanwhile the distorted death's head in the foreground, which serves as a memento mori, corresponds to James's theme of *carpe diem*: "live all you can."[52]

This death's head, elongated by a trick of perspective, decenters the gaze of the spectator, who is forced to look awry to make sense of the distorted image.[53] In this way the death's head marks the blindness constitutive of vision, by revealing that every point of view occludes as much as it commands. Shattering the illusion of faithful representation, this trompe-l'oeil demonstrates that the painting is a trap to catch the gaze, rather than a gateway to a prior, self-evident reality. What is more, the death's head opens up a perspective from which the looker may be looked at, eyed by the empty sockets of a skull. Far from seeing "the whole picture," the spectator confronts her own erasure: "Holbein makes visible to us something which is simply the subject as annihilated," Lacan declares in his famous discussion of this picture.[54]

At the same time, the death's head, by brandishing its artifice, exposes the canvas as a tracery of brushstrokes rather than a window to a pre-existent scene. This skull, moreover, intimates that there is nothing underneath this system of appearances but death. In a similar way, James's narrative draws attention to its own contrivances, with its repeated references to "fiction," "farce," "fable," and "performance." When Strether leaves Paris for his country jaunt, he may still believe that representations faithfully reflect reality, but by the time that he goes back, this illusion

has been shattered. His "sharp fantastic crisis" has revealed that the fascination of the picture lies in what it "wants," not what it shows. In the
realm of vision, everyone is framed and no one sees the whole. Rather than
comforting spectators with a mirror of their unity and mastery, the picture opens up the "want" where death inscribes its "intimate difference."

The position of Holbein's death's head, cutting through the foreground of
the painting, corresponds to the "line through the middle" of Lily Briscoe's
picture in *To the Lighthouse*, a line that divides its painted scene in half. Both
Lily's line and Holbein's skull are ways of making "nothing" visible. For
Lacan, this "nothing" signifies the absent penis, and Holbein's death's head,
with its phallic shape and thrusting posture, lends itself to this interpretation. Similarly Strether, faced with a lesion in his vision comparable to the
death's head in the painting, staggers as if he had been "cut." In his encounter with the lovers, the term "violence" recurs three times within a single
paragraph.[55] Glimpsing something "quite horrible" – that the boating lovers
are pretending not to see him – Strether greets them with gesticulations of
"surprise and joy." At this point "the boat … [goes] a little wild," but as
Chad steers it around, "relief … [supersedes] mere violence." Strether

went down to the water under this odd impression as of violence averted – the
violence of their having "cut" him, out there in the eye of nature, on the assumption that he wouldn't know it. He awaited them with a face from which he was
conscious of not being able quite to banish this idea that they would have gone
on, not seeing and not knowing … had he himself taken a line to match. That
at least was what darkened his vision for the moment. Afterwards … everything
found itself sponged over by the mere miracle of the encounter. (*A* 310–11)

Here Strether narrowly averts the violence of being "cut." Yet by knowing that the couple *would* have cut him, were it not for his tactful intervention, Strether finally renounces his New England innocence. His
foreknowledge of this "cut" releases him from his infantilism, from
"the assumption that he wouldn't know it," and enables him – in Miss
Gostrey's withering phrase – to "toddle alone" (*A* 192). While critics have
objected to Strether as a mere castrate, James more subtly suggests that
this "cut" is the only way his hero can become a man.[56] Being a man,
however, is not a matter of consolidating an identity – unified, coherent,
self-contained – but of acknowledging the want or cut or woundedness
of subjectivity. Strether's much-criticized passivity, a trait he shares with
many other Jamesian men, rather signifies an openness to otherness, and
an acceptance of what James describes as our "exposed and entangled"
state as "social creatures."[57]

In the Preface to *The Ambassadors*, James speaks of "the revolution performed by Strether under the influence of the most interesting of great cities." This revolution involves both a *bouleversement* and a return, since Strether ultimately turns full circle back to Woollett, thus rounding off the *nostos* of his odyssey. But Strether performs another kind of revolution by exposing the irrelevance of sovereignty in a world where power no longer descends from above, but circulates among the networks of deputed, represented surrogates. In this networked world (as James's shifty pronouns intimate), experience becomes vicarious, passion transferential, thought telepathic.

The most conspicuous of these networks in *The Ambassadors* is the telegraph system, which also plays an important part in the case history of the Rat Man, a patient obsessed with the idea of telegraphing middlemen while taking trains around the country in a complex "revolution" back to where he started from. As Mark Goble has pointed out, telegrams feature more prominently in *The Ambassadors* than in James's other late works – "nothing having ever been known like the cabling that goes on" (*A* 394) – with the exception of the novella *In the Cage*, in which an imaginative telegraph operator intervenes in the illicit correspondence that she mediates.[58] In *The Ambassadors*, Mrs. Newsome's only message directly quoted in the narrative arrives by telegram, with its brusque command: "Come back by the next ship" (*A* 192). This peremptory cable reaches Strether at the moment that Mrs. Newsome's lengthy letters cease, to be superseded by communication in the vengeful form of Sarah Pocock.

Far from retrieving Strether, Mrs. Newsome's cable convinces him to linger in Paris and to persuade the homeward-turning Chad to linger with him. From this point onwards Strether's letters expand as Mrs. Newsome's contract, as if the flow of words were vampirically distributed between them. Yet Mrs. Newsome is not the only source, nor Strether the only recipient of telegrams; Strether suspects Waymarsh of "wiring" Woollett behind his back, in order to catapult the Pococks into Paris. Meanwhile Mrs. Newsome, with her countless "wires" and "cables," administers her wire-pulling by "remote control" – an expression dated by the *OED* to 1904, one year after the publication of *The Ambassadors*.[59]

In this wired world, James's characters inevitably get their wires crossed, and find themselves transported into alien selves. Telegraphy coalesces with telepathy, as if thinking could be "wired" between minds. A striking instance of telepathy occurs in the opening chapters of *The Ambassadors*, where Maria Gostrey, having just met Strether, interpolates his mission from the slightest clues, crowning her intuitions with a verbal conjuration of the "moral swell" of Woollett. From this point onwards it is clear that Maria knows Strether's mind better than he knows his own; she "knew intimate things about him that he hadn't yet told her and perhaps never would" (*A* 22). In fact Miss Gostrey's contest with "the lady at home" could be seen as a tug-of-war between the sympathetic witchcraft of telepathy, which literally means "far-feeling," and the high-tech magic of telegraphy, that peremptory writing from afar associated in this novel with American managerialism. Strether never settles this contest; the fact that his desire circulates, never fixing on a single object, male or female, reveals the promiscuity implicit in a networked universe, where everyone is "tuned in" to each other's airways, and "relations stop nowhere."

Strether begins the novel with a "double consciousness," and by the end of his adventure this consciousness has multiplied, having partaken of the other minds that he has met (*A* 18). This idea of multiplicity is encoded in the title of the novel, *The Ambassadors*, where the plural intimates that delegates breed delegates. Not only does Strether's dithering demand a second deputation, but Strether himself is several ambassadors in one. By betraying Mrs. Newsome, he demonstrates how representatives necessarily escape their source, since every effort to ensure fidelity – to parents, spouses, countries, or the facts – fails to overcome the "inevitable deviation" and "exquisite treachery even of the straightest execution."

The Ambassadors reverses the traditional project of the *Bildungsroman*. Instead of tracing the evolution of a character, James shows how Strether unbecomes the relatively solid citizen he was. In this sense Strether undergoes an analysis in Paris, with Miss Gostrey acting as his primary analyst, aided by little Bilham, Madame de Vionnet, and even Chad – analysis, as we have seen, means loosening, unbinding. The reader is also placed in the position of an analyst, interpreting the hero's actions and inactions as responses to the unacknowledged and the disavowed. Strether pays through the nose for this analysis (a "nose of bold free provenance" frequently remarked by the narrator; Mamie Pocock's nose, by contrast, is "too small" [*A* 20, 212]). He earns his limited freedom from the past by giving up all possibility of gain, his aim being "not, out of the whole adventure, to have got anything for myself." In the end, there is no longer a "myself" to get things for, at least a "myself" in the sense that Woollett understands it, which Posnock characterizes as "the anxious Victorian ethos of strenuous masculinity."[60] This selfhood is unraveled in the novel and reconstructed in a looser, more absorbent fabric, and the novel never tells how Strether will "come out" (*A* 344). It is tempting to interpret this phrase anachronistically, since "coming out" – in today's parlance – would provide a facile explanation for many of Strether's temptations and abstentions, such as his susceptibility to the "glossy male tiger" Gloriani, or his rejection of two dazzling women. But Strether is queerer than gay, and his coming out involves an opening to otherness, rather than a bid for sexual identity. "Yes," James writes, "he goes back other – and to other things" (*A* 403).

CHAPTER 4

The Woolf woman

In the last decade of the nineteenth century, the five-year-old son of Russian aristocratic parents dreamed that six or seven wolves, sitting in the walnut tree outside his bedroom window, were staring at him in his cot. On the other side of Europe, a little English girl, four years older than the Russian boy, dreamed or imagined that the face of an animal was staring at her in the mirror.

By a curious coincidence, both these children were later to adopt the name of wolf, suggesting that their own identities were implicated in these early bestial visitations. Serge Pankejeff, better known as the Wolf Man, earned his lupine title through the psychoanalytic institution, Virginia Woolf through the institution of marriage. Yet both chose Wolf or Woolf as *noms de plume*, as if the act of writing had completed their lycanthropic metamorphoses.

Beyond the coincidence between their names, the Wolf Man and Virginia Woolf were near contemporaries who witnessed the cataclysms of the twentieth century: the First World War, the Russian Revolution, the rise of the Third Reich. Both contemporaries also played a crucial role in the development of psychoanalysis, the Wolf Man as Freud's most famous patient, and Virginia Woolf as publisher of the Strachey translations of Freud's works. And in both cases, their childhood visions of terrifying animals have been linked to the sexual traumas of their early years. As children, both were molested by their older siblings, Virginia Stephen by her half-brothers, George and Gerald Duckworth, and Serge Pankejeff by his sister Anna. Pankejeff blamed this premature seduction for all his future miseries: "This sister complex is really the thing that ruined my entire life," he declared (Obholzer, p. 37); although Freud insisted that the father's evident preference for Anna was to blame. Anna Pankejeff was a precocious child, groomed by her father as his intellectual successor, but she killed herself before his vicarious ambitions could be fulfilled, and Pankejeff's father also probably committed suicide. The Wolf Man never recovered from these deaths. On the contrary, it has been argued that this life-long analysand was possessed by the ghosts of his father and his sister, "encrypted" in the locked vault of his ego.[1]

While the Wolf Man was haunted by his father and sister, Woolf was haunted by her mother, Julia Stephen, who died when Virginia was only thirteen years old. In a much-cited passage of her memoir "A Sketch of the Past," Woolf recalls how writing *To the Lighthouse* quelled her mother's ghost:

> when it was written, I ceased to be obsessed by my mother. I no longer hear her voice; I do not see her.
>
> I suppose that I did for myself what psycho-analysts do for their patients. I expressed some very long felt and deeply felt emotion. And in expressing it I explained it and then laid it to rest. (*MB* 93)[2]

Despite this exorcism, Woolf's mental illness, whose onset coincided with her mother's death in 1895, persisted throughout her life, the worst attacks triggered by the completion of her novels.[3] These recurrences indicate that writing, despite its power to exorcize the dead, also creates a further object to be mourned – the book itself, which is torn from its author to be savaged by the critical establishment. In a diary entry of 27 June 1925, Woolf mentions "an idea that I will invent a new name for my books to supplant 'novel'. A new – by Virginia Woolf. But what? Elegy?" (*Diary* 3:34) This term "elegy" captures the persistent theme of mourning in her works, as well as the author's serial bereavement of her own creations.

Both Woolf and the Wolf Man struggled with the ambivalence of mourning, with the desire to preserve yet also to overcome the dead. Their grief, incurable and virtually professional, aligns them with the legendary werewolf, whose symptoms were often attributed to melancholia, as Robert Burton notes in the *Anatomy of Melancholy*.[4] Burton describes "lycanthropia" as a form of madness in which

> men run howling about graves and fields in the night, and will not be persuaded but that they are wolves, or some such beasts … This malady, saith Avicenna, troubleth men most in February … They lie hid most part all day, and go abroad in the night, barking, howling, at graves and deserts; "they usually have hollow eyes, scabbed legs and thighs, very pale and dry," saith Altomarus …[5]

Incidentally, the ancient tradition of the werewolf has revived in modern cinema, where wolf men greatly outnumber wolf women, suggesting that lycanthropy is a male-dominated vocation. Legend, however, is not so chauvinistic, but provides numerous instances of wolf women; numerous enough for one scholar to claim lycanthropy for feminism, arguing that women donned wolfskins and took to the woods in defiance of their housebound servitude.[6] Furthermore, the masculinity of wolf men is impugned by the lunar nature of their malady. The werewolf is a man with monthlies, suffering from a particularly beastly form of PMS. Does this mean that the wolf man is a wolf woman in disguise?[7] Does the myth of becoming wolf mask a fear of becoming woman, and demolishing the boundaries of gender?

Virginia Woolf challenges these boundaries through a different kind of canine transformation, becoming dog as opposed to becoming wolf. In *Flush*, her biography of Elizabeth Barrett's spaniel, the dog's gender, which is almost as malleable as Orlando's, is determined by environment rather than anatomy. A Lothario in his rustic youth, Flush is feminized by his allegiance to his urban mistress. Not only does Flush change sex, but he changes into everything he smells, thus evading the egotistical aloofness that Woolf attributes to the masculine mind. Like the androgynous Orlando, Flush enables Woolf to regress to the presexual – a frequent temptation in her life and work – and to embrace the dog of childhood, eluding the wolf of adult sexuality.

Both Woolf's writings and Freud's case history of the Wolf Man voyage back to "the prehistoric period of childhood," in Freud's resonant phrase: the period before the male is rigidly distinguished from the female, or the human from the animal (SE 17:18). "A child," Freud contends, "can see no difference between his own nature and that of animals … Not until he is grown up does he become so far estranged from animals as to use their names in vilification for human beings" (SE 17:140). For Woolf and the Wolf Man, the return to the prehistoric goes by way of animality, and in both cases the archaic animal assumes a canine form, alternately wolf, dog, or fox. In *Between the Acts*, for instance, Woolf describes the prehistoric as "the night before roads were made, or houses" when "the dogfox fights with the vixen, in the heart of darkness, in the fields of night" (*BA* 129–30).

In a famous misquotation in *The Waste Land*, Eliot substitutes the "the Dog … that's friend to men" for John Webster's "wolf … that's foe to men." Friend or foe, both these canines use their all-too-human "nails" to dig up corpses: "O keep the Dog far hence, that's Friend to men, / Or with his nails he'll dig it up again!"[8] Analogously, Woolf and Pankejeff invoke the dog-wolf or wolf-dog to dig their way into the mausoleum of prehistory.[9] But there is one chamber in this mausoleum that cannot be unlocked, its secrets immured in amnesia. This is the site of what Freud calls the "primal scene," the theater of seduction in which adult sexuality precociously intrudes into the child's world. Like the navel of the dream, discussed in the introduction of this book, the primal scene marks the point at which the past becomes "unplumbable." Having never been experienced, this lost event can only be imputed from its web of traces, from "the phantom net floating there to mark something which had sunk," to borrow an eerie image from *To the Lighthouse* (*TL* 57).

The next section of this chapter, "Wolf-gathering," investigates the role of canines (both *canis lupus* and *canis lupus familiaris*, the family wolf) in the phantasmatics of the Wolf Man and Virginia Woolf, exploring the connections between sexuality, trauma, lycanthropy, and cynanthropy.[10] A further section, "Analysis Interminable," pursues the theme of trauma in the Wolf Man's psychobiography, followed by "Postures and Impostures," which examines the traumatic structure of *To the Lighthouse*. I conclude by reconsidering the notion of the primal scene, the "sensational" climax of Freud's case history of the Wolf Man.[11] As many critics have observed, *To the Lighthouse*, with its two familial dramas divided by a ten-year interval, invites comparison to the compulsive repetition of the primal scene, as well as to Freud's notions of trauma, latency, and deferred action.[12] Developing this comparison, I propose that trauma consists in the violent irruption of the scene itself, rather than its cast of characters – the jealous child, the desired mother, the forbidding father. Trauma is a matter of "making scenes," in all the senses of the phrase, but what these scenes stage is the unrepresentable.

WOLF-GATHERING

It is hard to imagine anyone less wolfish than the Wolf Man. The patient who presented himself to Freud in 1910 was a pathetic victim of his incapacities, the most troubling of which was the inability to defecate without an enema delivered by a manservant. Defying the ministrations of Freud and subsequent doctors and analysts, the Wolf Man continued to relapse into mental illness throughout his long and miserable life. A sheep in wolf's clothing, this patient earned his honorific from a dream about wolves in sheep's clothing. In early childhood, little Serge dreamed that his bedroom window flew open to reveal a group of wolves, perched white and motionless on the branches of a walnut tree, transfixing the dreamer with their gaze.[13] However, Pankejeff's famous drawing of this dream, produced for Freud, portrays these animals as fluffy-tailed "sheepdogs," rather than bloodthirsty wolves.[14]

Sheepish though he was, Pankejeff took pride in his psychoanalytic nom de guerre; in later life he would answer the telephone with the announcement: "*Hier spricht der Wolfsmann*."[15] He also signed his memoirs "Wolf Man," thereby laying claim to his lycanthropic alter ego while retrieving his life-story from the jaws of Freud, who had published the case history in 1918. Freud's official title, *From the History of an Infantile Neurosis*, was quickly forgotten by his followers in favor of the Gothic frisson of "The Wolf Man." Thus the psychoanalytic establishment transformed Pankejeff into the Wolf Man, but the Wolf Man also transformed psychoanalysis, since many key Freudian concepts – castration, fetishism, anal erotism, incorporation, bisexuality, primal scenes and primal phantasies – were inspired or corroborated by this case.[16] The Wolf Man was at once Freud's "greatest prize *and* his archnemesis," as Lawrence Johnson has pointed out, since the patient's disorder ultimately defeated all his analysts. Paradoxically the edifice of psychoanalysis is built on its most famous failure.[17]

Virginia Woolf, on the other hand, often signed her letters as a dog. Dogs were fixtures of the Stephens' household – Leslie Stephen was "unthinkable" without a dog, according to Maitland, his biographer – and Virginia, obliged to dance attendance on her father's gloomy tyranny, had reason to identify herself with his companion animals.[18] Her position vis-à-vis her father resembles that of Flush, Elizabeth Barrett Browning's much-kidnapped pooch, who gave up sunshine, hares, and freedom to devote himself to an ailing mistress. "That silly book Flush," as Woolf described it, presents a dog's-eye view of the Brownings' love-affair.[19] After experimenting with transsexualism in *Orlando*, dedicated to her lover Vita Sackville-West, Woolf joked about trans-speciesism, promising another book "about turning into a rusty, clotted, hairy faithful blue-eyed sheepdog" (*Letters* 5:41). In the event Woolf morphed into a spaniel rather than a sheepdog; responding in October 1933 to a generous review of *Flush* by David Garnett (known to his friends as "Bunny"), Woolf signed herself, "Yours affectionate old English springer spaniel Virginia" (*Letters* 5:232).

It is true that *Flush* is often silly – whimsical and cute – and Woolf's doubts about the book have rubbed off on her critics, most of whom exclude this canine excursion from her canon.[20] *Flush*, as Woolf explained to Ottoline Morrell, "is only by way of a joke. I was so tired after the Waves, that I lay in the garden and read the Browning love letters, and the figure of their dog made me laugh so I couldn't resist making him a Life."[21] Woolf was embarrassed by the popular success of *Flush*: her best-selling book in England, it was a Book Society choice for October 1933, and was also chosen as a Book-of-the-Month Club alternate selection in America.[22] On the eve of publication, Woolf dreaded the kind of praise that she anticipated from reviewers: "They'll say its 'charming' delicate, ladylike" (*Diary* 4:181). Some did, of course. Yet if *Flush* is a joke, a money-spinner, and a silly novel by a lady novelist, it also opens up what Woolf, speaking of the unrecorded experience of women, describes as a "different order and system of life."[23] By giving voice to the voiceless, *Flush* defamiliarizes Victorian society from the perspective of the underdog, "seeing things – literally – from a low position," as Kate Flint has observed.[24] The snobbery of the Spaniel Club, for instance, with its disdain for topknots, curly ears, and light noses, mocks Victorian obsessions with human pedigree and genealogy.[25]

As an experiment in cynanthropy, *Flush* is also memorable for its romp through the canine "world of smell," those "myriad sensations" that the human nose cannot detect, and human words cannot approximate:

Where two or three thousand words are insufficient for what we see … there are no more than two words and one-half for what we smell. The human nose is practically non-existent. The greatest poets of the world have smelt only roses on the one hand, and dung on the other. The infinite gradations that lie between are unrecorded. Yet it was in the world of smell that Flush chiefly lived … He nosed his way from smell to smell; the rough, the smooth, the dark, the golden. (*Flush*, pp. 86–87)[26]

This sentiment echoes the dog's indictment of the human species in G. K. Chesterton's "Song of Quoodle" of 1914: "They haven't got no noses, / The fallen sons of Eve." Like Quoodle, Woolf laments the human repression of the sense of smell, which Freud identifies as the founding "organic repression" of civilization. In two famous footnotes to *Civilization and its Discontents*, Freud ascribes the rise of patriarchy to the triumph of the eye over the nose. Adopting Darwin's view that the cultural dominance of vision stems from "man's adoption of an upright posture," Freud argues that the erect male forfeited the sexual stimulus of scent, best appreciated on all fours, in favor of the vertical stimulus of vision.[27] Standing upright exposed the genitals to view, requiring them to be protected and concealed. As a result of this verticality, the periodic sexual stimulus of smell was subordinated to the constant stimulus of sight. According to Freud, "the deepest root of the sexual repression that advances along with civilization is the organic defence of the new form of life achieved with man's erect gait against his earlier animal existence" (SE 21:104n3). One consequence of this repression is the taboo against menstruation; another is a general depreciation of the sense of smell, extending to an embargo against all bodily odors.[28]

While Freud associates the feminine with the olfactory, via menstruation, Woolf allies the woman poet with her sharp-nosed companion Flush. Both are pampered captives of the stifling Victorian interior, where upright men literally look down on dogs and females. "Yes, they are much alike, Mrs. Browning and her dog," Woolf wrote to a delighted reader of *Flush* (*Letters* 5:234).[29] Noting the striking facial resemblance between the poet and the spaniel, their faces framed by heavy curls and heavy ears respectively, Woolf wonders if "each completed what was dormant in the other?" (*Flush* 18) Woolf herself seemed to feel completed by dogs, since she associated these pets with "the private side of life – the play side."[30] As Quentin Bell remarks in his biography of Woolf, "*Flush* is not so much a book by a dog lover as a book by someone who would love to be a dog."[31]

If Woolf wanted to become a dog, she also regarded dogs as cynanthropes, half-canine and half-human, by virtue of their intimacy with the human family. In her earliest published essay, an obituary of the Stephens' dog Shag, Woolf senses something "profane in the familiarity, half contemptuous, with which we treat our animals."

We deliberately transport a little bit of simple wild life, and make it grow up beside ours … How have we the impertinence to make these wild creatures forego their own nature for ours, which at best they can but imitate?

Woolf concludes, however, that Shag was thoroughly at home in human life: "I can see him smoking a cigar at the bow window of his club, his legs extended comfortably, whilst he discusses the latest news on the Stock Exchange with a companion."[32] In this passage, it is worth noting that Woolf transports the dog into the gentleman's club, a privilege from which women are debarred. Similarly Woolf's famous delusion, during her illness of 1904, that the birds were singing in Greek endows these creatures with the classical education denied to girls, a deprivation bitterly resented by the author.[33] These examples indicate that Woolf sees animals and women as fellow casualties of patriarchy, yet also envies animals their fun and freedom, imagining their options to be fuller than those allotted to the female sex.

There is a dark side, however, to Woolf's canine identification. If Flush belongs to "the playful side of life," her childhood vision of the beast in the mirror evokes the wolf rather than the dog. This lycanthropic trauma is recounted in Woolf's memoir *Moments of Being:*

I was looking in a glass when a horrible face – the face of an animal – suddenly showed over my shoulder. I cannot be sure if this was a dream, or if it happened … But I have always remembered the other face in the glass … (*MB* 83)[34]

In this dream or hallucination, the child confronts herself as animal, or more precisely as a double-headed monster, half girl, half beast. Roger Poole, among others, has attributed this vision of "the other face in the glass" to Virginia's early sexual abuse at the hands of her half-brothers, George and Gerald Duckworth.[35] It is worth noting that Woolf later depicts George as a "pug-dog," a dwarfed and mutant version of the shaggy sheepdog associated with the private playful side of life.[36] Woolf also avenges herself on her abusers by playing on their name: in her early novel *The Voyage Out* (1915), the ship's captain remarks that the most dreaded of navigational perils is *Sedgius aquatici* which, to the layman, is "a kind of duck-weed."[37] Through marriage, Woolf enlisted the leonine and lupine influence of Leonard Woolf to counteract this baleful zoomorphonym – the duck – and to overcome her anatine abusers. Together Leonard and Virginia invented bestiaries of pet names, sealing themselves into a private, duck-free world; the common endearment "duck" is conspicuously absent from their lovers' discourse.[38]

These animal monikers also belonged to a family tradition among the Stephens, whose nickname for Virginia, for example, was "the Goat." Leonard Woolf renamed Virginia "the Mandrill," a fierce gigantic African baboon, whom he also invoked as the "great Brute."[39] He confessed to his own "beastly qualities," a euphemism for lust, which Virginia deflected into childish fun by dubbing him the Mongoose, a thin flea-ridden rodent wildly enamored of the Mandrill (*Letters* 2:44). At other times she addressed her husband as a rabbit, hedgehog, antelope, and even as a swarm of marmots or high-mountain mice.[40] These endearments may have been devised to tame the beast in the mirror, or the "beastly qualities" in Leonard Woolf, yet there is something verminous about the way that epithet breeds epithet, about the pullulation of the whole menagerie.

In contrast to this proliferation of pet-names, it is only one name – Wolf – that reasserts itself throughout the Wolf Man's case history. This name is re-embodied in a series of father-figures – teachers, doctors, psychoanalysts. In Serge's childhood a German tutor by the name of Wolf punished the little aristocrat for errors in translation.[41] Later Pankejeff repeatedly consulted wolves in human form to treat his ravening afflictions – as if it took a wolf to know one. Dr Moshe Wulff treated him in Moscow before referring him in 1910 to Freud, himself the fond owner of a large grey police-dog that "looked like a domesticated wolf." In the 1930s the Wolf Man suffered from acute hypochondria about his nose and teeth (his muzzle?), and visited a series of dentists, including two named Wolf. From one Dr Wolf the patient learned that his "hard bite" would cause him to lose all his teeth, which confirmed the other Dr Wolf's diagnosis that the "violence of his bite" was responsible for his afflictions (Gardiner, pp. 277, 268). In addition to his violent bite, another of his wolfish symptoms was recurrent acne, which the analysts Abraham and Torok have connected to *lupus seborrheus*, *lupus* being the Latin word for wolf.[42] The *Oxford English Dictionary* defines *lupus* as "an ulcerous disease of the skin, sometimes erosive, sometimes hypertrophous," providing the following citation from 1590: "a malignant ulcer quickly consuming the neather parts, and it is very hungry like unto a woolfe." In the Wolf Man's pimples, this hungry wolf inscribes its signature into his flesh, blistering his skin with lycanthropic graffiti.

A recurrence of this acne, condensed into a single pimple on the nose, precipitated the Wolf Man's mental illness of the late 1920s. Obsessed with this blemish, he sought treatment from Freud, who referred his former patient to an American disciple, Ruth Mack Brunswick. At the same juncture Freud gave his daughter Anna an Alsatian named Wolf, possibly as a compensation-prize for conferring his most famous patient on a rival analyst.[43] For readers unfamiliar with the Wolf Man's story, the following section of this chapter provides an overview of Freud's case history and Brunswick's re-analysis.

ANALYSIS INTERMINABLE

On 13 February 1910, Freud wrote to Sandor Ferenczi:

> A rich young Russian whom I have taken on because of compulsive tendencies admitted the following transferences to me after the first session: Jewish swindler, he would like to use me from behind and shit on my head.[44]

With these admissions the Wolf Man probably expected to make a good impression on Freud, having received some coaching in psychoanalytic theory from his Russian psychiatrist, "Dr D" [Drosnes], who had accompanied the patient from Odessa to Vienna. Freud's po-faced letter does not divulge whether he took the Wolf Man's overtures seriously, but he was fully persuaded of his patient's incapacities. In addition to chronic constipation, Pankejeff suffered from de-realization, the sense that the world was hidden from him by a veil. This sensation disappeared only when his constipation was relieved by an enema administered by a man-servant. Freud traces this veil-delusion to the fact that Serge was born with a caul, which was regarded by his Russian family as an omen of good fortune – a superstition that could scarcely have been further from the truth.[45] Unbeknown to Freud, Slavic folk tradition associates the natal caul with the werewolf, as Carlo Ginzburg has discovered.[46] If the Wolf Man was aware that Freud was also born with a caul, the patient may have recognized a fellow lycanthrope.

Some commentators have contended that Freud exaggerated the severity of his patient's illness, partly to embellish the success of the analysis, since the young man's symptoms had already improved as a result of that old-fashioned remedy, a change of scene.[47] It is also possible that the hard-working Freud, driven by ambition and the need to make ends meet, over-looked the fact that indolence and apathy, far from symptoms of distress, are affectations cultivated by the upper classes. "Defecate? Our servants can do that for us" – the Wolf Man might have said.[48] Before consulting Freud, Pankejeff had been drifting in and out of sanatoria for a couple of years, undergoing hydrotherapy and other futile treatments. It was in Emil Kraepelin's Munich sanitorium in 1909 that Pankejeff fell in love with a nurse called Therese Keller, with whom he embarked on a tempestuous affair. Although Freud regarded this "breakthrough to the woman" as the patient's greatest psychic achievement, he advised the Wolf Man not to see Therese during the first stage of the treatment, but assented to a reunion the following year, granting the couple permission to marry at the close of the analysis.[49]

This conclusion seemed imminent when the Wolf Man, preparing to return to Odessa, visited Freud to say good-bye on 29 June 1914, one day after the Archduke Franz Ferdinand was shot in Sarajevo. The consequence, unforeseen by both doctor and patient, was that they would have no contact for the next four years. The Wolf Man and his wife returned to Odessa to enjoy an aristocratic life, but in May 1918 Pankejeff wrote to Freud complaining of Therese's broken health, and requesting a consultation at Semmering, the Freuds' summer resort. Meanwhile the Austrian invasion of Russia had saved Pankejeff's estate from the Bolsheviks, but this proved only a temporary respite. By the time the patient returned to Vienna, his vast fortune had shrunk to nothing, and even the cash he managed to smuggle out of Russia was valueless, having been converted into failing currencies. The Wolf Man was therefore penniless when he resumed analysis with Freud, who agreed to treat him free of charge, kicking Helene Deutsch out of her training analysis to make time for his famous patient.⁵⁰ In 1919 the Wolf Man considered the idea of returning to Russia to reclaim his estate, but Freud urged him to remain in re-analysis, no doubt suspecting that the patient was likely to be executed.

When the Wolf Man fell ill again in 1928, undergoing a lycanthropic reversal of his former character, he blamed Freud's advice for the loss of his estate (Obholzer, pp. 48–49). Thus swindled by his doctor, Pankejeff felt justified in accepting further gifts from Freud, collected from wealthy patients and disciples in Vienna, without informing his benefactors of his sizeable inheritance of jewels from Russia.⁵¹ The illness that drove him back into analysis was acute hypochondria focused on his nose and teeth, possibly aroused by anxiety about Freud's cancer of the mouth. In 1923 Freud had undergone his first minor mouth operation, and when Pankejeff collected his annual retainer, he was shocked by Freud's appearance (Gardiner, p. 268). Yet the Wolf Man's imitation of his doctor's illness failed to convince Freud to take his famous patient back. Instead, Freud referred the patient to Ruth Mack Brunswick – a gift that once again offended Helene Deutsch, who had coveted this mark of favor from the master.⁵²

The patient who presented himself to Brunswick was suffering from the delusion that his nose was permanently disfigured by a scar, perpetrated by medical malpractice. The Wolf Man had consulted several dermatologists about the pimple on his nose, and had undergone some mildly invasive treatments, which only aggravated his conviction that his nose was irreparably damaged. When one of his Wolf-dentists attributed the nasal inflammation to an infected tooth, the Wolf Man had two teeth extracted, one in error. Another doctor's ominous remark, "scars never disappear," drove the Wolf Man to despair. His mother's lament, which he had overheard in childhood, that she could not "go on living like this any more" (probably an allusion to gynaecological problems), came to represent his own predicament. Obsessed with the idea that "everybody was looking at the hole in his nose," the Wolf Man adopted the habit of carrying a little pocket-mirror in which he constantly scrutinized his nose, trying to determine the extent of his mutilation. Brunswick, however, insists that there was nothing visibly amiss about the patient's nose.⁵³

Her re-analysis reveals a tangle of motives for the Wolf Man's dental and nasal deliria: Freud's buccal cancer, tantamount to the castration of the father; the Wolf Man's feminine identification with his mother and his wife, whose noses were both blemished by warts; the patient's adolescent acne, an affliction he shared with his suicidal sister. Brunswick's short account of the analysis, deferentially entitled "A Supplement to

Freud's History of an Infantile Neurosis," reports that the patient's recovery came unexpectedly, when he suddenly found himself able to read novels again, a source of pleasure that had eluded him throughout his illness. The reason for this inhibition, he explained, was his reluctance to identify with the hero of a novel, since such a character was wholly in the power of his creator (Gardiner, p. 296). At this point the patient was also able to resume his Sunday painting, while making a modest living as a clerk in an insurance office.

Despite this apparent cure, however, the Wolf Man continued to seek treatment from Brunswick with interruptions until 1938, the year that his wife Therese committed suicide, the greatest tragedy of his unhappy life. After this catastrophe he intermittently consulted Brunswick's student Muriel Gardiner, who had first made his acquaintance in 1927. His amateur painting, which Brunswick had regarded as a sign of his recovery, later precipitated a psychotic fugue on his dead sister's birthday in 1951, when he wandered into the Russian zone of occupied Vienna in search of something to paint (Brunswick, pp. 326–28). Somehow the suburbs of Vienna reminded him of his Russian boyhood, and he was unaware of his mistake until he was arrested as a spy by Russian officers, who interrogated him for the next three days. This alarming delusion, which plunged the Wolf Man into mortal danger, persuades some commentators that his psychosis must have worsened since the days of his nasal mania. In any case, this life-long patient was evidently not curable through Freudian methods, and probably not even analyzable. From the 1950s onwards the Wolf Man sought treatment from dozens of doctors, both psychiatrists and psychoanalysts, until he died in the Psychiatric Hospital in Vienna at the age of 92.

These multiple treatments and analytic conversations produced the numerous texts that constitute the "Wolf Man" for posterity – a highly contradictory array of documents. One difficulty is that both Freud and Brunswick are unreliable narrators, who persistently overlook their countertransferential investments in the case. Subsequent investigation has revealed much Freud in the symptoms and associations imputed to the Wolf Man; as Frank Cioffi has observed, Freud "stood to his patients' associations, dreams, symptoms, reminiscences and errors more as the painter to his pigments than as the sleuth to his traces of mud and cigar ash."[54] Similar symptoms of countertransference emerge in Brunswick's supplement; her crusade to demolish the Wolf Man's pride in being Freud's favorite patient shows telltale signs of sibling rivalry.[55] No wonder the elderly Pankejeff told Karen Obholzer that he did not believe in psychoanalysis, although he did believe in transference.[56] Apart from this astute remark, Pankejeff's interviews with Obholzer indicate an obdurate resistance to psychoanalytic insight, and offer little evidence of the "first-class intelligence" that Freud admired in his patient.[57] One can only wonder why the Wolf Man invested so much of his time and words (if not his money) in a form of treatment that he ultimately debunks as a confidence trick.

In particular he repudiates Freud's reconstruction of the primal scene – "it's terribly farfetched," he claims (Obholzer, p. 35). According to Freud, this scene is encoded in the wolf dream that triggered off the patient's first neurotic illness at the age of four. The first transcription of this dream was published by Freud in 1913, in a brief essay entitled "The Occurrence in Dreams of Material from Fairy Tales":

I dreamt that it was night and that I was lying in my bed. (My bed stood with its foot towards the window: in front of the window there was a row of old walnut trees. I know it was winter when I had the dream, and night-time.) Suddenly the window opened of its own accord, and I was terrified to see that some white wolves were sitting on the big walnut tree in front of the window. There were six or seven of them. The wolves were quite white, and looked more like foxes or sheep-dogs, for they had big tails like foxes and they had their ears pricked up like dogs when they pay attention to something. In great terror, evidently of being eaten up by the wolves, I screamed and woke up. My nurse hurried to my bed, to see what had happened to me. It took quite a long time before I was convinced that it had only been a dream. (*SE* 12:283–84)

In the version published in the Wolf Man's case history, this account is followed by the dreamer's observations:

The only piece of action in the dream was the opening of the window; for the wolves sat quite still and without making any movement on the branches of the tree, to the right and left of the trunk, and looked at me. It seemed as though they had riveted their whole attention on me.

After this nightmare, little Serge developed a phobia about being stared at, and was also reluctant to go to sleep lest he see "something terrible" in his dreams (SE 17:29). Freud argues that the dream-wolves derived from an illustration in Serge's book of fairy-tales, which depicted a wolf standing upright. Serge's sister Anna, amused by her little brother's terror of this image, used to flash it at him to provoke his screams (SE 17:29–30, 39). Other fairy-tales enlisted by the dream include "Little Red Riding-Hood" and "The Wolf and the Seven Little Goats." According to Freud, the second of these stories provided the numbers of the "six or seven" wolves in Serge's dream, since six little goats were eaten by the wolf, while the seventh escaped by hiding in the clock-case.

Freud emphasizes that the patient's phobic animal was drawn from stories and picture-books, rather than from lived experience; indeed the little boy was sorely disappointed when he finally laid eyes on a real wolf.[58] Nonetheless the "lasting sense of reality" that Serge experienced after the dream, requiring his Nanya to dispel its terror, convinces Freud that the nightmare referred to "an occurrence that really took place," not merely to a fiction or fantasy (SE 17:33). Yet this putative occurrence, the "primal scene," is more improbable than many of the child's fairy-tales. According to Freud, little Serge, suffering from malaria at the age of one-and-a-half, witnessed his parents indulging in "coitus *a tergo* [from behind], three times repeated," at precisely five-o'clock one fateful afternoon – the same hour at which the adult Pankejeff regularly slumped into depression (SE 17:37). In the dream, the whiteness of the parents' rumpled sheets and nightclothes is memorialized in the whiteness of the wolves, whose fixed stare recalls the infant's own rapt gaze as he watched this X-rated movie from his cot.[59]

The ailing child interrupted his parents' passionate exertions by screaming and defecating, a detail Freud deduces from the patient's later bowel inhibitions. The Wolf Man's association of enemas with unveiling also refers back to the primal scene, when the child released his bowels in response to the unveiling of his parents' genitalia. At the age of eighteen months, Serge was too young to understand the meaning of this raunchy spectacle, but its traces lay dormant in his memory until they were reactivated by his nightmare. The "shock of the event" (to borrow a phrase of Woolf's) was registered through its deferred effects, the trauma apprehended only *après coup* (*TL* 169). The implication is that trauma resides neither in the primal scene, nor in its imaginary "new editions," but between the acts and in their very non-coincidence (SE 17:36).

How does Freud make the leap from the wolves to parental intercourse? And why does he insist on the time of day at which this steamy episode occurred? According to Freud, the lynchpin of the primal scene is the posture that the parents supposedly assumed in intercourse. The fact that copulation from behind – "*more ferarum*" – is the posture preferred by animals reinforces the lycanthropic motif of the case. As Peter Brooks has pointed out, these postures also represent the nodal points at which reality "plugs into" fiction, connecting the parents to the wolves of fairy-tales: "this connection is provided … by the postures and only by them," Freud declares.[60]

For Freud's purposes, the crucial fairy-tale behind the dream is "The Tailor and the Wolf."[61] In this story a tailor, sitting in his workroom, is startled when his window opens of its own accord – like the window in the dream – and a wolf leaps through the unprotected aperture. The tailor seizes the intruder by the tail, breaking it off, and the wolf bolts away in terror. Some time later, the tailor is walking through the forest when he glimpses a pack of wolves and scrambles up a tree for safety. At first the wolves are flummoxed, but the maimed wolf orders the others to climb on top of him and snatch the tailor from the branches. The tailor, recognizing his dismembered visitor, cries out "Catch the grey one by the tail!" – the same words he had shouted when he met this beast before. Terrified by the recollection, the tailless wolf takes flight, and his companions tumble down behind him (SE 17:30–31).

In the patient's fantasies, Freud argues, "his mother took the part of the castrated wolf, which let the others climb upon it; his father took the part of the wolf that climbed" (SE 17:47). But little Serge identified himself with the mother rather than the father, craving the passive rather than the active role. In anticipation of his birthday the next morning, which was also Christmas day, the child was hoping to receive a double share of presents, perched among the branches of the Christmas tree – a wish both represented and disguised by the image of the walnut tree bedecked with wolves (SE 17:15). At the core of the dream, Freud argues, was the desire to enjoy the father's penis as Christmas and birthday gift combined.

It is not surprising that the aging Wolf Man, together with many other commentators on the case, have balked at Freud's conjectures, which are presented with breathtaking assurance, in contrast to the patient's faltering testimony.[62] But it would be churlish not to appreciate the deftness with which Freud discloses – or invents – each tantalizing detail of the mystery. Particularly ingenious is his interpretation of the time of day, 5 o'clock, at which the Wolf Man's parents supposedly engaged in their strenuous love-making. Although the number five does not appear in the dream-text as reported by the patient, who remembers seeing "six or seven" wolves, this number is reduced to five in his subsequent drawing of the dream. Freud interprets this pictorial subtraction as a correction of the patient's verbal recollections. At 5 o'clock that long-lost afternoon, the short hand of the clock would have been pointing to the Roman V, an upside-down image of the splayed legs of the mother in the coital posture associated with the tailless wolf. This primal memory was later reawakened by a nursery-maid called Grusha, who was washing the floor on her hands and knees when Serge glimpsed her from behind. Her posture, reminiscent of his mother's in the primal scene, caused the little boy to urinate excitedly (SE 17:90–93).

Associations continue to proliferate, branching out into the intricate network of the world of thought, a world in which minds of analyst and patient are difficult to disentangle. The name Grusha, which sounds like the Russian word for a pear with yellow stripes, lies behind another childhood incident when Serge, chasing a butterfly, suddenly collapsed into hysterics. This was because the butterfly had spread its wings and revealed its yellow stripes, thus evoking the memory of Grusha, an association reinforced by the V-shaped position of its wings (SE 17:89–90). These stripes resurface in another of the Wolf Man's dreams, in which a man is tearing off the wings of an "Espe." Since Freud is puzzled by this term, the Wolf Man explains that an "Espe" is a yellow-striped flying insect with a sting in its tail; in other words a *Wespe*, which is the German word for wasp. By dismembering the *Wespe* of its W – a letter composed of two ominous V's – the Wolf Man inflicts upon the word the same kind of mutilation performed upon the insect in the dream. Furthermore, the term *Espe* is a homonym of S. P., the Wolf Man's initials in German, which identify the patient with the insect castrated of its wings, as well as with the name castrated of its W (SE 17:94). Ultimately, the W missing from *Espe* refers to that which is missing from the mother's body, the penis-less V between the open scissors of her legs.

The intricate artistry of this analysis justifies Lacan's remark that the Wolf Man is the "most sensational" of Freud's case histories.[63] Yet as many commentators have observed, Freud's reconstruction of the primal scene relies on some strategic oversights. One of these, divulged by the Wolf Man in his later years, is that children never shared their parents' bedrooms in Russian aristocratic families; on the contrary, little Serge slept in a cot beside his Nanya (Obholzer, p. 36). Freud, by contrast, shared his parents' bedroom up to the age of three. This detail suggests that the wolf dream opened up the window to Freud's primal scene, his real or imaginary observation of parental intercourse, as opposed to any wolfish rutting witnessed by his patient.[64] Other countertransferential evidence includes Freud's natal caul, his chronic constipation, and his daughter's name Anna, details that implicate the analyst in the "latent content" attributed to the analysand.[65] Otto Rank, moreover, argues that the Wolf Man produced his dream for Freud, regardless of its putative antiquity, since its imagery alludes to the contemporary scene of the analysis. The walnut tree, for instance, which Freud interprets as the Christmas tree of childhood, is identified by Rank as the walnut tree that stood outside the window of Freud's Viennese consulting room.

If Freud reads his own fantasies into the Wolf Man's deliria, he also manipulates the evidence to validate his theories, especially those of infantile sexuality and the castration complex. Contra Freud, Melanie Klein has argued that Serge's fear of being eaten by the wolves, which Freud dismisses as a euphemism for castration-phobia, represents a relic of a "primal anxiety" predating either of these fears.[66] More recently, Ricardo E. Bernardi has pointed out that Freud ignores the theme of wolves with open wombs (suggested by "Little Red Riding-Hood" and other fairy-tales), and also fails to notice the transferential implications of the little goat hiding in the clock-case.[67] Characteristically Freud pays more attention to phallic than to uterine images, and emphasizes the castration complex by downplaying the motif of cannibalism. These emphases arise from Freud's ongoing disputes with Jung and Adler, followers turned rivals whom Freud accused of perverting his discoveries. During this period Jung was reinterpreting the primal scene as the product of racial inheritance and retrospective fantasy; Adler, meanwhile, was attempting to substitute his own theory of "masculine protest" for Freud's castration complex. Contra Jung, Freud insists on the objective reality of the primal scene; contra Adler, Freud stresses the castration complex over other connotations of the lupine theme.[68]

The psychoanalysts Nicolas Abraham and Maria Torok revisit the theme of cannibalism in their study, *The Wolf Man's Magic Word: A Cryptonomy*, and their subsequent collection of essays, *The Shell and the Kernel*.[69] Taking their inspiration from Freud's essay "Mourning and Melancholia," which argues that the bereaved ego devours or "incorporates" the lost object, Abraham and Torok argue that incorporation hollows out a "crypt" within the ego where the lost object is preserved alive. In the case of the Wolf Man, this incorporated object consists of the incestuous dyad of his father and sister. Since the ego refuses to relinquish the object's reality, any symbolization of this object is tabooed. By creating a verbal substitute for the encrypted object, symbolic language implies the loss of the original, a loss the ego cannot tolerate. To acknowledge this loss would be to destroy the crypt in which the object must be kept alive.

Instead, the crypt protects this object by means of "demetaphorization," whereby symbolic language is displaced by "cryptonyms" or "magic words." According to Abraham and Torok, the Wolf Man's cryptonyms are composites of Russian, German, and English (the language of his childhood governess), designed to hold interpreters at bay. The wolf itself is such a cryptonym: it signifies the open fly [*goulfik*] through which Serge's sister Anna rubs [*tieret*] their father's penis. Excluded from their intimacy, Serge stands to the crypt as "cemetery guard," his cryptonyms contrived as distractions to mislead the curious.[70] As Lawrence Johnson has observed, the construction of the crypt means that "the Wolf Man could give to Freud – then to Brunswick, then to Gardiner, then to Eissler and to others – time and again, what analysis needed to perpetuate itself: something hidden, something left to analyze. In return, analysis enables the crypt to continue to fashion its enigmatic façade …"[71] The Wolf Man's psychoanalysts, addicted to symbol-hunting, merely play into the machinations of the crypt, which contrives to keep the Thing alive, protecting its obscene enjoyments by stonewalling all attempts at symbolization.

According to Abraham and Torok, Freud's mistake was to think the Wolf Man was speaking in his own voice, rather than the voices of the undead objects in the crypt. Be this as it may, what makes Freud's case history so compelling is not that it is right, but that it generates more possibilities than it acknowledges, with regard to both the Wolf Man and his analyst. Besides, conventional ideas of rightness – the truth about an object determined by a subject – fail to account for the intersubjectivity of transference and countertransference. The "Wolf Man" is a hybrid creature, composed of both the analyst and the analysand; like the legendary werewolf, he oscillates between these alter egos, his shape depending on the moonlight cast by subsequent interpreters. While Freud pays little attention to hints of cannibalism, for example, he makes it possible for readers to reinvestigate these intimations.

The theme of cannibalism lurks in several of the fairy-tales discussed by Freud, in which wolves devour grandmothers and children. Some of these wolves resemble male mothers, in that they carry children in their bellies, thus confusing the boundaries of gender. In "Little Red Riding-Hood," the Wolf is dressed in drag, disguised in the nightgown of the grandmother he ate for dinner; in "The Seven Little Goats," six kids are rescued from the Wolf's belly through a kind of posthumous Caesarian section. "Was the wolf a female creature, then," little Serge asked himself, "or could men have children in their bodies as well?" (SE 17:25) The Wolf Man's Nanya encouraged this fantasy of paternal birth by telling Serge that Anna was her mother's child, whereas Serge was his father's, a distinction cherished fiercely by the little boy (SE 17:17).

Nonetheless Freud dismisses the "phantasy of re-birth" as a Jungian aberration. In Freud's judgement, the Wolf Man imagined himself as the passive partner in the primal scene, a fantasy restaged in his ritual enemas, in which the patient "identified himself with his mother," the attendant "acting as his father," and the enema "repeating the act of copulation, as the fruit of which the excrement-baby (which was once again himself) would be born." Freud concludes that "the phantasy of re-birth was simply a mutilated and censored version of the homosexual wishful phantasy" (SE 17:100). Yet it is possible that Freud's own "homosexual wishful phantasy" towards Jung compelled the founder of psychoanalysis to "mutilate and censor" his apostate's theory of rebirth. In any case, Freud is denying any assistance from a male attendant (Jung) in the delivery of psychoanalytic theory (excrement-baby).

Regardless of Freud's denials, the theme of paternal parturition resurfaces insistently throughout the Wolf Man's case. In addition to the fairy-tales, the patient's desire to be born from the father found mythological support in Christianity, which is also based on the denial of the mother's role in procreation. It is therefore telling that the Wolf Man was obsessed with the all-male family of the Trinity – reputedly the only holy family in mythology without a mother goddess. Whenever he came across three heaps of dung lying together in the road he was compelled to think of Father, Son, and Holy Ghost (SE 17:68). Born on Christmas day, the Wolf Man identified himself with Christ, who was "begotten not made" (in the words of the Nicene Creed), the child of the father rather than the mother.[72] The patient's fantasy of paternal birth was symbolically fulfilled when Freud published the case history, thereby giving birth to the book in which the Wolf Man was delivered to the world. If Christ was the word made flesh, the Wolf Man was the flesh made Word, re-engendered in the text of Freud the father.

Brunswick's case history defers to Freud's in stressing symbols of castration over those of cannibalism and incorporation.[73] Her re-analysis focuses on a series of the patient's dreams, including the following nightmare, which evokes the proverbial wolf at the door:

In a broad street is a wall containing a closed door. To the left of the door is a large, empty wardrobe with straight and crooked drawers. The patient stands before the wardrobe; his wife, a shadowy figure, is behind him. Close to the other end of the wall stands a large, heavy woman, looking as if she wanted to go round and behind the wall. But behind the wall is a pack of grey wolves, crowding toward the door and rushing up and down. Their eyes gleam, and it is evident that they want to rush at the patient, his wife, and the other woman. The patient is terrified, fearing that they will succeed in breaking through the wall. (Gardiner, pp. 288–89)[74]

If the wolves in Serge's childhood nightmare stood for Christmas gifts, this wolf dream represents a rich gift from the patient to his analyst; oneirically speaking, he is "paying like a gentleman" (Gardiner, p. 275). Brunswick reciprocates with an ingenious analysis. She interprets the large woman as an image of herself, amalgamated with a female acquaintance of the patient's. This acquaintance has a tiny scar on her nose, which causes her no anguish, much to the surprise of the analysand; this woman is therefore "a courageous person who fears neither wolves nor scars – the juxtaposition indicating a connection between the two." This connection between wolves and scars implies that the Wolf Man's obsession with his non-existent nasal scar derives from its association with his phobic animal.

Brunswick argues that the "closed door" in this dream takes the place of the open window of the original wolf dream (Gardiner, p. 289). But the locked doors, walls, and wardrobes of the later dream also correspond to Abraham and Torok's conception of the crypt. A "cryptonymic" reading might identify the restless wolves with the incorporated object, whose vitality ("rushing up and down") contrasts to the death-like figures of the heavy woman, the shadowy wife, and the motionless dreamer, all of whom remain immobilized outside the cryptic walls. Brunswick links the pacing wolves to the Bolsheviks who broke into a wardrobe in the Pankejeffs' estate. But it is also possible that the dreamer's fear of the marauding wolves masks an urge to storm the crypt, to reclaim a room of one's own within the ghost-infested ego.

According to Brunswick, a "clarified wolf dream" heralded the Wolf Man's recovery. In this dream, the patient gazes through a window at a tree, marveling at the beauty of its intertwining branches, and wonders why he has never painted this scene before. Brunswick argues that this tree replaces the wolf-bearing tree of Serge's childhood dream, and represents the patient's reconciliation to the primal scene; his appreciation of the beauty, rather than the terror, of the sexual embrace (Gardiner, p. 291). As we shall see, it is also by re-imagining a tree that Lily Briscoe paints her way back to the primal scene in *To the Lighthouse*. The next section of this chapter investigates convergences between Woolf's novel and the Wolf Man's case, especially the relation between trauma and making scenes.

POSTURES

Lily's painting demonstrates Freud's principle that "the finding of an object is always a re-finding of it" (SE 7:222). For Lily is paralysed by the presence of her object, Mrs. Ramsay, who must be lost to be re-found in Lily's art. Thus Mrs. Ramsay perishes in order to be resurrected in the picture, just as the novel's opening domestic idyll shatters to be reassembled at the end, after the deathly interlude, "Time Passes." In this novel everything that takes place takes two places, since each event is interrupted and resumed, according to the logic of *Nachträglichkeit* or deferred action. In her "Notes for Writing," Woolf describes this structure as "two blocks joined by a corridor."[75]

The first of these "blocks" climaxes in Chapter 7, which presents the Madonna-like tableau of Mrs. Ramsay reading to her son, framed by the window of the drawing-room. Meanwhile Mr. Ramsay is galumphing around the grounds, reciting Cowper and Tennyson, and Lily Briscoe is trying to capture these "unrelated passions" in her painting (*TL* 123). The window, which provides the title of the first section of the novel, could be compared to the window that flies open in the Wolf Man's dream, insofar as both disclose incestuous fantasies, James for his mother, Serge for his father. Woolf's window positions the members of the family and organizes their symbolic space, placing James inside the circle of maternal sympathy and casting Mr. Ramsay out, "like a wolf barking in the snow" (*TL* 163). Stopping by the window, Mr. Ramsay looks down at the framed scene of mother and son, demanding the undistracted attention of his wife:

But his son hated him. He hated him for coming up to them, for stopping and looking down on them; he hated him for interrupting them … but most of all he hated the twang and twitter of his father's emotion which, vibrating around them, disturbed the perfect simplicity and good sense of his relations with his mother. (*TL* 33)

Here it is important that James hates his father for "interrupting them," because the paternal function in this novel – as in Lacanian psychoanalysis – is to interrupt. In this case, the father intrudes between mother and son, shattering their intimacy; elsewhere he barges in between the painter and her canvas, nearly knocking over Lily's easel; he also foists himself between speaker and utterance, "cutting off" his children's "right to speak" (*TL* 18). While Mr. Ramsay interrupts, Mrs. Ramsay knits, as if to repair the paternal lesions in the family web.

Mrs. Ramsay abhors any form of separation, from single women to disgruntled guests, and Lily, as an artist and a spinster, finds this maternal compulsion to connect as oppressive as the paternal compulsion to dissever.

This tension between knitting and cutting, uniting and dividing, as embodied in the Ramsay parents, resembles the double-sided notion of the omphalos, which implies both connectivity and separation. In *To the Lighthouse* these omphalic contradictions are battled out within the very texture of the prose: when Mr. Ramsay speaks, or the narrator speaks on his behalf, the sentences fragment into non sequiturs, ejaculations, and quotations uprooted from their context: "little words that broke up the thought and dismembered it ..." (*TL* 146). No sooner do these interruptions strike, however, than the opposing force re-knits them into the elastic fabric of the prose; thus "ruin [is] veiled."[76] Yet the ruins in the prose seem to resurface on the body of the landscape, where the mountainside is riven with "vast fissures," the pear tree scarred with "fissures and humps," and the sea disfigured by a purple stain, "as if something had boiled and bled, invisibly, beneath" (*TL* 23). In these disturbing images, the lesions in the family and the prose break out in the surfaces of the external world, much as the Wolf Man's psychic scars break out in the lupine ulcerations of his skin.

The fact that Mr. Ramsay reasserts his claim to James's mother at the same time that he forbids the lighthouse to his son implies that his paternal entitlement to one entails the other. That the lighthouse stands for the paternal phallus therefore seems embarrassingly obvious – "there it loomed up, stark and straight" (*TL* 165). But this Freudian truism dissolves on contact with Woolf's protean imagery:

Mrs. Ramsay, who had been sitting loosely, holding her son in her arm, braced herself, and, half turning, seemed to raise herself with an effort, and at once to pour erect into the air a rain of energy, a column of spray, looking at the same time animated and alive as if all her energies were being fused into force, burning and illuminating (quietly though she sat, taking up her stocking again), and into this delicious fecundity, this fountain and spray of life, the fatal sterility of the male plunged itself, like a beak of brass, barren and bare. He wanted sympathy ... Flashing her needles, confident, upright, she created drawing-room and kitchen, set them all aglow; bade him take his ease there, go in and out, enjoy himself. She laughed, she knitted. Standing between her knees, very stiff, James felt all her strength flaring up to be drunk and quenched by the beak of brass, the arid scimitar of the male, which smote mercilessly, again and again, demanding sympathy. (*TL* 34)

In this passage the "phallic ghost," to borrow Lacan's terminology, flits among the family triangle, alighting on one member after another, in what resembles a game of musical chairs, or musical phalloi.[77] First of all the mother seems "to raise herself," "to pour erect into the air a rain of energy, a column of spray," her phallic knitting needles flashing. Only then does her husband's "beak" begin to "plunge" into her fountain – a beak which, despite its phallic connotations in this passage, is associated with the "harpy," traditionally a female monster. Meanwhile James assumes the place of the maternal phallus, "standing between her knees, very stiff," like the organ missing from the V-shaped thighs in the phantasmatics of the Wolf Man. Woolf's imagery deranges the ostensible alignments of her characters: although James is seething with jealousy about his mother, his gestures tell a different story and implicate him with his hated father. Perceiving his father as a murderous "scimitar" – "lean as a knife, narrow as the blade of one" – the little boy himself is armed with scissors (*TL* 7). Thus equipped he is cutting out pictures of knives from an Army and Navy Stores catalogue; his mother worries that "the picture of a pocket knife with six blades … could only be cut out if James was very careful" (*TL* 17). In Kleinian terms, the violence imputed to the father represents a "projective identification" on the part of his sadistic son, whose allegiance to his mother is belied by the images of knives and scissors that align him with the cutting father.[78]

Smite and plunge though Mr. Ramsay does in James's fantasy, in reality the father touches his son only once, "whimsically" tickling the little boy's bare calf with a "sprig of something." Nonetheless this "tickling spray" leaves a sensory scar on James's leg that reawakens during the final journey to the lighthouse (*TL* 28–29); in psychoanalytic terms, this portion of his skin has been "hystericised." In the concluding section of the novel, the paternal interdiction of the lighthouse is reversed when the widowed Mr. Ramsay bullies his now reluctant children into resuming the interrupted journey. At this point the Oedipal triangle is rearranged, with Cam assuming the position of her mother in the former scene, obliged to mediate between the rival males. Sandwiched between her father and her brother James, like "the sandwiches among them" on the boat, Cam bears witness to the drama of inheritance in which her father delivers "the tablets of eternal wisdom" to his son, so that James can now become the "lawgiver" (*TL* 166, 138).[79] Meanwhile Lily rearranges the figures in her painting, having spent ten years – broken by the novel's corridor of dormancy – fretting over the position of the tree. Her obsession with position, with the need to fashion "some relationship between those masses," mirrors the Oedipal crisis of the Ramsays, forced to realign their own positions in relation to the absent mother.

The novel's primal scene begins to re-emerge when James, enraged at Cam's submission to Mr. Ramsay, remembers how his mother had capitulated to her husband's imperious demand for sympathy:

> She'll give way, James thought, as he watched a look come upon [Cam's] face, a look he remembered. They look down he thought, at their knitting or something. Then suddenly they look up. There was a flash of blue, he remembered, and then somebody sitting with him laughed, surrendered, and he was very angry. It must have been his mother, he thought, sitting on a low chair, with his father standing over her. He began to search among the infinite series of impressions which time had laid down, leaf upon leaf, fold upon fold, softly, incessantly upon his brain … (*TL* 139)

Here the postures of the parents trigger James's recollection of the earlier event, much as the similar postures imputed to the Wolf Man's parents triggered the wolf dream: "this connection is provided … by the postures and only by them," as Freud insists. Apart from their postures, James's parents have faded into metonymic shards of reminiscence: "scents, sounds; voices, harsh, hollow, sweet; and lights passing, and brooms tapping, and the wash and hush of the sea, how a man had marched up and down and stopped dead, upright, over them" (*TL* 139). Here the father, "upright," assumes the same posture as the upright wolf in little Serge's picture-book, the posture also adopted by the father in the primal scene – "*more ferarum.*" In Woolf's novel, as in the Wolf Man's case, the postures of the father, upright, and the mother, physically debased, have come to represent the child's violent exclusion from their intimacy (SE 17:94).

James's recollection of the primal scene coincides with the reactivation of his sensory scar, the tickle of the sprig on his bare leg, but this sprig is now confounded with the penetrating beak of a "fierce sudden black-winged harpy, with its talons and its beak all cold and hard, that struck and struck at you (he could feel the beak on his bare legs, where it had struck when he was a child) …" (*TL* 151).[80] By imagining Mr. Ramsay as a harpy, James performs a sex-change on his father, transforming him into a kind of phallic mother. This gender-ambiguity endorses James's view that "nothing was simply one thing" (*TL* 152). Both male and female, father and mother, Mr. Ramsay is a monster, but he is also "a figure of infinite pathos" (*TL* 128), a sad old man who never reached the letter R.

"Nothing was simply one thing." The final section of the novel stages this duality by juxtaposing scenes on land to scenes on sea, thereby inflicting on the reader Lily's sense that staying with the Ramsays "was to be made to feel violently two opposite things at the same time" (*TL* 83). While the Ramsays' boat travels forwards, *to* the Lighthouse, Lily travels backwards through her painting: "She went on tunneling her way into her painting, into the past" (*TL* 142).[81] Lily's conception of the painting as a tunnel to the past resembles the Wolf Man's psychotic fugue, when he wandered into the Russian zone to paint his way back home to childhood. But Lily cannot finish with the past until the Ramsays have arrived at the long-awaited lighthouse. This arrival is presented by proxy, coinciding with the moment when Lily moves the tree to the middle of her canvas, a realignment planned but interrupted ten years earlier.[82]

This newly centralized position of the tree corresponds to the position of the lighthouse in the novel; as Woolf explains, "One has to have a central line down the middle of the book to hold the design together." By moving the tree, Lily inscribes "a central line down the middle" of the canvas, an omphalic scar that cuts the scene in half, creating a "razor edge of balance" (*TL* 158). Furthermore, this divided canvas reflects in spatial form the temporal disjunction of the novel, split by the central "corridor" of "Time Passes." This middle section joins and separates the novel's halves, while providing an umbilical passageway to the lost mother. As Laura Marcus has pointed out, "Time Passes" records the slow deterioration of the house as a means of contemplating the decomposition of the mother's body in the grave.[83]

Woolf writes in her diary on April 18, 1926: "I have to give an empty house, no people's characters, the passage of time, all eyeless & featureless with nothing to cling to ..." (*Diary* 3:76).[84] Like Wallace Stevens's cold observer in "The Snow Man," "who, nothing himself, beholds / Nothing that is not there and the nothing that is," Woolf attempts to present nothing from the point of view of nothing. This nothing, "creeping in at keyholes and crevices," also spreads into the parenthetical reports of family deaths – including Andrew Ramsay's death in the Great War – which riddle the sentences with tiny crypts. During the protracted interval of "Time Passes," only servants venture into the decaying house, but their subjectivity is too attenuated to impinge upon this "world seen without a self" (*Waves* 221). Rather than a seeing self, or a narrating subject, the servant Mrs. McNab is reduced to the quintessence of the dust that she disturbs.

In the final section of the novel, the surviving Ramsays fill the house again, yet without dispelling the nothing that is – for this nothing is displaced onto the lighthouse. "I meant nothing by the Lighthouse," Woolf famously declared, and nothing is precisely what the lighthouse means: it functions as the gap of gaps, the totem of the intermittent and interstitial. "There it loomed up, stark and straight, glaring white and black, and one could see the waves breaking in white splinters like smashed glass upon the rocks" (*TL* 165). This apocalyptic image of smashed glass suggests that "The Window" has been shattered: the window in which Mrs. Ramsay sat enfolded with her son until Mr. Ramsay "loomed up, stark and straight," and interrupted them; and also the window to reality supposedly provided by the realist novel. Similar images of smashed glass reappear in Woolf's last novel, *Between the Acts* (1941), where the village children, dressed as elves and demons, flash broken mirrors at the audience, distorting and dismembering the startled faces. In this way the mirrors "shiver into splinters the old vision; smash to atoms what was whole" (*BA* 109). Like the waves that splinter on the rocks in *To the Lighthouse*, the broken mirrors of *Between the Acts* herald the emergence of a violent new art, pledged to rupture rather than to reparation.

Daniel Ferrer has drawn attention to the sadism involved in Lily's art, the "violent aggressive and libidinal drives" that transform what was inscription on a surface into "spasm, coitus, excretion, a struggle, doomed to failure, against a jealous and implacable divinity."[85] To cite a few examples: "the mass loomed before [Lily]; it protruded; she felt it pressing on her eyeballs"; "striking, she scored her canvas with brown running lines"; "those lines cutting across, slicing down"; "as if some juice necessary for the lubrication of her faculties were spontaneously squirted" (*TL* 130–31). The images of cutting in this passage (striking, scored, cutting across, slicing down) reinvoke the scene in Part I Chapter 7, where the furious James is cutting up a catalogue in lieu of Mr. Ramsay, a tableau that reveals the unconscious alliance between the cutting father and his son. The echoes of this scene in the description of Lily's painting associate her art with the paternal principle of cutting, as opposed to the maternal principle of unifying.

Lily's last "stroke," however, complicates this opposition, since the term "stroke" may denote either a blow or a caress, and also refers back to the Lighthouse's pulsating beam, the "third stroke" of which belongs to the dead mother ("[Mrs. Ramsay] looked out to meet that stroke of the Lighthouse, the long steady stroke, the last of the three, which was her stroke …" [*TL* 47]). Lily's final stroke is to move the tree to the middle, thereby inscribing the central line that cuts the painted scene in half.[86] At once sadistic and reparative, this stroke completes the murder of the mother but also brings her back in substitutive form. This ambivalence is captured in Lily's final words, "I have had my vision": I have possessed, enjoyed, accomplished my vision, but I have also got rid of it at last.

The Wolf Man makes a similar adjustment to a tree in the final dream discussed in Brunswick's *Supplement*, the dream in which the patient is enchanted by the intertwining branches of a tree. This tree has shed its wolves and moved to the center of the Wolf Man's vision. Yet this vision, like Lily's painting, is communicated only in the form of words; the analyst can never see the patient's dream, but relies upon the patient's verbal recollections, just as the reader cannot see the painting that Woolf portrays in words. In Woolf, this absorption of painting into narrative smacks of sibling rivalry, suggesting the ambivalent desire to incorporate yet also to outdo her sister Vanessa's visual art. In the Wolf Man's case, the dream-tree also testifies to sibling rivalry, and to his sister Anna's posthumous control over his mind. As a child, Anna was the better artist of the siblings, and particularly good at drawing trees – so good, in fact, that Serge gave up trying to draw them (Brunswick, 9). Nonetheless he persists in this sibling competition in his dreams, creating first the wolf tree and finally the self-embracing tree, shed of its strange fruit, which convinces Brunswick of his recovery.

Brunswick argues that the wolf-free tree reveals the patient's reconciliation to the primal scene, and his acceptance of parental sexuality. However, the sad fact that the Wolf Man never conquered his illness casts doubt on Brunswick's optimism. Her interpretation of this pretty tree fulfills her own wish, rather than the dreamer's: a wish to cure the incurable, and to succeed where Freud had failed in banishing the lupine spectres of the Wolf Man's past. It could be argued that Brunswick's analysis reproduces the Wolf Man's family triangle, with the female analyst standing in for the suicidal sister (Brunswick later died of a fall resulting from her opium addiction), and Freud for the Wolf Man's father – a father who preferred his daughter to his son.[87] The de-wolved tree, with its beautiful branches, pays homage to the trees that Anna used to draw so skilfully, in contrast to little Serge's clumsy imitations. This dream-tree also serves to propitiate Brunswick, as a stand-in for the Wolf Man's sister, by affirming the analyst's power to heal, thus humoring Brunswick's fantasies of omnipotence.

If the tree-borne wolves of the first dream represented the father's gifts to Serge, the wolf-less tree could be seen as the Wolf Man's belated gift to Anna, a gift received by Brunswick in Anna's place. One reason why the Wolf Man may have persisted in his painting, despite Freud's disapproval of this hobby, was to perpetuate the art of the dead sister. Another possibility, implied by Abraham and Torok's interpretation of the case, is that the incorporated sister was directing her brother's paintbrush from her crypt, through a kind of manual ventriloquism. Remember that Anna's birthday was the date that the Wolf Man wandered into the Russian zone in search of something to paint (a tree?), as if he were compelled to paint a birthday present for his sister. Brunswick has argued the motif of the gift "runs like a red thread" through the Wolf Man's psychobiography. The next section of this chapter investigates the theme of gifts in relation to the economy of trauma.

Making Scenes

The "to" in the title *To the Lighthouse* indicates direction, but also hints that the novel is a gift, dedicated "to" its central image, as a literary work is often dedicated to a loved one or a muse. In the novel, the lighthouse itself represents a gift in the possession of the father, a gift withheld for ten long years. As a paternal gift, the lighthouse corresponds to the wolves in Serge's dream, which signify the father's undelivered presents. In both cases the paternal gift, whether of the lighhouse or the Christmas presents, is withheld and postponed. Instead of being given or exchanged, for instance, the gift of the lighthouse is invested, saved up for an unrainy day. It is investment that brings about deferred "returns," whether in the form of long-term dividends or compulsive repetition of the past. In this sense, the economics of investment therefore correspond to those of trauma, in that both involve deferred returns. In trauma, pain is invested in the mind or body, such as the sensory scar on James's calf, to be reactivated at a future time, with a usurious increment of anguish.

If the economy of *To the Lighthouse* is dominated by the notion of investment, the Wolf Man was not an investor but a gambler. The two activities are not dissimilar, but gambling is a form of investment that attempts to short-circuit the delay between the outlay and the profit. The Wolf Man was introduced to gambling by the Russian doctor who accompanied him to Vienna, along with the versatile manservant who made a third at cards, as well as administering enemas. (In view of the connections between faeces and money that Freud maps out in his essays on anal erotism, these enemas could be seen as the excremental equivalent to winning the jackpot.[88]) As compulsive gambler, the aristocratic Wolf Man bears a striking resemblance to the Russian landowners in

Dostoevsky's story *The Gambler*, who squander vast family fortunes at roulette. Dostoevsky's gamblers play to lose; the fantasy of profit serves as a pretext for the thrill of waste, for the "exhilaration at losing possessions," as Woolf described her feelings when her London flat was bombed in 1940 (*Diary* 331).

The Wolf Man's gambling may be traced back to his childhood dream, which arose from the desire to maximize his Christmas presents. In his analysis with Brunswick, the theme of gambling re-emerges in a dream in which the Wolf Man's father warns the assembled company about his son's "tendency to speculate."[89] It is ironic that the father should discourage speculation in the dream, since it was this father who provoked his son's first bet, the wolf dream itself. As we have seen, this dream gambled on the father's power to multiply the presents on the Christmas tree, as well as to give birth to sons.

Elsewhere Freud identifies paternity itself as the "speculation" underlying the symbolic fabric of civilization. "Family Romances" (1909), for example, argues that maternity is founded on the evidence of the senses – the incontrovertible testimony of the umbilical cord – whereas paternity is founded on "inference" and "speculation." A great advance in civilization was achieved when "men" renounced the fact of motherhood in favor of the gamble of paternity (SE 9:232). In this sense, little Serge's gamble on paternal parturition could be seen as an exaggeration of the founding fantasy of patriarchy. In his analysis, moreover, the Wolf Man gambles on the father of psychoanalysis, betting on Freud's power to provide him with rebirth, as a new book, if not as a new man. The Wolf Man's "tendency to speculate" therefore led him not only to the gambling table but to the couch, ensuring his addiction to psychoanalysis. A particularly seductive form of gambling, psychoanalysis offers patients the opportunity to stake their all, with no assurance of return, on the chance that Freud's speculations may be true. More reckless still, these punters gamble that Freud's truth can cure. On the basis of this wager, patients squander money, words, and time, to be rewarded with the gift of silence – which is the only gift one can be certain to receive from God.

Freud notoriously flouted the rule of analytic silence, a rule retrospectively established in his name. Instead his case histories expose his indefatigable efforts to talk his patients into something, to submit themselves to his "penetrating interpretations coming from behind," as Patrick Mahony puts it.[90] The patients meanwhile interject, resist, digress, consent, or slam the door on psychoanalysis, as Dora did, but mainly listen to Freud talk.

Beyond this talk, however, lies the silence of the primal scene, a phantom space conjured up by the transference itself, belonging to neither the past nor the present, neither the analyst nor the analysand, and yet more real than any lived or liveable experience. Unknown and unremembered, the primal scene corresponds to that which Lacan calls the Real, and Freud calls the navel of the dream: the "unplumbable" abyss of the unrepresentable.

Both Woolf and the Wolf Man reveal an impulse to make scenes, to conjure up the stage of this impossible event, as if the mise-en-scène were more compelling than the deed supposedly performed within its frame. Woolf persistently invokes such empty scenes: in "Time Passes," she presents the house bereft of its inhabitants; in *Jacob's Room*, the room without its tenant; in "The Mark on the Wall," the wall without the characters who marked it. When writing "The Mark on the Wall" in 1917, Woolf was elated with the discovery that she could do away with narrative duration, presenting "violent moments of being" instead of interposing the contrived continuities of the conventional novel.[91] This discovery enabled her to act on her impulse to make scenes, instead of recapitulating their history and aftermath. Her obsession with scene-making strains against the temporality of narrative, causing her novels either to be set within a single day, as in *Mrs. Dalloway* or *Between the Acts*, or to be broken into two days, as in *To the Lighthouse*, where the first and third parts of the novel form the torn halves of a single odyssey. Between these days, "Time Passes," but the kind of time that passes is cordoned off within the central section, like a condemned corridor within the narrative.

Woolf's preference for "violent moments," as opposed to the passing time of narrative, may explain why *To the Lighthouse* portrays the female artist as a painter striving to create a scene, rather than a writer striving to narrate a story.[92] The Wolf Man also resorted to painting as a way of making scenes, a hobby that Freud, with his marauding countertransference, urged his patient to forego in favor of a verbal form of sublimation. Yet the Wolf Man seemed to know that only painting could express the petrifaction of his inner world, frozen as the white wolves of his dream.[93] Freud's interpretation of this dream pays less attention to the silence and stillness of these wolves than to the sound and fury of the primal scene: the child's screams, the parents' motion. Yet elsewhere Freud argues that silence in dreams symbolizes death, a meaning he also attributes to Cordelia's silence in *King Lear*.[94] Wolves are usually associated with noisy aggression and destruction, but Serge's dream-wolves seem to represent the outcome of the death-drive as opposed to its destructive means, embodying the dumbness of inorganic matter.

It is important that the dream makes a scene out of this dumbness, the bedroom window flying open much as the curtain rises in a theatre. The Wolf Man's dreams, together with his paintings, attempt to reproduce this silent scene, as opposed to its sexual commotion. These attempts suggest that there is something contagious about primal scenes, something that demands repeated scene-ification. Freud's ingenious reconstruction of the primal scene fails to banish the suspicion that nothing actually happened to the little boy, or nothing that could be reintegrated into an objective history. But this nothing left a scar, in the form of the compulsion to make scenes, to visualize a place for that which never literally "took place." The Wolf Man's dream-scenes, like Lily's elegiac painting, summon up this placeless, timeless non-event, this rupture in the flow of history. Their visions suggest that trauma, rather than the impulse to restore a lost original event, represents the drive to make a scene of nothing. "I meant nothing by the Lighthouse," Woolf declared; the Wolf Man might have echoed, "I meant nothing by the wolf-tree." By making scenes, the writer and the dreamer strive to frame this nothing, to stage the unoccurred and unoccurable.

CHAPTER 5

The darkened blind: Joyce, Gide, Larsen, and the modernist short story

> Night after night I had passed the house (it was vacation time) and studied the lighted square of window: and night after night I had found it lighted in the same way, faintly and evenly. If he was dead, I thought, I would see the reflection of candles on the darkened blind for I knew that two candles must be set at the head of a corpse.
>
> (*D* 9)

In this famous passage from "The Sisters," the first story in Joyce's *Dubliners*, the child-narrator gazes upward to the window to figure out if Father Flynn, the paralytic priest, is dead. But instead of seeing through this window, the child's gaze is obstructed by the "darkened blind." This blind transforms the window into a surface to be read, as opposed to a transparent portal to the death-chamber. That the boy is searching for a sign of death, rather than the living presence of the syphilitic priest, implicates the blind in the ascendancy of signs, and the sign in the downfall of father-figures.

In Chapter 3 I argued that a central blindness organizes Strether's visual field, both obstructing and enhancing his perception of Chad's love affair: obstructing, in the sense that Strether's idealization of the romance conceals its carnal element; enhancing, in the sense that Strether alone appreciates the moral benefits of the liaison. The Pococks see through Chad's refinement, as if he were an unobstructed window, but Strether regards him as a darkened blind, marked with "signs and tokens ... too thick for prompt discrimination" (*A* 120). In this sense Strether plays a similar role to Joyce's juvenile narrator, who is too young to understand the priest's disgrace or the conspiracy of silence that surrounds it. Both observers are blinded to sexual scandal, either by the innocence of youth or by the quixotism of regretful middle-age.

Dubliners is haunted by the theme of blinds and blindness, beginning with the darkened blind of "The Sisters" and culminating in the blinding snowstorm of "The Dead": "snow was general all over Ireland" (*D* 223).

Furthermore, *Dubliners* is organized around a central blind spot, the absent father, in much the same way that James's network of ambassadors fans out from the absent mother, Mrs. Newsome. In *Ulysses* Stephen Dedalus announces that the Church is founded on the "legal fiction" of paternity, "and founded irremovably because founded, like the world, macro and microcosm, upon the void. Upon incertitude, upon unlikelihood" (*U* 170:841–43). The world of *Dubliners* is also founded on the void of fatherhood. This void cannot be held at bay, but seeps into the gaps and ellipses of the narrative. Repeated references to blinds and blindness, along with equally insistent references to silence, mark the paternal dereliction at the core of *Dubliners*.

In *The Blind Short Story* (2004), a special issue of the *Oxford Literary Review*, the authors point out that the theme of blindness frequently recurs in the short story, as if the dangers of obscured or baffled vision were somehow endemic to the genre. A surprising number of short stories feature blind protagonists, and their blindness is the flipside of the "blind" they present to the reader, the opacity with which they fend off the psychologizing gaze. Joyce's story "Eveline" in *Dubliners*, for instance, concludes with this chilling image: "Her eyes gave him no sign of love or farewell or recognition" (*D* 41). Here Eveline's blind and blinding stare epitomizes the way that the short story thwarts the reader's desire for a "sign" of inner life.

The next section of this chapter investigates the theme of blindness in the history and theory of short stories, ranging from Poe to Elizabeth Bowen, and focusing on Gide's novella *The Pastoral Symphony* (1919), the story of a blind girl "cured" by cataract surgery. Notice that Gide's title alludes to a work of music written by a deaf man, for *The Pastoral Symphony* reveals that blindness and vision, like deafness and hearing, are not the opposites they seem; indeed, the blind and deaf may see and hear more clearly for the reason that their eyes and ears are free of sights and sounds. Moreover, blindness is inextricable from vision; we see only what we learn to see, what we can bear to see, what we can look at without blushing, retching, fainting, dying. As James Elkins has written: "Each act of vision mingles seeing with not seeing, so that vision can become less a way of gathering information than avoiding it … Blindness is like a weed that grows in the very centre of vision, and its roots are everywhere."[1]

The discussion of Gide is followed by an investigation of the theme of blindness in *Dubliners*. Joyce, who started out as the shortsighted master of the short story, ended up as the blind punster of *Finnegans Wake*: "till

allearth's dumbnation shall the blind lead the deaf!" (*FW* 68:34). Roy
Gottfried, in *Joyce's Iritis and the Irritated Text*, makes an ingenious case
that Joyce's puns were inspired by his eye disease, which caused the letters of the word to wander off on independent odysseys.[2] Borges, who
was also blind, praises Joyce's valorous lie that "of all the things that have
happened to me, I think the least important was having been blind." Yet
it was Joyce's "gift" of blindness, Borges argues, that enabled him to bring
"new music" to the English language, the loss of vision having sharpened
his attention to the sounds of words.[3]

The concluding part of this chapter, "Color-blindness," turns to the
optics of race in the African American short story, particularly in the
work of Joyce's contemporary Nella Larsen (1891–1964). In American culture, to be "colored" is to be too visible, because whiteness is regarded
as an absence rather than another shade of color; but also to become
invisible, because color functions as a surface for projections, concealing the humanity of those it marks. As we shall see, Nella Larsen's story
"Sanctuary" (1930) probes the lethal forms of blindness arising from the
fiction of the visibility of race.

BLIND STORIES

In 1960 Elizabeth Bowen gave a course on the short story at Vassar, in
which she asked her students how a short story differs from a novel. The
obvious answer is "shortness." But "what is shortness"? "*Not* a *negative*
quality," Bowen writes in her class notes:

> Not mere stripping-off
> Not exhaustion
> Not constriction.

On the contrary, shortness is an art of "concentration." There is "a sense
of pressure – of immediacy – of something happening within the – grip
of *our* senses – under our eyes." What the short story gains, however, in
intensity of focus, it loses in development of character. Instead of eluci-
dating human motives, it deepens their mystery. "There is a touch of the
Sphinx in many human beings," Bowen comments:

and this "sphinx" quality is one which – quite often – the S.S. – legitimately –
exploits[.] The S.S. – in its small, spotlit zone – may "exhibit" characters of a
kind which might not be "interesting enough to pursue" through the greater
length of the novel. In fact, the short-storyist often makes an instinctive choice
of the *type* of character most likely to profit by *brief*, brilliantly-lit treatment.[4]

Here Bowen implies that the short story shines a spotlight on the human sphinx, not to solve its riddle but merely to "exhibit" its opacity. If the mission of the realist novel is to make the reader see, Bowen's metaphors suggest that the short story aims to make the reader blind, by casting such a glaring light on character that everything before, beyond, or underneath this incandescent surface vanishes. Bowen's image of the "small, spotlit zone" could be compared to Beckett's drama of elimination, especially his play *Not I*, in which "character" is reduced to a brilliantly-lit mouth babbling wildly in the darkness. In this play, what we see depends on what we don't see; the world is blotted out to spotlight speech in all its salivating muscularity. In a comparable way, Bowen intimates, the short story blots out more than it illuminates: its spotlight makes the sphinx too dazzling to see, the world too dark.

In a BBC broadcast of 1956, Bowen wonders if "the study of individual character" has exhausted itself in the novel, to be replaced by "the symbolic, the masked speaker."[5] If this is so, then the novel has been revolutionized by the short story, in which characters exist to implement the action, not to upstage it with their own star turns. This is why they must be masked – to baffle the novel-gazing habits of the reader, accustomed to peering through the surface to the depths of personality. Yet the mask, which deflects the reader's prying eyes, also seems to obstruct the vision of the characters themselves, who typically suffer some defect of sight or insight. Many are literally blind, and their blindness renders them impenetrable to the sighted.

Thus the blind cannot be seen; the blind blind us. This reversibility is built into the very word, for "blind" is noun, verb, adverb, and adjective at once. What we look for in the other is an answering gaze, an affirmation of our own visibility; Narcissus was enchanted by his mirror-image not just because it was good-looking, but because it could look back at him. In blind eyes, on the contrary, we see ourselves unseen, obliterated from the field of vision. In effect, we see ourselves dead. Hence it is traditional to shut the eyelids of the dead to spare the living from the sight of sightlessness. It is worth noting that until the 1930s dark glasses were worn only by the blind, not to protect their eyes but to conceal them from the sighted.

Why does blindness, both literal and metaphorical, recur so frequently in the short story? Is this theme the symptom of a blindness inherent in the form? One answer is that the short story typically begins and ends *in medias res*, thereby blinding the reader to before and after, as well as to the wider world beyond its spotlit zone. The novel, by contrast, demands continuity, and for this reason Bowen argues that British novelists have gained the edge over their Irish counterparts, the continuity of British life having been purchased at the cost of Irish havoc. Bowen claims that her early transplantation to England made her a novelist, whereas her native Ireland inclined her towards short stories. The novel is "too life-like, humdrum" for the apocalyptic spirit of the Irish, but "we do not do badly with the short story, 'that, in a spleen, unfolds both heaven and earth' – or should."[6] Joyce's *Dubliners*, however, confounds this distinction by combining the humdrum with the epiphanic. What is more, its stories are always printed in the same order, thereby breaking the conventions of the genre. Beginning with tales of childhood and ending with those of disappointed middle-age, *Dubliners* aspires to the condition of the novel; conversely, it could be argued that *Ulysses* is a novel aspiring to the condition of short stories.

Other Irish masters of the short story include Bowen's friend Frank O'Connor and her sometime lover Sean O'Faolain, both of whom were also pioneering critics of the genre. O'Faolain attributes the Irish flair for the short story to the shambolic state of Ireland, proposing that "the more firmly organised a country is the less room there is for the short-story, for the intimate close-up, the odd slant, or the unique comment."[7] O'Connor, in his famous study *The Lonely Voice* (1963), argues that the short story depends on a "submerged population group," and seeks protagonists among the humble and the dispossessed, often focusing on "outlawed figures wandering about the fringes of society." Characterized by "an intense awareness of human loneliness," the short story reflects an atomized society, its characters islanded within their spotlit zones. The novel, on the contrary, is "bound to be a process of identification between the reader and the character."[8] For this reason, its hero cannot be what Wilde called a "sphinx without a secret" – a blind with nothing hidden underneath – for the novel depends upon the promise of an inner life to be revealed.[9]

In case my emphasis on Irish writers conveys the false impression that Ireland invented the short story, an invention often claimed by the United States, it should be pointed out that neither country actually deserves the credit. The short story in its modern form arose out of the periodical literature of the eighteenth century, and in the same period that Irving, Hawthorne, Longfellow, Poe, and Melville were Americanizing the short story, British writers such as Thackeray, Dickens, Trollope, Gaskell, and George Eliot also produced masterworks of short fiction. Edgar Allan Poe, however, is generally agreed to be the first critical theorist of the short story. In his famous 1842 review of Nathaniel Hawthorne's *Twice-Told Tales*, Poe defines the prose tale as a narrative that can be read at a single sitting, "requiring from a half-hour to one or two hours in its perusal."[10] It is intriguing – à propos of blindness – that the Hawthorne stories singled out for praise in Poe's review revolve around concealment, especially concealment of the eyes.[11] In "The Minister's Black Veil," the veil that hides the minister's eyes terrorizes his parishioners because they cannot see him seeing them. In this sense the minister's black veil performs a similar function to the dark glasses worn by the Sicilian Mafia, which "conceal the most revealing parts of the body and prevent others from detecting either the direction of the gaze or any lapses into sentimentality or absent-mindedness," as Diego Gambetta has observed. "Cover up the mirror of the soul, and people begin to doubt whether a soul is there at all."[12] Similarly, the cloaks and veils that hide the eyes of Hawthorne's characters cause the gaze to boomerang on the beholder, exposing his or her corrupted soul.

Later American theorists of the short story include Edith Wharton, who argues that this genre differs from the novel in subordinating character to plot. "The test of a novel," she declares, "is that its people should be *alive*." Does it follow that the characters of the short story must be dead? Not quite – but dead enough to subordinate themselves to the "chief affair" of action. According to Wharton, the short story harks back to "the old epic or ballad," whose characters, "if they did not remain mere puppets, rarely became more than types."[13] But the epic and the ballad derive from the oral tradition, whereas the self-conscious artistry of the short story draws attention to its writtenness. It is telling that critical studies of the short story tend to focus on the craft rather than the theory of the genre: Sean O'Faolain's *The Short Story* (1951), for example, is a how-to book, based on his experience of teaching would-be writers. This preoccupation with technique, together with the emphasis on epiphanic moments and the material intrusiveness of formal artifice, associates the short story with the modernist tradition: in fact it has been argued that "the short story encapsulates the essence of literary modernism."[14] Also typical of modernism is the close attention required of short-story readers, who need to be alone and undistracted in order to appreciate the writer's craft. In this sense the short story's lonely hero reflects its implied reader, compelled to concentrate in solitude and silence.

The hero's isolation often stems from a mental or physical defect that limits his or her participation in the world. Bowen considers the short story well adapted to depicting what she calls the "Simple Soul," a category that includes:

(a) the *young* child
(b) the "arrested" character
(c) the defective (idiot)
(d) [*sic*] the simpleton
(e) the abnormally *submissive*[15]

The term "simple soul" harks back to Flaubert's "Un Coeur Simple" (1872), the poignant story of a servant-woman enchanted by a parrot, whose exotic plumage brightens her grey life.[16] According to Bowen, the short story profits from the limitations of the simple heart or "innocent character," who catalyzes action rather than controlling it. This simple soul is often trapped in a blind body, which has the effect of immunizing innocence against the corrupting influence of light.

Take Arthur Schnitzler's story "Blind Geronimo and his Brother" (1902), which traces the destruction of the innocent trust between two brothers. The younger of these brothers was blinded by the elder in a childhood accident, and to expiate his guilt, Carlo has devoted his life to caring for Geronimo. Together the two beggars wander the resorts, the blind man strumming his guitar while his brother takes care of the money. Their symbiotic dyad is shattered, however, when a stranger's practical joke persuades Geronimo that Carlo has been cheating him. Although the brothers are reconciled in the end, their quarrel has revealed the faultline in their union, and the illusion of innocence can never be restored.[17]

In Conrad's novella *The End of the Tether* (1902), the simple soul is Captain Whalley, "big and quiet," who has dedicated his old age to rescuing his daughter from the horrors of poverty. Having realized that his sight is failing, he conceals his blindness from the crew of the *Sofala* in order to redeem the money invested for his daughter in the ship. But Massy, the bankrupt owner-engineer, deliberately sinks the ship for the insurance pay-off, and the blind captain goes down with the *Sofala*, his black world engulfed in a "black sea."[18] In this work, blindness is presented as a journey into darkness, not as a foregone conclusion, and the narrative extends beyond the usual limits of the short story, in terms of length and development of character. Some heroes are born blind, some become blind, and some have blindness thrust upon them, but those whose blindness remains static are best suited to short stories; those whose vision dims or brightens tend to strain of the limits of the form. As Captain Whalley's vision gradually fails, Conrad's short story stretches to the end of its own tether, lengthening and deepening into a novel.[19]

Other long-short sea-stories in which blindness is presented as a process rather than a premise of the narrative include Melville's *Benito Cereno* (1856) and *Billy Budd* (written 1888–91, published posthumously 1924). Whereas Conrad's story traces a voyage from light into darkness, Melville's stories trace voyages from blindness into sight, a blindness that arises from innocence rather than from ocular impairment. In the case of Billy Budd, "innocence [is] his blinder," closing his eyes to the machinations of his nemesis Claggart. In *Benito Cereno*, Captain Delano's sentimental conception of "the negro" scotomizes his perception that Cereno's ship has been taken over by the slaves. In both these works, the passage from blindness to vision unsettles generic categories, making the short story long – *Benito Cereno* is a novella, while *Billy Budd* is story, novel, and Greek tragedy at once. And in both works, the price of sight is death: Billy is hanged when the scales of innocence fall from his eyes; Benito Cereno perishes under the "shadow" of "the negro" soon after the mutiny that makes this darkness visible.[20]

Historically the association of blindness with innocence goes back at least as far as the Gospel of St. John, but it gained new force in the Enlightenment, when William Molyneux asked John Locke the famous question whether a man born blind, whose vision was miraculously restored, would recognize by sight the cube and sphere that he had learned to identify by touch. The Cartesian answer would be yes, because geometrical ideas such as cubeness and sphericity are knowable by reason alone, whereas the Lockeian answer would be no, because the blind man would have to learn how to process the information transmitted by his eyes. Incidentally Locke seems to have been right, judging by the few recorded instances of people "cured" of lifelong blindness. Oliver Sacks discusses the case of a blind man who became much more disabled when he gained his sight, because he had no means of interpreting visual stimuli. Wilkie Collins imagines a similar awakening for "poor Miss Finch," in his novel of that name; Miss Finch decides that she is better off without eyesight when an operation to restore her vision reveals that her lover's face has improbably turned blue – a color she cannot tolerate.[21]

Molyneux's question fascinated the French philosophers, including the "sensationalist" philosopher Condillac, who replaced Molyneux's hypothetical blind man with the model of a statue whose senses could be unlocked one by one to demonstrate how knowledge is constructed out of sense experience.[22] The eighteenth century also witnessed the first successful cataract operations, which inspired Diderot's famous *Letter on the Blind* (1749), whose originality lies in re-conceptualizing blindness not as a defect but as a different and in some ways wiser form of knowing. One notable instance of this wisdom, cited by Diderot, is a blind man's response to the question whether he wants eyes: "I would just as soon have long arms."[23] In the Enlightenment, both philosophy and medicine contributed to the process described by William Paulson as the "*desacralisation* of the blind*,*" whereby long-standing myths in which the blind person was seen as saint and sinner, singled out by God for punishment but also for compensatory second sight, gave way to new myths in which the blind person was seen as inexperienced and innocent, a *tabula rasa* untainted by the spectacle of human turpitude.[24]

If innocence is a "blinder," as Melville says of Billy Budd, the function of blindness in short stories is often to preserve the innocence of childhood intact – sometimes well beyond its sell-by date. A number of short stories, such as Kipling's "They" (1904), feature heroines whose innocence has been immured in blindness, and there is something pornographic in this image of a child in a woman's body, unable to look back at the male gaze. The same could be said of Gide's *The Pastoral Symphony*, in which the heroine is mute as well as blind, a feral child rescued – or stolen – from the wilderness. Originally entitled *L'aveugle* or "the blind one" – as if her gender were yet to be determined – this child is discovered by a pastor in a snowbound cottage where her only caretaker has died. Huddled in the shadows of the deathbed, scarcely distinguishable from the darkness, the child is described as "opaque," "an uncertain being," "an involuntary mass," "this package of flesh without soul."[25] In Jean Delannoy's beautiful film version of 1949, the blind girl makes her first appearance staggering across the moonlit snow to be presented with a bowl of soup, which she laps up like an animal.

The unnamed pastor, who narrates the story in his journal like a psychoanalyst recording case notes, takes this "lost sheep" into his home, forcing his family to adopt her in defiance of his wife's presentiments of doom (41/162–63). He then becomes obsessed with educating the young beauty, now renamed Gertrude, coaxing smiles from her "statue-like face" ["visage de statue"], much as Condillac imagined animating his insensate statue (42/163). In his mission to bring light to Gertrude's darkness, the pastor is egged on by the story of Laura Bridgeman (1829–89), born deaf and blind, whom Dickens wrote about in his *American Notes* (1842), and recreated in his story "The Cricket on the Hearth" (1945). In this story, the penniless father of a blind girl, Bertha Plummer, does everything he can to make his daughter happy and conceal their wretchedness: "a deception which Dickens exerts all his art to present as an act of piety," Gide's pastor comments, "but which, thank God, I won't have to use with Gertrude" (38–39/160).[26] Despite this protestation, the pastor proceeds to copy Bertha Plummer's father by shielding Gertrude from any knowledge of the evil of the world.

Blinder than Gertrude, he cannot see what is all too visible to his family, as well as to the reader – that his act of mercy is motivated by sexual desire for his protégée. "We can't all be blind," his wife says bitterly (113/211).[27] Blinder still, the pastor ostracizes his son Jacques, who wants to marry Gertrude, using casuistical interpretations of the scriptures to justify his own adulterous relationship with her. When a doctor suggests that an operation might restore her sight, the pastor conceals the information, fearing that her newly opened eyes would be attracted to his handsome son. His fears come true when the operation is eventually performed, and Gertrude realizes she loves Jacques's face, not his father's. At this point she attempts to drown herself, and although she briefly revives, the pastor fails to save her from the fever she contracted in the icy water. On her deathbed she reproaches him with her last breath for tearing her away from Jacques. Even her death, however, fails to cure the pastor of his blindness, for he remains oblivious to his destructiveness, thinking only of his own loss and the arid desert of his heart: "J'aurais voulu pleurer, mais je sentais mon coeur plus aride que le desert" (145/233).[28]

At the beginning of his journal, the pastor writes: "Je profiterai des loisirs que me vaut cette claustration forcée …" (12/141).[29] These words refer to his enforced confinement by the snow, which has blinded all the roads, much as Gertrude's blindness blocks all traffic to and from her mind: "The snow has been falling continuously for the last three days and all the routes are blocked" (12/141).[30] The short story also profits from such "forced claustration," but *The Pastoral Symphony* overspills the boundaries of the genre. Longer than a story, shorter than a novel, this work is usually described as a *récit*: a first-person narrative in which the reader is invited to see through the narrator's self-justifying ruses, as in Browning's dramatic monologues. Gide's other *récits* (*L'immoraliste*, *La porte étroite*, and *Isabelle*) are much the same length as *The Pastoral Symphony*, but the shortness of the latter troubled Gide; having been haunted by "l'aveugle" for so long, he was disconcerted that the story came so quickly to an end.[31] Its generic ambiguity is embodied in the heroine, whose blindness belongs to the short story, while the restoration of her vision opens up the promise of a novel, which is promptly aborted by her death. In this tale of failed Pygmalionism, Gertrude's "visage de statue" reverts to stone.

Derrida remarks that statues' eyes are "always closed," like the eyes of the dead: "'walled up' in any case … or turned inward, more dead than alive … more dead than the eyes of masks."[32] Gertrude is dead at the beginning of *The Pastoral Symphony*, and she dies at least twice before it ends, despite the pastor's efforts to reanimate her through ventriloquy. Described by Gide as the critique of "a form of lying to oneself" ["un forme de mensonge à lui-même"], this *récit* was written soon after his passion for an adolescent boy, Marc Allégret, had exposed the falseness of his marriage to Madeleine, and it is a scathing portrait of the pedagogue as pederast.[33] But it is also a portrait of the artist as an Orpheus whose desire to look back at the blindness of Eurydice exceeds his desire to convey his knowledge to the light of day. As Maurice Blanchot has written, Orpheus "does not want Eurydice in her daytime truth and her everyday appeal, but wants her in her nocturnal obscurity, in her distance, with her closed body and sealed face – wants to see her not when she is visible, but when she is invisible …"[34]

Dubliners

In *The Pastoral Symphony*, Gertrude's blindness functions as a "blind" in the sense of an obstacle to vision, a decoy that distracts the pastor from his blindness to himself. It is he, as much as she, who is "l'aveugle." In the figure of the pastor, Gide provides a double of the reader's interpretative efforts to endow the "opaque" body of the story with a soul. Joyce's "The Sisters" also presents a double of the reader in the child-narrator, who attempts to read the darkened blind. This blind, among its many meanings, denotes a feint or decoy, which deflects the child's gaze from the deathbed concealed behind its enigmatic surface.

The term "blind" is also used to mean a decoy in the "Cyclops" episode of *Ulysses*, a chapter strewn with references to blinds and blindness in homage to the blinding of the one-eyed Cyclops by Odysseus. Towards the end of Joyce's "Cyclops" episode, when Bloom beats a speedy exit from the pub, proffering the alibi of visiting the courthouse, Lenehan scoffs, "The courthouse is a blind" (*U* 274:1550). In *Dubliners*, Joyce throws out "blinds" analogous to Bloom's, baiting the reader with the promise of a destination never to be reached: "The blinds would be drawn down …" (*D* 222). With the exception of "The Dead," Joyce's stories stop rather than end, and could therefore be described as "blind stories," defined by the *Oxford English Dictionary* as stories with no point. "Araby," for instance, begins in a "blind" street, suggesting a narrative blind alley:

North Richmond Street, being blind, was a quiet street … An uninhabited house of two storeys stood at the blind end, detached from its neighbours in a square ground. The other houses of the street, conscious of decent lives within them, gazed at one another with brown imperturbable faces. (*D* 29)

The term "blind" features twice within this opening paragraph, while the curious phrase "being blind," immured in commas, signifies not only a dead end but a failure of vision. If the houses are "conscious," the street is "blind," its blank stare contrasted to the mutually congratulating gazes of the terraces.

Bowen likens the short story to a house – each "has a structure" – and many of her own short stories begin by crossing the threshold of a house, often by illicit means. The reader crosses the threshold of the story at the same time that the characters invade the house, implying an analogy between the act of reading and the thrill of trespass.[35] A comparable analogy between the house and the short story may be found in "Araby," where the terraced houses of Richmond Street reflect the semi-detached stories of *Dubliners*, while the empty house at the blind end suggests the abandonment of ends or teleology. That this house has "two storeys" may be a deliberate pun, reminding us that we are reading two stories at once, one about Dublin and one about the structure of the narrative itself. The phrase also draws attention to other forms of twoness or doubling at work in *Dubliners*: the doubles of the absent father, such as the two expected candles in "The Sisters"; the doubled characters of "Two Gallants" and "Counterparts"; the double meanings that pervade the whole ensemble. Here it is worth noting that Joyce in *Finnegans Wake* spells Dublin with an inaudible "o," creating "doublin" – a retrospective clue to the duplicities of *Dubliners* (*FW* 13:8, 572:14).

These double meanings begin with the darkened blind of the first story, and images of blinded or obstructed vision proliferate throughout the text. In "Counterparts," Farrington's eyes are repeatedly described as "dirty" (*D* 86). Other characters are blinded by their clouded spectacles: Bob Doran in "A Boarding House," Gabriel Conroy in "The Dead," and Little Chandler in "A Little Cloud" each wipe their spectacles at moments of crisis. In "Clay," Maria's tipsy brother cannot find the corkscrew because his eyes are blinded with maudlin tears. In "Araby," the lovelorn narrator welcomes blindness – "I was thankful that I could see so little" – in order to protect his fantasies against the violation of the light. "All my senses seemed to desire to veil themselves … " (*D* 31). He crouches in the shadows, like a hunter in a "blind" – a hiding-place concealed from the prey – and peeks at his beloved through a slit between the sash and the window-blind:

if Mangan's sister came out on the doorstep to call her brother in to his tea we watched her from our shadow peer up and down the street … Every morning I lay on the floor in the front parlour watching her door. The blind was pulled down to within an inch of the sash so that I could not be seen. (*D* 30)

This peephole could be compared to a device known as an anorthoscope, which was employed by the nineteenth-century theorist of perception Hermann von Helmholtz to investigate the processes involved in the recognition of forms. As Simon Stevenson has shown, an anorthoscope consists of two rotating discs, the first scored with a series of slits through which a figure on the second is gradually revealed. Helmholtz's experiments demonstrated that observers succeeded in recognizing forms through the slits, even though these forms were reduced to slivers. This result implies that form-recognition has more to do with cognition than with seeing per se.

Stevenson suggests that the anorthoscopic gaze corresponds to V. S. Pritchett's definition of the short story as "something glimpsed out of the corner of an eye, in passing."[36] With regard to "Araby," the short story might be re-described as a slit in a blind that beckons towards a missing picture. In *Dubliners* Joyce performs anorthoscopic experiments in language by reducing sentences to slits in which the reader is obliged to interpolate the missing sense: "Did he … peacefully?" (*D* 15). In his later writing, Joyce's most startling anorthoscopic effects occur in the "Sirens" episode of *Ulysses*, where words, pulverized by music, retain their sense despite the fragmentation of their syllables. For instance, Bloom's thought, "Must be the bur," appears incomprehensible, yet in context the reader recognizes "bur" as burgundy, and understands that Bloom is blaming his flatulence on lunchtime wine (*U* 239:1287). As Paul Virilio says of Helmholtz's anorthoscopic experiments, Joyce's ellipses raise the question: "how far you can take blindness and still maintain form recognition?"[37]

The narrator of "Araby," peering through the slit, has no difficulty recognizing the idealized form of his beloved. Evoked throughout the story by synecdoche, this obscure object of desire is reduced to slivers by the narrator's anorthoscopic vision: her swinging hem, the "soft rope" of her tossing hair, "the white border of a petticoat, just visible as she stood at ease." "Just visible," this girl is always half-concealed by encroaching shadows in "Araby," most of which takes place at night, which is typical of Joyce's darkened stories. "Touched discreetly by the lamplight," only the margins of her figure can be seen, "defined by the light from the half-opened door" – an aperture reminiscent of the half-opened slits of the anorthoscope. If her presence is veiled in darkness, however, her remembered form has a blinding effect on the narrator: "her image came between me and the page I strove to read." Looking over at "the dark house where she lived," he can see "nothing but the brown-clad figure cast by my imagination," haloed in remembered lamplight. At the "blind end" of the story, when the boy's attempt to buy a love-token at the Araby bazaar has come to nothing, he gazes into the darkness, his eyes "burning with anguish and anger." In this way darkness, which had formerly cocooned his wistful fantasies – "all my senses seemed to desire to veil themselves" – now mocks him with his own futility, burning his eyes with mortification: "Gazing up into the darkness I saw myself as a creature driven and derided by vanity" (*D* 30–35).

The most explicit case of blindness in *Dubliners* occurs in "Clay," which climaxes in a game of blind man's buff, where the blindfolded Maria is tricked into handling "a soft wet substance with her fingers." This clammy substance is hastily removed, and its name is never uttered in the story. "Somebody said something about the garden, and at last Mrs. Donnelly said something very cross to one of the next-door girls and told her to throw it out at once: that was no play" (*D* 105). By leaving this lacuna, Joyce blindfolds his readers, forcing us to grope for the open secret in the title of the story – clay. And this blind spot tricks us into thinking the obscene.[38]

"*Clef*," pronounced "clay," is French for key, and the key to this story is hidden like Wilde's sphinx without a secret, right before our eyes. In other stories words themselves perform the role of blinds, debarring access to their referents. The word "paralysis" in "The Sisters" blinds the narrator to its meaning, taking on a perverse life of its own.

Every night as I gazed up at the window I said softly to myself the word *paralysis*. It had always sounded strangely in my ears, like the word *gnomon* in the Euclid and the word *simony* in the Catechism. But now it sounded to me like the name of some maleficent and sinful being. It filled me with fear, and yet I longed to be nearer to it and to look upon its deadly work. (*D* 9)

Here it is the word "paralysis," rather than its meaning, that mesmerizes the narrator, as if paralysis were not only the name of a disease but the disease itself – a malady of language that petrifies the word and dissolves its connection to its referent. These antithetical ideas of petrifying and dissolving both inhere within the term "paralysis," which "etymologically conveys an idea of dissolution, of an unbinding … coupled with an anguishing immobility," as Jean-Michel Rabaté has pointed out.[39] Joyce famously described Dublin as a "centre of paralysis," but he also recognized its glamor and charm, admitting that his admiration for the city had been twisted by the "mischievous" spirit of his pen.[40] Yet his best effort to capture the vitality of Dublin produced "The Dead," whose title speaks for itself. In this story, the living change places with the dead, becoming blinds or surrogates for furious ghosts: Gabriel Conroy learns that he is deader to his wife than her long-buried lover Michael Furey. Thus the book concludes with a dead lover, just as it begins with a dead priest, yet both these deaths are stand-ins for a death that never literally "takes place" but creeps like a paralysis through the "deadly work" of the invisible and the inaudible in *Dubliners*.

This death makes itself felt in the absence of fathers, but also in the multiplication of paternal substitutes, each double more degraded than the last. Even fathers who are technically alive are missing or impotent in Joyce's Dublin, often because they are blind drunk – the most lethal form of blindness in these stories. The child-narrator of the first three stories seems to have lost both parents, enabling first the syphilitic priest and then the masturbating pervert to fill the patriarchal vacuum. I say *the* child, but because he (or she) is unnamed there is no way of knowing whether the narrator of "The Sisters" reappears in "An Encounter" or "Araby." Such namelessness, along with the distortion of the proper name, recurs like a chronic symptom in the text, marking the absence of a credible symbolic father to anchor persons in their patronymics. In Lacan's terms, the "*nom-du-père*," or name-of-the-father, succumbs to the double affliction encoded in the word "paralysis," alternately petrifying as a fetish or dissolving into anonymity.

Lacan's "*nom-du-père*" puns on "*non-du-père*," meaning "not-of-the-father," hinting that the symbolic father never coincides with the real father, who is always insufficient to his role. But Lacan's fallen father is an abstract function, a geometrical position, whereas Joyce's is all too vulnerable to history. The paternal void of *Dubliners* harks back to two contemporaneous events in the life of the author and the Irish nation – the bankruptcy of Joyce's father and the fall of Parnell, whose absence looms so large in "Ivy Day in the Committee Room." The first of these paternal falls sent the Joyce family tumbling down the social ladder; the second marked the collapse of the aspirations of the Catholic middle class, which had hoped to flourish under Home Rule.

This double downfall of John Joyce and Parnell, of the real and the symbolic father, reverberates in *Dubliners* in the form of mutilated patronymics. In "The Dead," Lily pronounces Conroy with three syllables; in "Two Gallants," Corley aspirates "the first letter of his name after the manner of the Florentines"; in "Counterparts," Farrington miscopies the name Bernard Bodley as Bernard Bernard, and also loses his own name to anonymity when the narrator demotes him to "the man" (*D* 177, 52, 86–98). In "The Dead," Mr. Browne – a drunkard of "the other persuasion" – puns on his surname, reducing the *nom-du-père* into an adjective evocative of filth. When Aunt Julia worries that the goose may not be brown enough, Mr. Browne pipes up: "Well, I hope, Miss Morkan … that I'm brown enough for you, because, you know, I'm all brown." This stupid pun accrues sinister overtones at the end of the story, when Aunt Kate asks someone to close the door to keep out the cold.

– Browne is out there, Aunt Kate, said Mary Jane.
  – Browne is everywhere, said Aunt Kate, lowering her voice. (*D* 194, 200, 206)

The phrase "Browne is everywhere" looks forward to "snow was general," the weather forecast for the celebrated snowstorm of "The Dead." Snow was general, Browne is everywhere: both phrases imply an all-encompassing erasure, in which names, distinctions, and identities succumb to a white-out or a brown-out.

While surnames are repeatedly effaced or defaced, given names also succumb to distortion and erasure. The nameless narrator of "Araby" insists that his beloved's name is "like a summons to all my foolish blood," but the reader knows her only as "Mangan's sister" and never learns her "magical name." Its magic is displaced onto the name of the bazaar, whose orientalism bewitches the narrator: "The syllables of the name *Araby* were called to me through the silence in which my soul luxuriated and cast an Eastern enchantment over me" (*D* 30–34). Like the word "paralysis," the name "Araby" is petrified and fetishized, blinding the narrator to its referent by exercising an attraction stronger than the treasure-trove for which it stands.

A similar fetishization occurs in "A Painful Case," where Mr. Duffy is haunted by the name of Mrs. Sinico, the loving friend whom he abandoned to a lonely death. He learns from the newspaper that Mrs. Sinico has been killed by a train, having probably committed suicide, like Anna

Karenina. But the coroner's report gives the cause of death as "shock and sudden failure of the heart's action," recalling Mr. Duffy's own failure of heart when he brusquely rejected her caresses. After her death, when his paralyzed emotions briefly thaw, Duffy is tormented by "the laborious drone of the engine reiterating the syllables of her name" (*D* 117). By implication, the chugging syllables of Sinico identify her name with the engine of her death.

Another talismanic name occurs in "A Mother," in which O'Madden Burke's "magniloquent western name" is described as "the moral umbrella upon which he balanced the fine problem of his finances." This metaphorical umbrella harks back to the invisible sign mentioned in "The Sisters": "on ordinary days a notice used to hang in the window, saying *Umbrellas Re-covered*. No notice was visible now for the shutters were up." The recurrence of the umbrella in the story suggests that Joyce is playing on the verb "re-cover," meaning to cover up again but also to retrieve (recover). O'Madden Burke's umbrella is wittily "recovered" in the final sentence of "A Mother," which finds him "poised upon his umbrella in approval," and by this point it is hard to tell if he is leaning on his literal umbrella or the "moral umbrella" of his name (*D* 145, 11–12, 149). The fact that his magniloquent *nom-du-père* conceals his debts ("the fine problem of his finances") implies that the patronymic is founded "on the void," as Stephen Dedalus asserts in *Ulysses*. This void is constantly re-covered and recovered in *Dubliners*, concealed and revealed in the paralysis inflicted on the father's name.

Furthermore, this void instigates a network of substitution, supplanting originals with simulacra. This structure corresponds to the form of blindness that Freud, in his essay on "Fetishism," identifies as "scotomization": the blotting out of one perception through the substitution of another, a fetish which at once erases and memorializes the intolerable sight that there is "nothing" to be seen.[41] In *Dubliners*, such substitutes perform the role of blinds, at once re-covering and recovering the absence of the father. The words "gnomon" and "simony" that magnetize the boy-narrator in "The Sisters" provide a clue to the dynamics of loss and substitution in Joyce's stories. In Euclidian geometry, a "gnomon" designates that part of a parallelogram that remains when a similar parallelogram is taken away from one of its corners. Simony, derived from the name of Simon Magus, means the worldly traffic in sacred things, which is condemned in the Roman Catholic Catechism as a sin against the First Commandment. In *Dubliners*, the absent father functions as the gnomon or the missing corner that instigates the simoniac traffic in false fathers.

To pursue these interconnections between "gnomon" and "simony" – between lack and substitution, blindness and fetishism – the next section of this chapter turns to "Two Gallants."

En-garde

Co-written with Marilyn Reizbaum

Joyce once said that "Two Gallants," along with "Ivy Day in the Committee Room," was the story that pleased him most in *Dubliners*. When his publisher Grant Richards threatened to omit "Two Gallants" on the grounds of sexual impropriety, Joyce retorted that he would sooner sacrifice five other stories than allow this masterpiece to be amputated. Given Joyce's sense of the importance of the story, "Two Gallants" demands close attention.

The story is mercilessly simple. Two depraved companions strike a shady deal: Corley the gigolo wins a bet with Lenehan the leech by cheating a hard-working "slavey" out of a substantial sum of money. Or so we suspect, because the obliquity of the narration blinds the reader to the facts. It is this blindness that breeds suspicion, both for the reader and for Lenehan, since both are excluded from the scene of Corley's sexual conquest. Just as Lenehan is forced to "read the result from their walk," and impute the seduction from its signs, so the reader, excluded from the off-stage act, substitutes prurient imaginings for visual evidence. In this way the story confronts us with our own dirty minds, reflected in what Joyce called his "nicely-polished looking-glass" (*L* 1:64). Like Corley, possible pimp and probable police-informer, readers are obliged to play the supergrass against themselves, exposing their own desires instead of seeing through the story's darkened blind.

As noted earlier, most of the stories of *Dubliners* take place at night or twilight, when vision is impeded or impossible. "Two Gallants" accordingly begins at dusk, when the "pale disc of the moon" is "nearly veiled," blinded by "the grey web of twilight across its face." The "grey warm air" enveloping the city seems to emanate from the obscene and the unspeakable, like the miasma that descends on Thebes in retribution for Oedipus's crime. In this pernicious atmosphere, the narrator sets out to seduce us with "deep energetic gallantries" of prose – the aerial view of Dublin in the opening paragraph, where the city is transformed into a living texture, "changing shape and hue incessantly," and the lyrical description of the harpist filling the miasmal air with Ireland's eternal lamentation – only to exploit our gullibility to sentiment. Willing victims of this "gay

Lothario" of a narrator, we surrender to his tricks with a contented leer, paying dearly for our own violation.

These gallantries about the city and the harp suggest an elegiac attitude to Irishness. Yet this nostalgic nationalism functions as a blind or decoy, diverting our attention from the hints that Ireland is enervated, flaccid, out of shape. Lenehan, with his outfit of breeches, white rubber shoes, and jauntily slung waterproof, puts on a performance of youth, but the narrative suggests that he is falling both morally and physically, dragged earthwards by his own dead weight. His hair, "scant and grey," is falling out; his figure has fallen "into rotundity at the waist," and his face falls after "waves of expression" have passed over it, giving it "a ravaged look." All these falls allude to other falls in *Dubliners* – the fallen chalice in "The Sisters," the falling coins in "Araby," the final snowfall in "The Dead" – as well as looking forward to the fall of Finnegans. Even the harp in "Two Gallants" is depicted as a fallen woman:

a harpist stood in the roadway, playing to a little ring of listeners. He plucked at the wires heedlessly, glancing quickly from time to time at the face of each new-comer and from time to time, wearily also, at the sky. His harp, too, heedless that her coverings had fallen about her knees, seemed weary alike of the eyes of strangers and of her master's hands.

Disheveled and heedless, like the slavey with her "straggling mouth" and "ragged black boa," this feminized harp recalls the traditional image of the Shan van Vocht, the poor old woman, who serves as a blind or secret codename for Ireland in rebel balladry.

The harp-music has a spellbinding effect on the two gallants, striking them dumb; only when they cross the street at Stephen's Green does "the noise of trams … [release] them from their silence." The reader also runs the risk of being spellbound by the symbolic implications of the harp, lured into mistaking this instrument for something other than a sphinx without a secret. For this reason Margot Norris describes the harp as a "blind," a distraction from the "unsentimentalized degradations of the story," which pose a gritty resistance to the consolations of allegory.[42] In the scene quoted above, the national dirge is traded in for tips, just as sex is later traded in for the gold coin. The harpist is busking, and his heed-less music prostitutes itself to the winds: "The notes of the air throbbed deep and full."

Thus the harpist could be seen as a simoniac who traffics in the nation's sacred myths, his heedless indifference passing for a gallant act of national pride. "She" – the harp – is also "heedless" but knowing, like the leering slavey with whom the harp is associated by the feminine pronoun and the image of slovenly undress: "heedless that her coverings had fallen about her knees." Indeed the slavey's abrupt appearance in the wake of the ballad – "There she is!" – suggests that this "fine decent tart" has been conjured up by the mournful music of the harp. This conjunction implies that both the slavey and the harp are stuck in the same old song of exploitation: just as the harp is "weary alike of the eyes of strangers and of her master's hands," so the slavey is shunted between hands and eyes, between the treacherous caresses of her master Corley and the voyeurism of the stranger Lenehan.

Yet Lenehan barely catches a "squint" of the slavey before she disappears with Corley. Left in the dark, Lenehan begins to turn into a harp himself, an instrument both played upon and playing. His feet, controlled by the movement of the music, trudge to the mournful melody, while his fingers strum the railings of the Duke's Lawn: "The air which the harpist had played began to control his movements. His softly padded feet played the melody while his fingers swept a scale of variations idly along the railings after each group of notes." The fact that Lenehan the would-be "player" – playboy, gambler, conman, "toreador" – finds himself the puppet of the music exposes the flimsiness of his delusions of agency. His automatism offers an ironic counterpoint to the young narrator of "Araby," who revels in the sense of his body as a harp vibrating to his idol's fingertips: "my body was like a harp and her words and gestures were like fingers running upon the wires" (*D* 23). In "Two Gallants," by contrast, the transformation of the harp-strings into railings hints that the Irish are imprisoned by their heartstrings, railed in by the seductive music of national self-pity.

Most of Joyce's stories preserve some distinction between victim and victimizer, however compromised. But the image of Lenehan played by the music he is playing on the railings intimates that this distinction no longer holds. Even the slavey, the obvious victim of the story, plays along with the familiar tune of seduction and betrayal. Her knowing leer makes it hard to view her as an ingénue, and even harder to view her as an allegory of her downtrodden nation, violated by the British Empire, as some critics have proposed.[43] On the contrary, the story shows how the colonial condition belies any simple opposition of oppressor and oppressed. In Dublin the exploited exploit each other in a world reduced to debt and doubt. Debt generates exchange, while doubt generates suspicion; thus exchange and suspicion are founded "on the void," on the dearth of wealth and information. Yet the mechanics of exchange persist even in the absence of production, just as the mechanics of suspicion thrive on blindness; no one "makes" money in Dublin, but everyone steals, leeches, inveigles, or extorts it. This parasitical economy resembles Primo Levi's account of Auschwitz, in which prisoners developed elaborate systems of exchanging almost nothing: a spoon, an egg, a shoe.[44] Similarly, the economy of Dublin is "running on empty," yet its inhabitants still go through the motions of exchange, devising ingenious means of cheating fellow indigents. As Lily puts it in "The Dead," "The men that is now is only all palaver and what they can get out of you" (*D* 178). And not just men – the slavey's leer suggests that she is trying to get something out of Corley, presumably a husband to release her from wage-slavery or prostitution, the career options open to a woman of her class.

However, the story never reveals exactly what the characters are trying to get out of each other, but deflects the reader's gaze with darkened blinds. "Two Gallants" poses a riddle which, like Stephen's riddle in the "Nestor" episode of *Ulysses*, has a ready-made solution – the gold coin. Yet this blinding revelation raises more questions that it answers. The coin is the narrative pay-off that the reader, like Lenehan, has been "panting" for, yet its significance remains opaque. Why is Lenehan so obsessed with Corley's transaction with the slavey? Does Corley owe him money, as Margot Norris speculates?[45] How does the slavey acquire the gold coin? Does Corley really extort this trophy from the slavey, or does he pull it out of his long pocket to hoodwink Lenehan? Is Corley himself caught up in a game of blind man's buff, in which "filthy lucre" takes the place of clay, the gold coin in Corley's fist corresponding to Maria's handful of mud? Has Corley conned the girl into paying him for sex, or is she "on the turf," with Corley running her? (Remember that Corley's former squeeze has resorted to prostitution, apparently "ruined" by Corley, although this gallant claims "there was others at her before me.") Whether the slavey stole the money from her master, or earned it on the game, she is defenceless against Corley, who is likely to inform on her for either misdemeanor; in fact it is possible that Corley is blackmailing her about her moonlighting.

Does the gold coin therefore represent the price of sex or the price of silence? Joyce mentions this gold coin in a letter to his publisher Grant Richards, protesting at the "one-eyed" Cyclopean printer's objections to his stories. "I am sorry you do not tell me why the printer, who seems to be the barometer of English opinion, refuses to print *Two Gallants* and makes marks in the margin of *Counterparts*. Is it the small gold coin in the former story or the code of honour which the two gallants live by which shocks him?" (*L* 2:132–33).[46] Like many of Joyce's protestations to his publisher, this statement has the paradoxical effect of reinforcing, rather than assuaging, any suspicions aroused by the enigmatic coin.

Don Gifford points out that this coin would be equivalent to six or seven weeks' wages for a slavey. Most critics surmise that Corley has charmed the girl into paying him for his caresses, in a reversal of the traditional gender roles of prostitution.[47] Yet although some villainous transaction seems to have occurred, the reader never sees the coin change hands, nor ascertains what it is paying for. The exchange value of money disappears, leaving only its fetishized materiality, blinding in its spotlit visibility: "A small gold coin shone in the palm." When he opens his fist to reveal this prize to his "disciple," Corley is momentarily transformed into a magician or an alchemist, conjuring gold out of the empty air, rather than a tawdry conman caught up in the strandentwining debts of Dublin's lowlife. With Lenehan's encouragement, he builds up the dramatic tension through his performance of suspense – the grim stare, the grave gesture, the extended hand, and the smile. His final revelation could be compared to the so-called "money-shot" in porn photography, in which the ejaculating penis is exposed, coming – but going nowhere. Likewise the coin displayed in Corley's greasy palm has been withdrawn from circulation, its "shine" blinding all parties to its exchange value. This coin harks back to another round and shiny object described at the beginning of the story, namely Corley's "large, globular, and oily head," on which his hat sits like "a bulb that had grown out of another." This inimitable description, planted in the sentence like a banana skin to trip up Corley's striding gait, alerts the reader that the balding Corley is not so "hairy" as he boasts. Was the one-eyed printer sufficiently hairy to perceive the double entendre linking the shiny coin to the oily head with its extended phallic bulb?

"Shine" also plays a crucial role in Freud's account of fetishism, where his unidentified patient (recognizable from other writings as the Wolf Man) is aroused by a certain "shine on the nose" (*Glanz auf der Nase*). According to Freud, this fetish originated in the patient's childhood, when the little boy "glanced" at his English governess's genitals and discovered that she lacked a penis. The German term "*Glanz*," a homonym of the English "glance," and also of the Latin *glans* or foreskin, memorializes this traumatic glance, but replaces the absent penis with the child's last-but-one perception – the shiny nose (SE 21:149–57). Like the shiny nose, the shiny coin in "Two Gallants" stands in for the void – the absent phallus – whose surrogates circulate among the characters, Corley having inveigled the *Glanz* out of the slavey in order to display it to the glance of Lenehan.

This is a glance that fails to see, a shine that blinds. Here it is worth noting that Marx and Freud both conceive of fetishism as a form of blindness: in Marx's theory of the commodity-fetishism, the fetish takes the place of human labor; in Freud's theory of sexual fetishism, the fetish takes the place of gender difference, but in either case reality is censored out of vision – "scotomized" – in order to endow an object with subjective agency. In a telling analogy, Marx associates the fetishism of commodities with the blindness constitutive of vision, whereby "the impression made by a thing on the optic nerve is perceived not as a subjective excitation of that nerve but as the objective form of a thing outside the eye."[48] This statement implies that sight depends on the seer's blindness to the act of seeing; to see is to substitute the object for the subject, the shine for the look, the *Glanz* for the glance.

A similar substitution takes place in "Two Gallants," where shining takes the place of seeing, the gold coin standing in for the sexual transaction occluded in the narrative. Fetishization also operates within the narrative itself, in which the coldness of the reportage is interrupted by the two shining epiphanies – the lyrical opening paragraph and the evocation of the Irish harp. These passages advertise themselves as fine writing, yet also stand as fetishes to the romantic sensibility they elegize, a sensibility excoriated by the ruthless naturalism of the prose. Like Corley's gold coin, these showy set-pieces seem extorted from another story, the shiny fragments of a foreclosed scene.

"Then with a grave gesture [Corley] extended a hand towards the light and, smiling, opened it slowly to the gaze of his disciple. A small gold coin shone in the palm."[49] Postponing this exposure like a wily flasher, Corley melodramatically reveals the coin – but what does the coin reveal? Its shine is set against the darkness much as the Freudian fetish is set against the void, serving as a dam against castration. What speaks in fetishism, according to Jean Baudrillard, is not the desire for substances but "the passion for the code."[50] In Joyce's story, the code embedded in the coin consists of neither the exchange value of the money, nor the labor power that the money represents, but "the code of honour which the two gallants live by," a code that prides itself on circumventing legitimate circuits of exchange. If the coin had been designated as a "sovereign," its implications would be quite different; not only would it signify a monetary value, but it would evoke the colonial predicament of Ireland, whose depleted economy is shackled to the sovereign across the Channel. In the epithet "a small gold coin," however, these political and monetary codes are "paralysed," trumped by the "code of honour" whereby promises to men are kept by breaking promises to women. This code of honor substitutes false magic – Corley's Midas-touch – for wealth and sovereignty, powers to which the gallants have no hope of aspiring. Instead they prey upon the lumpen slaveys of the "sovereign," flaunting "hairiness" as a cheap substitute for agency.

We have been prepared for this mercenary climax from the beginning of the story, when Corley boasts about the slavey having paid his expenses in tram fares and cigars, and later when Lenehan imagines how "some good simple-minded girl with a little of the ready" might redeem his weary life of "shifts and intrigues." "A little of the ready" conflates sexual availability with financial solvency, in a kind of simoniac transference between economies. A similar transference takes place in the gallants' discussion of the slavey, in which such terms as "close," "ticklish job," and "bring it off" refer to either financial or sexual extortion:

"– But tell me, said Lenehan again, are you sure you can bring it off all right. You know it's a ticklish job. They're damn close on that point. Eh? … What?"

Corley's answer is to swing his shiny bulbs: "I'll pull it off, he said. Leave it to me, can't you?" Far from leaving it to him, Lenehan's anxiety about the "outcome" intensifies throughout the story like the build-up to an orgasm, his impatience mounting as the darkness deepens: "he took his stand in the shadow of a lamp … and kept his gaze fixed on the part from which he expected to see Corley and the young woman return … His eyes searched the street: there was no sign of them." At the beginning of the story, Lenehan and Corley are detected at a distance miming conversation – Lenehan wears "an amused listening face" as he waits for the end of Corley's monologue – but by the end, the two gallants seem to be miming the sex-act. Lenehan "start[s] with delight" when he catches sight of the returning Corley, yet crumples a split-second later, and even the language stops and starts, rollercoastering between the thrill of power and the dread of impotence.

Some hours earlier, Lenehan had tried to soothe his anxieties about the "outcome" by summoning up Corley's bulbous head rolling in its pantomime of speech: "the memory of Corley's slowly revolving head calmed him down; he was sure he would pull it off all right." If Corley's spectral talking head is reassuring, his silence has the opposite effect, plunging Lenehan into despair as the returning lovers loom into his field of vision: "They did not seem to be speaking. An intimation of the result pricked him like the point of a sharp instrument. He knew Corley would fail; he knew it was no go." Thick with double entendre, such expressions as "slowly revolving head," "pull it off," "fail," "no go," and "pricked him like the point of a sharp instrument," allude to the occluded sex scene. The last of these expressions positions Lenehan as the prickee of the metaphorical "sharp instrument," a homoerotic innuendo reinforced by the frictional rhythms of the prose. Meanwhile the intimation that the slavey has tipped her own seducer reverses the conventional roles of prostitution, confusing the grammar of the story: who is the gallant, the prostitute, the base betrayer?

What is clear is that a three-sided network has been formed by the circulation of money, desire, and the gaze. Confirming Adam Phillips's principle that "two's company but three's a couple," each of the three characters in "Two Gallants" plays the role of the third person who unites the other two into a couple.[51] Lenehan serves as the third person whose gaze emboldens Corley to exploit the slavey, while the slavey also makes a couple of the two gallants by providing an erotic currency between them. Lenehan's desire is "mimetic," like his movements to the rhythm of the harp: he wants what Corley wants, he wants to desire his desires.[52] This triangle resembles the erotic geometry of "The Dead," where Gabriel Conroy suffers torments not so much because his wife Gretta has loved another man, but because Michael Furey loved her with a greater passion than Gabriel can muster. It is Furey's fury that Gabriel envies, rather than its object. Likewise Lenehan desires to desire the desire of the "gay Lothario," rather than seeking to possess the girl herself.

This triangle anticipates Joyce's later works, in which the contest between two men for a woman often serves as a blind for the mutual attraction between male rivals. In *Ulysses*, Poldy panders to Blazes Boylan's designs on Molly, vacating the house at 7 Eccles Street to make way for his virile cuckolder. René Girard has argued that the European novel repeatedly evokes erotic triangles in which the woman serves as an object of exchange between two gallants, creating an unacknowledged bond between the men.[53] Stephen Dedalus anticipates this theory in his disquisition on Shakespeare in the "Scylla and Charybdis" episode of *Ulysses*, where Shakespeare is portrayed as "bawd and cuckold" to his wife Ann Hathaway (*U* 174:1021). Speculating that the virginal Will Shakespeare was seduced by Ann – "If others have their will Ann hath a way" – Stephen proposes that Ann later committed adultery with her husband's brothers, Richard and Edmund, which provided Shakespeare with the names of two of the worst villains in his plays (*U* 157:256–57). Meanwhile Mr. W. H., commissioned to play go-between for Shakespeare with the Dark Lady of the *Sonnets*, stole her heart. It was these betrayals by his mistress and his wife, as well as by his brothers and his closest friend, that produced the fury of the tragedies. Yet Shakespeare secretly engineered his own betrayal, for reasons both voyeuristic and artistic: jealousy and doubt were the energies that fueled his creativity.

Stephen admits that he doubts his own theory, and evidently it was Joyce himself, rather than Shakespeare, who needed this fantasy of cuck-oldry to spur him into creativity. Nora told Frank Budgen in 1918, "Jim wants me to go with other men so that he will have something to write about" (*JJ* 445). Some years earlier, in 1909, Joyce belatedly discovered that his friend Vincent Cosgrave had been pursuing Nora in 1904, when Joyce was also courting her. This discovery plunged Joyce into jealous torments, and even when Nora managed to assuage his doubts, Joyce insisted on picking at the wound. This picking persists in his fiction, which repeatedly invokes erotic triangles in which a husband yields his wife to a "conquering hero" (*U* 217:340). In Joyce's play *Exiles* (1918), Richard Rowan urges his wife Bertha to embark on an affair with his best friend (and her former lover) Robert Hand, Rowan hoping that jeal-ousy will galvanize his genius and inspire Shakespearean tours de force. But inspiration is merely the fringe benefit of this scenario, for Rowan also yearns to be betrayed, and to be blinded to this act of darkness: "In the very core of my ignoble heart," Rowan confesses to Hand, "I longed to be betrayed by you and by her – in the dark, in the night – secretly, meanly, craftily."[54]

In the hallucinatory "Circe" episode of *Ulysses*, Boylan invites Bloom to watch him fornicate with Molly:

BOYLAN (To Bloom, over his shoulder.) You can apply your eye to the keyhole and play with yourself while I just go through her a few times.
BLOOM (His eyes wildly dilated, clasps himself) Show! Hide! Show! Plough her! More! Shoot!

Here Bloom's keyhole view recalls the anorthoscopic vision of the narrator of "Araby," who spies on his beloved through the slit beneath the blind. Bloom's response to the spectacle – "Show! Hide! Show!" – implies that his vicarious excitement depends on both the showing and the hiding, on the frictional alternation of vision and blindness. Concealed from the lovers, Bloom occupies a similar position to Lenehan in "Two Gallants," who also wants to see without being seen. Instead of competing for the affections of the slavey, Lenehan merely wants "a squint of her." When Corley snaps, "Are you trying to get inside me?" Lenehan insists that his intentions are purely scopophilic: "All I want is to have a look at her. I'm not going to eat her." He eats a meager dish of peas instead, while Corley gets inside her.

In Lenehan's lonely meal, a degraded or simoniac sacrament, food provides a substitute for off-stage sex in the same way that the gold coin stands in for the absent phallus. Throughout *Dubliners*, food, sex, words, and money function as symbolic equivalents for one another, much as florins, rats, and excrement become equivalents for one another in the deliria of Freud's Rat Man (SE 10:213–16). In "Two Gallants," Corley exchanges sex and gallantries for money, whereas Lenehan exchanges words for drink. No one knows how Lenehan achieves "the stern task of living," but we learn that his tongue is "tired" from entertaining fellow drunkards in the hope of being treated to their rounds. Here it is worth noting that Joyce also paid his way with words, "armed with a vast stock of stories, limericks, and riddles," as he writes of Lenehan. Joyce achieved the stern task of living by sponging off acquaintances, flaunting a Lenehanian economy of freeloading in defiance of bourgeois thrift. Lenehanian, too, was Joyce's interest in the sexual exploits of his rivals. Lenehan could therefore be seen as Joyce's portrait of the artist as a young man gone to seed – as a scrounger, wordmonger, and peeping Tom.

The erotic triangle in "Two Gallants" resembles Freud's account of dirty jokes, in which the woman functions as the blind or pretext rather than the partner of the "smut" exchanged between two men. Smut, Freud argues, originates in sexual aggression directed at a woman, but the presence of a male third person diverts this impulse into the detour of a dirty joke. In polite society, men "save up" their jokes for times when they can be "alone together," excluding women from their smutty talk. Thus the woman, originally the addressee, latterly the butt, and finally the sacrificial victim of the joke, vanishes from the scene of masculine pleasure, reduced to the ghost of a deflected rape.[55]

In the course of Joyce's evolution as a writer, however, the woman increasingly asserts her independence, refusing to be blotted out by injokes between men. It is in Molly Bloom's soliloquy that the slavey finally talks back; here it is worth remembering that Nora Barnacle was working as a slavey or (more politely) a chambermaid in Finn's Hotel when Joyce first fell for her. Up to the last chapter of *Ulysses*, women tend to be relegated to the sidelines, figuring at best as incentives for male repartee. But Molly Bloom has the last word and the last laugh in the novel; her blithe autoerotism exposes the French triangle as a masculine defence against the fear of female jouissance.

Does the slavey's "contented leer" also intimate a secret jouissance, incalculable to her male manipulators? Although it would be extravagant to suppose that the slavey had outsmarted Corley – it is clear she is more sinned against than sinning – her leer could be seen as the dangerous supplement to her slavish position in the triangle. Her "straggling mouth," lying "open in a contented leer," anticipates what Molly calls the "hole in the middle" of the female body, the genital and ontological abyss that threatens to engulf the disappointed bridges between men (*U* 18:151). A "leer," however, normally refers to an expression of the eyes, rather than the mouth; according to the *Oxford English Dictionary*, to leer is to look askance, or cast side glances, in a gesture reminiscent of V. S. Pritchard's definition of the short story as a glimpse out of the corner of the eye. To leer may also mean to "look or gaze with a sly, immodest, or malign expression in one's eye," which captures the flavor of the slavey's leer, as well as the appraising "squint" that Lenehan casts over her. That the slavey leers with her mouth rather than her eyes renders these organs curiously interchangeable, suggesting that her eye is a devouring orifice, while her mouth is "gaping" like a greedy eye.

Both her eyes and mouth, however, remain blind to Lenehan, and it is he who does the active leering, squinting at the girl out of the shadows. Since the reader glimpses the slavey only through Lenehan's anorthoscopic gaze, it is hard to judge whether her unpleasant leer is merely the projection of Lenehan's voyeurism. And this is the only close-up that we get of her; for the rest of the story the slavey is largely occluded, first by her absence, then by Corley's broad figure which "hid[es] hers from view," and finally by the door that "close[s] on her" when she withdraws into the house.

Garry Leonard, in a Lacanian study of *Dubliners*, proposes that the bunch of red flowers, pinned stem-upwards on the slavey's bosom, provides "the tiniest suggestion that a real woman ex-ists [*sic*] behind the masquerade," since it is a detail spotted only by the narrator, not by the two gallants for whom she functions merely as an object of exchange.[56] These flowers also bring to mind Lacan's famous schema of the inverted bouquet, in which a complex play of mirrors produces the illusion that a vase of flowers is hanging upside-down. Similarly, the slavey's upsidedown corsage subverts the gallants' visual command over the scene, since these spectators fail to register its presence. As a detail that sticks out, these sloppy flowers correspond to her straggling mouth, at once conspicuous and abyssal. This mouth, "which lay open in a contented leer," could be compared to the gaping mouth in Munch's *The Scream* (1893), a vacuum that seems to be engulfing its surroundings. As Mladen Dolar comments on this painting, "we see the void, the orifice, the abyss, but with no fetish to protect us or to hold on to."[57] The slavey's open mouth is equally vertiginous, for we never learn the meaning of its leer, and it is from this vacuum that every inference unravels, leaving all the questions of the story "lying open." Furthermore the leer makes it impossible to sentimentalize the slavey as a victim, or by analogy to sentimentalize her nation, to indulge in the mawkish lamentation of the Irish harp. The leer implies that the slavey is something other than the currency of patriarchy; the slavey has something up her sleeve. Has she somehow outwitted her gallant, or fobbed him off with a shiny substitute for a gold coin? We never know, since we are forced, like Lenehan, to squint anorthoscopically, rather than to gaze directly at the scene.

Snow-blindness

"Two Gallants" exemplifies how blindness pervades the narratives of *Dubliners*, where characters are glimpsed askance – like the skull in Holbein's *The Ambassadors* – rather than beheld directly. These characters, leering at one another in the dark, mirror the reader's efforts to discern their motives through the slits of Joyce's narrative. Paradoxically the moment of revelation in "Two Gallants" is also the moment of the greatest blindness, when the gold coin shines forth without illuminating any of the story's mysteries. As we have seen, its shine is more blinding than the darkness, its message as opaque as the "darkened blind" in "The Sisters."

If *Dubliners* begins with the black-out represented by the darkened blind, it concludes with the white-out of the snow.

Yes, the newspapers were right: snow was general all over Ireland. It was falling on every part of the dark central plain, on the treeless hills, falling softly upon the Bog of Allen and, farther westward, softly falling into the dark mutinous Shannon waves. It was falling, too, upon every part of the lonely churchyard on the hill where Michael Furey lay buried. It lay thickly drifted on the crooked crosses and headstones, on the spears of the little gate, on the barren thorns. [Gabriel's] soul swooned slowly as he heard the snow falling faintly through the universe and faintly falling, like the descent of their last end, upon all the living and the dead. (*D* 223–24)

In this passage, the pronoun "he" is deliberately ambiguous, like the "he's" that crowd into Molly Bloom's final rhapsody in *Ulysses*, rendering her lovers indistinguishable. The "he" in the closing paragraphs of "The Dead" refers to Gabriel himself, but it could also refer to his dead rival Michael Furey, as well as to "the vast hosts of the dead" encroaching on the living; here it is worth noting that the term "ghost" derives from a Teutonic word for "fury." All these hes dissolve and dwindle: Gabriel's "own identity was fading out into a grey impalpable world: the solid world itself which these dead had one time reared and lived in was dissolving and dwindling …" As the snow thickens, so do Gabriel's tears, blinding him to everything except the ghost of Michael Furey, the fury of whose passion puts Gabriel to shame. "He had never felt like that himself towards any woman but he knew that such a feeling must be love. The tears gathered more thickly in his eyes and in the partial darkness he imagined he saw the form of a young man standing under a dripping tree" (*D* 223–24).

"Snow was general": this blizzard resembles the snowstorm in *The Pastoral Symphony*, which covers up the landscape like white lies: "The snow has been falling continuously for the last three days and all the roads are blocked," Gide writes (11/141).[58] Furthermore Joyce's snow enacts the loosening and dissolution implicit in the word "paralysis." In this ultimate dissolve, Joyce buries the boundary between the living and the dead, and he also buries Ireland, erasing it in snow in order to inscribe a new kind of writing on its whitened surface. For the whiteout in "The Dead" also buries the short story – Joyce never published one again.

Beckett's parody of the snowy ending of "The Dead" in his rainy story "A Wet Night" offers a clue to Joyce's transformation as an artist:

But the wind had dropped, as it so often does in Dublin when all the respectable men and women whom it delights to annoy have gone to bed, and the rain fell in a uniform untroubled manner. It fell upon the bay, the littoral, the mountains and the plains, and notably upon the Central Bog it fell with a rather desolate uniformity.[59]

The word "littoral" literally means the shoreline. But Beckett hints that Joyce's snowfall also abolishes the "literal," marking the end of the naturalist aesthetic and the beginning of a new kind of fiction, in which the littoral between the living and the dead is overthrown. Enter the ghosts of Stephen's mother, Bloom's son and father, and Joyce's literary forefathers: in *Ulysses* and *Finnegans Wake*, the vivacentric world of naturalism gives way to a magic theater where the dead rise up among the living, defying both the "literal" signification of the word and the "littoral" or bourn from which no traveller supposedly returns. "The Dead" already exceeds the littoral of the short story, in terms of length and development of character; although it takes place on a single evening, it is thronged with extravagant and erring spirits from the past and the beyond. After "The Dead," Joyce seems to have decided that the short story is too blind, too dead-ended to accommodate those furies who have passed over the littoral of death and life.

COLOR-BLINDNESS

There are many different kinds of blindness, only some of which are caused by inability to see. Merleau-Ponty insists that blindness is not the opposite of vision but its necessary precondition: visibility always "involves a nonvisibility."[60] Taking up this proposition, Derrida argues that this nonvisibility is thematized in Western art by drawings of blind men and (infrequently) blind women. The groping fingers of the blind man, or the antenna of his tapping wand, allude to the artist's hand and drawing tool contending with the hungry darkness. "Every draughtsman is blind," Derrida declares, for drawing is haptic as opposed to visual, driven by the implement rather than the eye. "At the instant when the point at the point of the hand … moves forward upon making contact with the surface, the inscription of the inscribable is not seen." The draughtsman cannot see this "originary, pathbreaking [frayage] moment," any more than we can see ourselves seeing. By the same token, Derrida argues, "the visibility of the visible cannot, by definition, be seen, no more than what Aristotle speaks of as the diaphanousness of light can be."[61]

In the "Proteus" episode of *Ulysses*, Stephen considers Aristotle's theory that objects would be invisible unless they were enveloped in a colored "diaphane."

Ineluctable modality of the visible: at least that if no more, thought through my eyes … Snotgreen, bluesilver, rust: coloured signs. Limits of the diaphane. But he adds: in bodies. Then he was aware of them bodies before of them coloured. How? By knocking his sconce against them, sure. (*U* 31:1–6)

In this elliptical passage, Stephen is remembering Aristotle's work *Sense and Sensibilia*, in which the philosopher defines the colored "diaphane" (translated below as the "Translucent") as the "bounding extreme" or "external limit" of bodies:

But it is manifest that, when the Translucent is in determinate bodies, its bounding extreme must be something real; and that colour is just this "something" we are plainly taught by facts – colour being actually either at the external limit, or being itself that limit, in bodies.[62]

"But he adds: in bodies," Stephen echoes. Then he wonders which came first in Aristotle's mind, the idea of bodies or the sight of them. "Modality" means form as opposed to substance, and in saying that the modality of the visible is "ineluctable," Stephen is asserting that the form or structure precedes the substance of the visible. In other words, we think before we see: "My eyes do not see it: they think it rather than see," Joyce wrote in the earliest extant version of the passage.[63] Stephen concludes that the idea of bodies must have preceded the empirical perception of their colored diaphanes: for this reason Aristotle was "aware of them [as] bodies before of them coloured." How did he become aware of them? By collision, not vision: "By knocking his sconce against them." Even if bodies were invisible, Aristotle would have bumped his head against them, thus ratifying the existence of matter, much as Samuel Johnson kicked a large stone to refute the idealist philosophy of Bishop Berkeley.

Aristotle also argues that vision is the superior sense for "the primary wants of life," but that hearing "contributes most to the growth of intelligence."

For rational discourse is a cause of instruction in virtue of its being audible, which it is, not directly, but indirectly; since it is composed of words, and each word is thought-symbol. Accordingly, of persons destitute from birth of either sense, the blind are more intelligent than the deaf and dumb.[64]

Stephen tests this theory by shutting his eyes to "see" if he is smarter in the dark: "Shut your eyes and see … I am getting on nicely in the dark. My ash sword hangs at my side. Tap with it: they do." Here Stephen tells himself to tap with his "ash sword," his ashplant walking stick, in the same way that the blind tap with their canes to navigate the dark – "they do." With his eyes shut Stephen wonders, "Has all vanished since?" Is he caught forever in the "black adiaphane," an anti-world divested of its colored membranes? Is the darkness inside or outside his eyes?[65] When he reopens his eyes, he finds that the visible has been "there all the time without you: and ever shall be, world without end" (*U* 31:9–28). The visible therefore persists without the viewer, yet the viewer cannot see without imposing a cognitive structure or modality upon the seen: "thought through my eyes." In Derrida's terms, there is no visuality without the symbolic, no "ergon" without "parergon," no figure without frame.[66]

Stephen's notion that his eyes "think rather than see" could be extended to the sphere of race relations, where the colored diaphane of human bodies is at issue. Racism reverses what Stephen perceives as Aristotle's sequence of awareness, since the racist eye is "aware of them [colored], before of them [bodies]." Not only does thought (or prejudice) precede vision, but the racist mind can think the visible away, casting the unseen into the black adiaphane. "I am an invisible man," Ralph Ellison writes:

I am invisible, understand, simply because people refuse to see me … When they approach me they see only my surroundings, themselves, or figments of their imagination – indeed, everything and anything except me.[67]

Ellison goes on to dramatize the way the white man blinds himself to everything except the color of black skin, a dark screen that he peoples with his own chimeras. But is it preferable to be color-blind? Charles W. Mills points out that for blacks, color "becomes central in a way it does not for whites, since this is the visible marker of black invisibility." To ignore this marker is to deepen the invisibility of those it stigmatizes. For this reason Mills mocks the "liberal commitment to bringing about a colour-blind society by acting as if it already exists, not seeing race at all, and congratulating oneself on one's lack of vision."[68] This form of liberalism "scotomizes" the reality of racial inequality, making a fetish of its own blindness.

Patricia J. Williams illustrates this scotomization with an amusing anecdote about her son, whose nursery-school teachers suspected him of being color-blind. An ophthalmologist who tested him, however, pronounced his vision perfect. Yet when Williams asked her son what color the grass was, the little boy replied, "It makes no difference." At this point Williams realized that the teachers at his nursery school, which was predominantly white, had been coaching the children to be color-blind, assuring them that "it doesn't matter … whether you're black or white or red or green or blue."[69]

Of course it does matter – but skin color is not the litmus test of race. A long tradition of American fiction about "passing," extending from Mark Twain's *Pudd'nhead Wilson* (1894) to Philip Roth's *The Human Stain* (2000), wrestles with the paradox that race can be invisible or indistinguishable. One of the most intriguing works in this tradition, Nella Larsen's long story or short novel *Passing* (1929), concerns two women who are passing, one as black and one as white, although both look white and middle-class enough to get away with taking tea at the Drayton Hotel in Chicago. When Claire Kendry, who is passing as white, is finally unmasked as black, she falls out of a window to her death. We never find out whether she jumped out of her own accord, or was pushed out by

Irene, her jealous rival, or bellowed out by Bellew, her rampaging hus-band.[70] But her disappearance intimates that being black and white at the same time removes her from the field of visibility, making her unseeable at all.

Larsen's story "Sanctuary," first published in *Forum* in 1930, also deals with color-blindness and color fetishism. A black man running from the law knocks on Annie Poole's door, begging her to hide him from the white avengers. He confesses that he shot a man, but was unable to dis-cern whether his victim was black or white, dead or alive. When he men-tions his friendship with her son, Obadiah, Annie reluctantly agrees to hide the fugitive under the laundry. In this "suffocating shelter," he lis-tens to the footsteps of the posse advancing on the house, the knuckles rapping on the door, and the sheriff stammering the news to Annie that Obadiah has been killed, and by the very wretch that she is sheltering. But when the sheriff asks if she has seen the murderer, she feigns blind-ness: "No, Ah ain't sees nobody pass. Not yet." As soon as the white men leave, she throws the murderer out, crying "don' nevah stop thankin' yo' Jesus he done gib you dat black face."[71] In this disturbing conclusion, loy-alty to color takes precedence over maternal love.

This story involves many forms of blindness: the killer Jim Hammer is a blind man with a pistol who cannot see the color of the man he shoots down in the dark. His blindness is redoubled by the "blind" or hiding-place in which he swelters – a blindness also imposed upon the reader, who witnesses the drama in the next-door room from the same blind position as the fugitive. Meanwhile, the white men are too blind to see the culprit right under their eyes, and never dream that Annie, blinded to everything but racial reflexes, could be harboring the man who killed her son. When she claims not to have seen the murderer, this is true to the extent that she cannot see beyond his skin-color – "not yet," in any case: "No, Ah ain't sees nobody pass. Not yet." That perception must await an age of justice.

Larsen herself passed out of the literary scene when she was accused of plagiarizing "Sanctuary," and thereby passing as another author, who happened to be white. In 1922 Sheila Kaye-Smith had published a short story called "Mrs. Adis" in the journal *Forum* under its previous title *The Century*. Although Kaye-Smith's story is set in northeast Sussex, the plot and characters of Larsen's story are the same, differing only in names and dialects, and even words and phrases from "Mrs. Adis" reappear in "Sanctuary." In Larsen's American short story, however, race-loyalty takes the place of class-loyalty in Kaye-Smith's British version of the tale.

Mrs. Adis protects the poacher from the "keepers," despite the fact that he has killed her son, in the same way that Annie protects her son's killer from the great white terror. Larsen wrote a self-defence explaining that her story came from "an old Negro woman," who claimed to be the prototype of Annie. At first Larsen believed her informant, but "lately, in talking it over with Negroes, I find that the tale is so old and so well known that it is almost folklore."[72] This defence failed to convince skeptics, and the probable explanation is that Larsen plagiarized the story blindly, forgetting she had read the phrases that resurfaced in her prose. Like Clare Kendry in *Passing*, Larsen disappeared from the literary scene because she could not pass as two authors of two races at the same time.

COUNTRIES OF THE BLIND

The Pastoral Symphony begins with the sun setting as the pastor is transported to an unknown destination, the shadows deepening as his sleigh approaches the "pays perdu" [lost land] of the blind (15/143). Similarly, "Mrs. Adis" and "Sanctuary" both begin with darkness falling, making every sound "distinct, intensified."[73] These journeys into blindness parallel the reader's journey into the short story, this unknown territory stripped of the familiar landmarks of the novel. As the visible world dissolves and dwindles, a world of "soundsense" is revealed, to borrow Joyce's coinage from *Finnegans Wake*: a country of the blind in which the sound of language is intensified (*FW* 121:15, 138:7). As Borges says of Joyce's loss of vision, the blind short story finds "new music" in the English language by shutting out the light of day.

But this is also an old music that recalls the short story's roots in the oral tradition. Perhaps the best-known example of the blind short story is Conrad's *Heart of Darkness*, where the story-teller Marlow disappears into the evening shadows, while his disembodied voice goes on talking through the night. "No more … than a voice," the story-teller can be heard even in the heart of darkness where the printed word becomes invisible. Thus the theme of blindness in short stories draws attention to the sound of words, the audible modality of narrative. "Sound," Levinas written, "is a ringing, clanging scandal. Whereas, in vision, form is wedded to content … in sound the perceptible quality overflows so that the form can no longer contain its content. A real rent is produced in the world …"[74] Similarly, sound is the rent through which the short story overflows the "forced claustration" of its form.

If Levinas equates sound with the disruption of the visible, other thinkers argue that vision is the sense that disrupts the complacency of hearing. Derrida, for instance, has argued that writing, the visible dimension of language, tends to be scotomized in favor of the supposed immediacy of speech. This contest between eye and ear, sight and sound, has occupied French thought for the last century, and the blind short story might be understood as a symptom of the trend that Martin Jay describes as the "denigration of the eye" in twentieth-century theory.[75] What I would propose, however, is that seeing and hearing are both haunted by the unassimilable stuff of language, its material resistance to signification. The short story seems peculiarly attuned to – and tormented by – the sight of writing and the rattle of speech – those asemantic sights and sounds that blind and deafen us to meaning. Often regarded as a truncated or disabled novel, the short story is associated with the classroom and the magazine, distinctively modern forms of pedagogy and dissemination. But the short story's affinity to modernism also lies in its preoccupation with the waste products of meaning, those blinding, deafening remains of sense.

CHAPTER 6

The name and the scar: identity in The Odyssey *and* A Portrait of the Artist as a Young Man

and Rouse found they spoke of Elias
in telling the tales of Odysseus   ΟΎ ΤΙΣ
           ΟΎ ΤΙΣ
'I am noman, my name is noman'
but Wanjina is, shall we say, Ouan Jin
or the man with an education
and whose mouth was removed by his father
        because he made too many things
whereby cluttered the bushman's baggage
vide the expedition of Frobenius' pupils about 1938
          to Auss'ralia
Ouan Jin spoke and thereby created the named
          thereby making clutter
             – Ezra Pound, Canto 74[1]

According to Australian aboriginal legend, the demi-god Wondjina cre-ated the world of things by giving them names. Intoxicated with his power, he named and made so many things that his father "cut out his mouth" to stop the clutter. Depictions of Wondjina show a mouthless face, the orifice wiped out without a trace.

In Pound's *Pisan Cantos*, the figure of this mouthless god, punished for naming and creating too many things, serves as a double for the silenced poet. Pound was also punished for his crimes of speech, specifically his fascist propaganda broadcasts for Rome Radio. Caged by the American army at Pisa, and subsequently committed to a mental asylum, Pound took a vow of silence, thereby sentencing himself to the punishment inflicted on Wondjina by his father.

In Canto 74, Pound amputates Wondjina's name into two halves – "Ouan Jin" – which is a French transliteration of a Chinese ideogram meaning "man of letters." The pun underlines the fallen deity's affinity to Pound, who also calls Ouan Jin "the man with an education."[2] In this

Canto, the splitting of Wondjina's name is preceded – and apparently triggered – by the intrusion of another severed name into the text: Ού τΙΣ, meaning "no man," which Pound mistook as a pun on Odysseus's name. In this way Odysseus slips into *The Cantos* under the same alias he used to trick the Cyclops: "I am noman, my name is noman."

By inserting these broken names into the poem, Pound sets up a resonance between the silenced namer (Wondjina) and the nameless hero (noman), overleaping the centuries, continents, and cultural traditions that divide these figures. If such myth-hopping seems implausible, Pound justifies it by reference to the scholar W. D. Rouse, who discovered when retracing Odysseus's itinerary through the Mediterranean that Greek islanders continued to retell the Odyssean legends, but cast the prophet Elias in Odysseus's role. Canto 74 could therefore be read in two antithetical ways. On the one hand, Pound seems to be anticipating Lévi-Strauss's theory that myths thrive on difference-in-repetition, so that their constant re-namings and re-spellings ensure their eternal renewal. Yet at the same time the Canto undermines this reassuring theory, since the movement from Odysseus to Elias to Ού τΙΣ to Wondjina to Ouan Jin traces an odyssey to anonymity.

Joyce's story "Grace" in *Dubliners* presents an Irish version of Wondjina, but there is little grace in Mr. Kernan's fall from vocal prowess. Reminiscent of Tim Finnegan, the tipsy hero of a vaudeville song who died by falling off a ladder but was resurrected by a shot of whiskey at his wake, Kernan tumbles drunkenly downstairs and bites off a piece of his tongue in his descent. Such images of verbal impotence recur in many forms in Joyce's fiction: in *Dubliners*, Little Chandler, Farrington, and Mr. Duffy suffer from an inability to write, while Humphrey Chimpden Earwicker, the fallen father of *Finnegans Wake*, speaks with an incriminating "hasitatense."[3] Stephen Dedalus also fails to overcome his writer's block, embodying throughout his fictional career the promise of a writing – and an exile – evermore about to be. Apart from one lame villanelle in the *Portrait*, and the fragmentary vampire-poem in "Proteus," Stephen never takes the risk of exile in writing. In *A Portrait of the Artist*, words fall apart before his eyes, disintegrating into the primeval chaos of their elements:

He could scarcely interpret the letters of the signboards of the shops. (*P* 92)

… he found himself glancing from one casual word to another on his right or left in stolid wonder that they had been so silently emptied of instantaneous sense … (*P* 178)

The letters of the name of Dublin lay heavily upon his mind, pushing one another surlily hither and thither with slow boorish insistence. (*P* 111)

Squalid, boorish, insubordinate to sense, the alphabet no longer seems constitutive of language but engaged in a guerrilla war against the word.

Why do these letters mutiny? And why do Joyce's would-be writers fail or fall? If language has no origin, no Adam, but a dumb Wondjina at its source, there is no power to bind names to things, or letters to names. The mutilation of Wondjina and his name raises questions about wounding, identity, and paternity that the present chapter traces through Homer's *Odyssey* and Joyce's *A Portrait of the Artist as a Young Man*. Both these works associate the name with a primal scene of scarification. In Homer, the exposure of Odysseus's scar precipitates a flashback that recounts how the hero received his name and scar, respectively the verbal and the bodily stigmata of identity. In the *Portrait*, Stephen Dedalus is searching for his father's name in the Cork anatomy theater when he discovers the word "Foetus" "cut several times" into a desk, and undergoes a crisis of masculinity, as if it were he who had been "cut." Why is Stephen so disturbed by this graffiti? The next section of this chapter shows how Stephen's anxiety arises from doubts about paternity analogous to those expressed by Telemachus at the beginning of *The Odyssey*.

ODYSSEUS'S SCAR

When the goddess Athena asks Telemachus if he is truly Odysseus's son, this simple question elicits a curiously roundabout reply:

> My mother says indeed I am his. I for my part
> do not know. Nobody really knows his own father. (*O* 1:215–16)

"*Pater semper incertus est*," Freud writes, quoting an old legal tag: fatherhood is always uncertain. Motherhood, by contrast, is "*certissima*."[4] This is because maternity is certified by the evidence of the senses, whereas paternity depends on verbal testimony: "my mother says indeed I am his." In effect, the father is created by the mother's word. Elsewhere Freud proclaims that a tremendous advance of civilization was achieved when the fact of maternity was subordinated to the fiction of paternity. Yet he overlooks the paradox that this fiction relies upon the mother's word.[5]

In a famous passage from "Scylla and Charybdis," previously discussed in Chapter 5, Stephen argues that the Roman Catholic Church is founded on incertitude about paternity.

Fatherhood, in the sense of conscious begetting, is unknown to man. It is a mystical estate, an apostolic succession, from only begetter to only begotten. On that mystery and not on the Madonna which the cunning Italian intellect flung to the mob of Europe the church is founded and founded irremovably because founded, like the world, macro and microcosm, upon the void. Upon incertitude, upon unlikelihood … Paternity may be a legal fiction. Who is the father of any son that any son should love him or he any son? (*U* 170:837–45)

This set piece belongs to Stephen's mission to be father to himself, self-made and self-begotten. To achieve this end, he repudiates the mother, dismissing the Madonna as a sentimental pretext thrown to the mob of Europe to sugar the patriarchal pill. At the same time, he insists on the "mystery" of paternity to disavow the father's sexual relation to the mother, and to mask the uncomfortable knowledge that "they clasped and sundered" (*U* 32:47). Through this stratagem, Stephen atones for the desire to castrate the father, to oust him from the mother's bed, by endowing him with the stupendous potency of fictionality. In Lacanian terms, he compensates the father for the loss of the penis by according him the "phallus" – a "mystical estate" indeed.

In *The Odyssey*, the father's absence from the first four books also makes a mystery of paternity. With a kind of scrupulous meanness, Homer defers the introduction of the father by opening the poem with the son. "Fit out a ship with twenty oars," Athena instructs Telemachus:

> and go out to ask about your father who is so long absent,
> on the chance some mortal man can tell you, who has listened to Rumour
> sent by Zeus. She more than others spreads news among people.
> (*O* 1:280–83)

Placed in a similar position to Telemachus, the reader finds out about the father only indirectly: by means of Rumour, the legends of the poets, and the stories that Odysseus invents about himself. For Odysseus is "a praiser of his own past" (*P* 241) (as Stephen describes his father Simon Dedalus), whose epic consists not only of his trials at sea but of his exploits in autobiography. When Odysseus regales the Phaiacians with the tales of his Great Wanderings, the reader also catches up with his adventures retrospectively, his words having substituted themselves for his deeds.

In addition to the authentic story of his life, Odysseus adopts a series of counterfeit identities. In Book 13, fencing off Athena's questions about his name, birthplace, and genealogy, he claims to be a murderer from Crete, fleeing retribution for his crime (*O* 13:256–86). Later on he attempts to deceive Eumaeus, Telemachus, Penelope's suitors, and even

Penelope herself with bogus autobiographies. The wildest of these tales is Odysseus's roundabout attempt to borrow a mantle from the swineherd Eumaeus. Having returned to Ithaca incognito, Odysseus needs this mantle to disguise himself so that he can seize possession of his house and storm the suitors. But instead of asking Eumaeus directly for the garment, Odysseus invents a lie about Odysseus lying to acquire a mantle on behalf of the present liar (*O* 14:459–506). These "tales within wheels" leave Eumaeus understandably perplexed (*FW* 247:3). Nonetheless the gentle swineherd encourages his guest to while away the night in story-telling:

> These nights are endless, and a man can sleep through them,
> or he can enjoy listening to stories, and you have no need
> to go to bed before it is time. Too much sleep is only
> a bore …
> … we two, sitting here in the shelter, eating and drinking
> shall entertain each other remembering and retelling
> our sad sorrows.
>
> (*O* 15:392–400)

Like Scheherezade in *The Arabian Nights*, who staves off death by telling stories, Odysseus's existence lasts only so long as he tells lies about it. These lies often seem more plausible than the truth, in that they steer clear of the monstrous and supernatural features of his actual adventures. The hero presents himself, with variations, as a nobleman misused by fortune, condemned to wander from the land of his fathers. All his lies serve as answers to the question, spoken or unspoken, which is raised by his arrival as a stranger: "Who are you and where do you come from?"[6] When he finally regains his true identity, having retrieved his kingdom, wife, and name, he vanishes with all his pseudonyms into the silence that is Ithaca.

If his mouth tells lies about his name and origins, Odysseus also has a secret orifice that speaks only the truth. This is his famous scar, which is discovered by his old nurse Eurycleia when she washes his feet, little suspecting that the weary stranger is her long-lost master in disguise.

> … the old woman took up the shining basin
> she used for foot washing, and poured in a great deal of water, the cold
> first, and then she added the hot to it. Now Odysseus
> was sitting close to the fire, but suddenly turned to the dark side;
> for presently he thought in his heart that, as she handled him,
> she might be aware of his scar, and all his story might come out. (*O* 19:386–91)

"She might be aware of his scar, and all his story might come out" – the translation suggests that the story literally "comes out" of the scar.[7] In fact, two fragments of Odysseus's story do come out or issue from the mention of this scar, for a long digression follows, recounting two apparently disjointed episodes from the hero's infancy and youth. This flashback, a rare technique in Homer, occupies almost a hundred lines before the narrative returns to the present. It is as if Odysseus's scar had scarred the narrative itself, which plunges into memory and self-dismemberment.

The two events hinged together in the flashback concern two signs that identify the subject, word and flesh – his name and scar. In the first episode, the infant hero receives his name from his maternal grandfather, Autolykos, who finding the kingdom of Ithaca "distasteful" decides to name his grandchild "Odysseus," which means "distasteful" – a curiously inauspicious name to bear (*O* 19:399–409). The second episode involves the hunting accident in which the youth Odysseus is wounded by a wild boar: "too quick for him the boar drove / over the knee, and with his tusk gashed much of the flesh …" (*O* 19:449–50). Thus the story of Odysseus's naming is closely followed by the story of his scarring, and both emerge out of the rupture in the narrative produced by the disclosure of the scar. Name, scar, and story all "come out" of one another, in the pattern mapped out in the diagram below:

The first movement (reading clockwise from the top right) is from the *scar* to the *story* that "comes out" of it. This is the story of Autolykos's naming of Odysseus, which is triggered by Eurycleia's recognition of the scar. And scarcely has Autolykos pronounced the name "Odysseus" when another story issues from the *name*: the story of the *scar* (the hunting accident). This *scar* then brings forth a further story about Odysseus's story-telling, when the hunter triumphantly reports the escapade to his proud parents:

> his father and queenly mother
> were glad in his homecoming, and asked about all that had happened,
> and how he came by his wound, and he told well his story … (*O* 19:462–64)

This sequence suggests that in order to accede to his identity, Odysseus's *name* has to be inscribed into a *scar*, but the *scar* must then be reinscribed into a *story*. Only when this cycle is complete does the hero truly "make his name." The flashback culminates with the story of Odysseus's story-telling, in which he overcomes the wild boar a second time, with words instead of spears, mastering nature with culture: "he told well his story …"

This cycle of name, scar, and story is accompanied by cycle of stage-settings. The scene of naming takes place in domestic space, the scene of scarring in the wilderness, but the scene of story-telling takes place in the public arena of the court, in which Odysseus assumes his position in the social order by accounting for his wound with words. Yet all these long-past scenes of naming, scarring, and story-telling are reconstructed in the present scene of foot-washing, which recalls the original domestic setting where the infant Odysseus received his name. The flashback concludes by restaging the moment when Eurycleia sees the scar and identifies her long-lost master. Her recognition of his name seems to seal the wound within the poem itself, restoring the continuity of narrative after the irruption of the past within the present.

This sequence implies that the scar is the generative principle of narrative, because it represents a breach in the symbolic fabric that has to be repaired by story-telling. It is important that the scar repeats: a living scar, it resurfaces both on the body of the hero and in the corpus of the text. Secondly, the scar secretes – in the double sense of letting stories out but also sealing them in secrecy. Finally, the scar irrupts into the narrative itself, so that linear progression suddenly gives way to cycles of remembering and dismembering.

Erich Auerbach has argued that Homer's style is "of the foreground"; despite the use of flashbacks and anticipations, whatever is narrated appears to be "the only present, pure and without perspective."[8] Extending this insight, one could argue the past inheres within the present of *The Odyssey* in the same way that the scar is imprinted on the surface of Odysseus's flesh, latent rather than concealed. Potentially the scar can re-emerge at any moment, unleashing the hemorrhage of that which was. But why is the scar introduced into the narrative so late, just before the showdown with the suitors? It is strange that these stories of

identification, which belong to the prehistory of the hero's fictional existence, should be reserved for this eleventh-hour revelation. Through this
narrative procrastination, Odysseus eludes the reader, just as he eludes his
mythical pursuers, by dropping his disguises only when his story is about
to close.

This belatedness inheres within the scar itself, which presides over a
logic of doubling, deferral, déjà vu. The scar makes its impact après coup
in both the story and the narrative, through the process Freud describes
as *Nachträglichkeit* or "deferred action," as discussed above in Chapter 2.
Note that Odysseus achieves identity through the deferred effects of language and violence: first his grandfather speaks his name, then the wild
boar tattoos his flesh. This sequence could be understood as a transition
from voice to writing – in effect, the scar is that which *writes* the name
onto the flesh. This signature in turn demands a reader to be recognized,
and reading is a retrospective act. Without a reader, the scar cannot release
its story; sealed in silence on the body, it awaits a Eurycleia to reactivate
its narrative. Only the second instance, the return, the re-cognition can
awaken the scar and make it speak. Eurycleia's cry of recognition restores
speech to the scar, re-assuming the writing on the body into the voicing
of the name.

If naming involves scarification, as this pattern of events suggests, the
subject is threatened with extinction by his own signature. The scar dis-
members that which it identifies: although it sets a seal upon the subject,
it also represents a seam through which identity escapes. The next section of this chapter examines this double logic in Joyce's *Portrait*, showing how Stephen's efforts to establish an identity are undermined by the
resurgence of the scar.

Disremembering Dedalus

A fan once accosted Joyce in Zurich and cried, "Let me kiss the hand that
wrote *Ulysses*." Joyce refused his hand, replying, "No, it did lots of other
things too" (*JJ* 110). In *A Portrait of the Artist as a Young Man*, Stephen
worries that his mouth, like Joyce's hand, is tainted by the "other things"
that it has done. The lips that chant Hail Marys are also lips that munch
and suck and kiss and spew profanities.

If ever his soul, re-entering her dwelling shyly after the frenzy of his body's lust
had spent itself, was turned towards her whose emblem is the morning star,
bright and musical, telling of heaven and infusing peace, it was when her names

were murmured softly by lips whereon there still lingered foul and shameful words, the savour itself of a lewd kiss. (*P* 105)

Stephen is dismayed that the highest and lowest sentiments are both expressed, "pressed out," through the same bodily members: the hand, the mouth.[9] Whether spoken or written, language passes through the body, corrupted by the physicality that Stephen is struggling to transcend. Words can never purify the flesh, since they are fashioned by the flesh – tongued by the mouth, scrawled by the hand.

How can these members remember? Among the things the hand that wrote *Ulysses* did was to write *A Portrait of the Artist as a Young Man*. In fact, it wrote three portraits of him: a brief essay of 1904, which was extended into *Stephen Hero*, which was then abandoned in favor of the novel regarded as the final text.[10] As for this last version, the indefinite article of its title suggests a Wordsworthian prelude to autobiography, rather than a definitive account: it is *a* portrait, not *the* portrait. If autobiography entails the repetition of the author's life, Joyce's portrait repeats itself, producing identity after identity. What is it about self-portraiture, for Joyce as for Wordsworth, which makes them reluctant to conclude?

In the case of *The Prelude, or, The Growth of a Poet's Mind*, Wordsworth must read his own life backwards to understand how he became the poet that he is. Yet the past can be recovered only through the present work of memory. In autobiography memory constructs the past in order to determine how the past constructed memory. As Gertude Stein puts it, "At any moment when you are you you are you without the memory of yourself because if you remember yourself while you are you you are not for purposes of creating you."[11] In "Scylla and Charybdis," Stephen speaks of the artist weaving and unweaving his own image, and the same could be said of the autobiographer, who must account for his existence in the present by unraveling the fabric woven by the past (*U* 9:376). In this sense, he decomposes what the past composed, unwrites the hand that writes. Remembering entails dismembering, or more precisely "disremembering" – to borrow Davin's Irishism from the *Portrait* (*P* 181).

If the *Portrait* borrows from the *Prelude* any model of the poet's mind, it is not the metaphor of growth but the principle of "spots of time." Described by Wordsworth as "islands in the unnavigable depth of our departed time," these spots could be interpreted as snags in temporality, which act like scratches on a broken record, introducing a subversive logic of repetition into the teleology of growth. A spot denotes a point in space or time, but it can also mean a blemish, mark, or scar. It is therefore appropriate that the spots of time passage in the *Prelude* climaxes in the discovery of a scar in the shape of a name. In Book XI Wordsworth writes:

> There are in our existence spots of time
> That with distinct pre-eminence retain
> A renovating virtue …

This claim for the renovating virtue of these spots of time sits oddly in this spooky episode, in which the young Wordsworth, rambling on horseback through the rough and stony moor, loses his companion to find himself confronted with the name of a murderer, carved into the earth to mark the spot at which the miscreant was hanged:

> The gibbet-mast was mouldered down, the bones
> And iron case were gone; but on the turf,
> Hard by, soon after that fell deed was wrought,
> Some unknown hand had carved the murderer's name.

Neither the name, nor the hand that wrote it, is revealed. What fascinates the poet is the act of cutting the inscription, and the uncanny "renovation" of its characters:

> The monumental writing was engraven
> In times long past; and still, from year to year,
> By superstition of the neighbourhood,
> The grass is cleared away, and to this hour
> The letters are all fresh and visible.[12]

As we shall see, the *Portrait* also presents identity as a scar that periodically reopens, so that its letters may remain "all fresh and visible."

To understand the dynamics of this scar, it is important to grasp how the body is depicted in the *Portrait*. In this regard the scandalized reactions of Joyce's early critics are particularly revealing. H. G. Wells famously accused Joyce of a "cloacal obsession," and the scatological motif crops up repeatedly in early criticism (Deming 86). One review, entitled "A Study in Garbage," describes the *Portrait* as an "extraordinary dirty study," whose author would be better suited to writing "a treatise on drains." The author of "A Dyspeptic Portrait" complains that Joyce "drags his readers after him into the slime of foul sewers" (Deming 85, 98). "Mr. Joyce can never resist a dunghill," another critic fulminates, while yet another deplores the "privy-language" of the *Portrait* (Deming 100, 97). Joyce's "preoccupation with the olfactory," particularly when it takes the form of Stephen's "passion for foul-smelling things," also comes in for much abuse (Deming 100, 93). More temperately, Clutton Brock detects in Stephen a "conflict of beauty and disgust" – and one could argue that this conflict continues to be battled out by critics, with the disgusted lining up on one side, and those enraptured with the novel's beauty on the other (Deming 90). Only Wyndham Lewis seems to find the *Portrait* insufficiently disgusting, with "far too tenuous an elegance for my taste" (Deming 120).

Other early critics complain that the novel has no plot, that Stephen Dedalus has "no continuum, no personality," and that "thoughts pass through his mind like good or bad smells. He has no control of them" (Deming 110, 90). The character is too "thin-skinned" to keep good thoughts in, or bad thoughts out (Deming 97). One hostile critic argues that "Samuel hewed Agag to pieces, but the pieces were not Agag; and the fragments here offered of the experience of Stephen Dedalus are no substitute for a 'portrait of the artist as a young man.'"[13] As far as Joyce's style is concerned, Edward Garnett regrets the "longueurs" of the *Portrait*. Arguing that Joyce has "failed to discredit the inverted comma," Wells complains that the dialogue flickers "blindingly" between dashes that confuse the speakers with their speech (Deming 81, 87).[14]

This critical hostility corroborates Gertrude Stein's view that when a masterpiece is born, "for a very long time everybody refuses and then almost without a pause almost everybody accepts," yet "when it is still a thing irritating annoying stimulating then all quality of beauty is denied to it."[15] Those who "accept" the *Portrait* today tend to neglect its "irritating annoying stimulating" features, especially its scatological dimension. Sympathetic criticism has traditionally focused on the concept of transcendence, arguing that Stephen transcends squalor by means of art, while Joyce transcends Stephen by means of irony. But it is precisely the absence of transcendence that shocked the first reviewers of the book, the intensity of whose reactions suggests a fear of contamination by the novel's filth. Yet these critics are right to point out that Stephen's character is inconsistent, porous, plural – Stephen leaks. While sucking up the voices, sights, and particularly the smells of his environment, his own emissions trickle out into the atmosphere. His discharges dissolve the boundary between body and language, for it is verbal as well as bodily effusions that Stephen sweats, exhales, urinates, defecates, ejaculates, and vomits.

Early critics were also right in pointing out that the novel is obsessed with smell, particularly of the putrid or excremental kind. As discussed above in Chapter 3, Freud argues that vision superseded smell in the hierarchy of the senses when the human animal began to stand upright, and

visual beauty took the place of body odor as the dominant sexual stimu-
lant.[16] Smell differs from vision in dissolving the distance between subject
and object, for the nose imbibes the very substance of the smelt, and the
smell rubs off on the smeller, causing him or her to smell in turn. This
intimate two-way exchange differs from the impact of sound-waves on
the ear, or light-waves on the eye, where subject and object supposedly
remain discrete and uninfected by each other.

In the *Portrait*, the predominance of the olfactory implies that personal
identity cannot contain itself; instead, the subject functions as a conduit
for the odors of the city. It is revealing that images of drainage, sewers, and
cloacae reappear throughout the early criticism, for Joyce depicts the subject as a drainage-system, absorbing and recycling the leftovers of others.
This system may be divided into three economies. The first is an economy
of flow, in which the subject issues forth in verbal and bodily secretions:

His sins trickled from his lips, one by one, trickled in shameful drops from his
soul festering and oozing like a sore, a squalid stream of vice. The last sins oozed
forth, sluggish, filthy. (*P* 144)

This account of Stephen's confession equates his words with blood, pus,
urine, semen, excrement. Elsewhere breath, money, and saliva feature as
currencies in the economy of flow. Throughout his adolescence, Stephen
oscillates between two states described as "unrest" and "weariness," a
cycle punctuated by "ejaculations," both verbal and corporeal – for the
novel persistently confuses these domains (*P* 96, 103, 176, 147).

Such moments passed and the wasting fires of lust sprang up again. The verses
passed from his lips and the inarticulate cries and the unspoken brutal words
rushed forth from his brain to force a passage. (*P* 99)

The term "pass," used twice in these two sentences and echoed in "passage," becomes a kind of signature for the economy of flow. In this
instance, passion has to pass through language, passing out of Stephen
in the form of verse, while the wasting fires of lust spring up to force a
passage, both visceral and verbal. If any of these flows is blocked, a fin-
de-siècle weariness results:

The old restless moodiness had again filled his breast as it had done on the night
of the party but had not found an outlet in verse … and all day the stream of
gloomy tenderness within him had started forth and returned upon itself in dark
courses and eddies, wearying him in the end … (*P* 77)

This obstructed flow could consist of either verse or semen, for the
term "stream" confounds these categories. Everything that passes out

of Stephen's mind or body liquefies: money "runs" through his fingers, confessions "trickle" from his lips, while poems ooze or stream or burst orgasmically:

A soft liquid joy like the noise of many waters flowed over his memory … A soft liquid joy flowed through the words where the soft long vowels hurtled noiselessly and fell away, lapping and flowing back … (*P* 97, 225–26)

Many bodily rhythms orchestrate these flows, from peristalsis to the beating of the heart. The rhythms of systole and diastole, inhalation and exhalation, tumescence and detumescence, recur in Stephen's cycles of unrest and weariness, as well as in paired words and phrases: "opening, closing, locking, unlocking"; "click, click: click, click"; "passing, passing"; "pick, pack, pock, puck"; "term, vacation; tunnel, out; noise, stop"; "bucket and lamp and lamp and bucket"; "ever, never, ever, never" (*P* 20, 41, 59, 17, 187, 132). In the following passage, Stephen's unrest issues from him in a tidal "wave of sound":

The sentiment of the opening bars, their languor and supple movement, evoked the incommunicable emotion which had been the cause of all his day's unrest and of his impatient movement of a moment before. His unrest issued from him in a wave of sound: and on the tide of flowing music the ark was journeying, trailing her cables of lanterns in her wake. (*P* 75)

The term "tide" associates this flow of sound with the lunar rhythms of menstruation, flouting the difference between the sexes, for every orifice – mouth, nostrils, anus, genitals – is enlisted as an outlet in the economy of flow. Stephen's outpourings may be verbal, respiratory, seminal, menstrual, urinary, faecal, salivary, vomitory, or all of these at the same time:

He stretched out his arms in the street to hold fast the frail swooning form that eluded him and incited him: and the cry that he had strangled for so long in his throat issued from his lips. It broke from him like a wail of despair from a hell of sufferers and died in a wail of furious entreaty, a cry for an iniquitous abandonment, a cry which was but an echo of an obscene scrawl which he had read on the oozing wall of a urinal. (*P* 100)

This cry is literally a dirty word: it breaks out of the subject orgasmically or diarrhetically, or spurts like blood from a reopened wound.

Note that this spontaneous overflow is not original: Stephen's dirty word is merely the echo of an obscene scrawl oozing on the wall of a urinal. Most of Stephen's outbursts are repetitions of previous ejaculations, hinting that everything that issues out of him passes into him before. The economy of flow therefore depends on a reverse economy of influence.

A major form of influence is food – including food for thought – and transubstantial victuals in particular. In the ritual of Holy Communion, the body and the blood of Christ are consumed in a totem feast, and the *Portrait* imitates this recipe. Depending on the cooking, words can turn into a Eucharist or Irish stew. "Stuff it into you," Stephen's belly counsels him, and in his greed he gobbles up words as eagerly as food (*P* 102). At other times, however, his rapacity is hindered by disgust, or by discriminations worthy of the fin-de-siècle connoisseur: "he tasted in the language of memory ambered wines, dying fallings of sweet airs … (*P* 233).

The *Portrait* makes a meal of almost anything: here Stephen literally eats his words, savoring the language of his memory. But he rarely gets the chance to sample anything so mellow. Most of the food and words that he consumes are old and stale, the rotting crumbs that other eaters, other speakers left behind:

Mr. Dedalus pushed his plate over to Stephen and bade him finish what was on it. (*P* 71)

[Stephen] drained his third cup of watery tea to the dregs and set to chewing the crusts of fried bread that were scattered near him, staring into the dark pool of the jar. The yellow dripping had been scooped out like a boghole … (*P* 174)

In the second passage, Simon Dedalus's bankruptcy has reduced his family meals to scraps and pickings, which are inventoried with a ravenous attention to detail:

Tea was nearly over and only the last of the second watered tea remained in the bottom of the small glassjars and jampots which did service for teapots. Discarded crusts and lumps of sugared bread, turned brown by the tea which had been poured over them, lay scattered on the table. Little wells of tea lay here and there on the board and a knife with a broken ivory handle was stuck through the pith of a ravaged turnover. (*P* 163)

Meanwhile language, like food, reaches Stephen half-devoured: "Old phrases, sweet only with a disinterred sweetness like the figseeds Cranly rooted out of his gleaming teeth" (*P* 233).

Where food is concerned, Stephen exercises some free will in deciding what he takes into his body. But he lacks the power to resist the influence of smell. In his ascetic exercises, he figures out ingenious ways of mortifying all his sense organs except his nose:

To mortify his smell was more difficult as he found in himself no instinctive repugnance to bad odours, whether they were the odours of the outdoor world such as those of dung and tar or the odours of his own person among which he had made many curious comparisons and experiments. (*P* 151)

It is largely through nasal or pneumatic means that Stephen's precursors exert their influence on their ephebe: "the spirit of Ibsen," for example, blows through Stephen "like a keen wind" (*P* 176). Less clean and less Norwegian, however, is the language that the artist is obliged to breathe most frequently:

A smell of molten tallow came up from the dean's candle butts and fused itself in Stephen's consciousness with the jingle of the words, bucket and lamp and lamp and bucket. (*P* 187)

His last phrase, soursmelling as the smoke of charcoal and disheartening, excited Stephen's brain, over which its fumes seemed to brood. (*P* 246)

In the first passage, words that smell of molten tallow jingle stupidly in Stephen's mind; in the second, soursmelling phrases seep into his nostrils. In both cases the economies of flow and influence converge in Stephen's lungs: the verbal gases that he breathes condense into his flows of verse to be discharged into the fetor of the atmosphere. In an image that looks forward to Anna Livia Plurabelle – the personified River Liffey that evaporates into a cloud in *Finnegans Wake* – the vapor of Stephen's sexual fantasy liquefies into the wet dream of his villanelle:

Conscious of his desire she was waking from odorous sleep, the temptress of his villanelle … Her nakedness yielded to him, radiant, warm, odorous and lavish-limbed, enfolded him like a shining cloud, enfolded him like water with a liquid life: and like a cloud of vapour or like waters circumfluent in space the liquid letters of speech … flowed forth over his brain. (*P* 223)

Here influence is converted into flow: the odorous vapors emitted by the temptress precipitate a waterfall of "liquid letters."

As a belated poet, Stephen finds it difficult to separate the air he breathes from the airs of prior masters of the art. Most of his verses are reported indirectly, but the few fragments recorded in the text are liberally seasoned with quotation. "Stale creampuffs" – the epithet that Ezra Pound applied to his juvenile imitations of the decadents – also pertains to Stephen's derivative effusions. The word "weariness," for instance, which issues from his crises of "unrest" is recycled from Shelley and Ben Jonson, and wearily reiterates the weariness of imitation (*P* 96, 176). When this quotation fails to come to Stephen's relief, the "soft speeches of Claude Melnotte" rise to his lips to "[ease] his unrest" (*P* 99). Even his dirty word is a quotation, the "echo" of graffiti in a urinal, where writing – the "wake" of the word – is stained with urine, the wake of the flesh. One way or another, almost every word that passes in or out of Stephen derives from other people's writings.

This means that the economies of influence and flow presuppose a third economy of literature.

Scar-letters

– One difficulty, said Stephen, in esthetic discussion is to know whether words are being used according to the literary tradition or according to the tradition of the marketplace. I remember a sentence of Newman's in which he says that the Blessed Virgin was detained in the full company of the saints. The use of the word in the marketplace is quite different. *I hope I am not detaining you.*
Not in the least, said the dean politely.
No, no, said Stephen, smiling, I mean …
Yes, yes: I see, said the dean, I quite catch the point: *detain*. (*P* 188)

At the time this passage was written, Joyce could scarcely have predicted the modern usage of the term "detain" to denote the imprisonment without trial of suspected terrorists in Northern Ireland. When Newman uses it, the term "detain" carries no sense of being held by force: the Virgin is "detained" among the saints, much as Burton in *The Anatomy of Melancholy* is "detained and allured with … grace and comeliness" (the citation given for this usage of "detain" in the *Oxford English Dictionary*). Stephen goes on to explain that words have one meaning in "the literary tradition," and quite another in the "marketplace" (*P* 213). The word "detain" enters the literary tradition when Stephen withdraws it from the marketplace of the vernacular. Literature itself "detains" language as a miser detains money, or constipation faeces: in fact, "detain" is an antiquated term for constipate. In the *Portrait*, the economy of literature consists of words and flesh detained, held back, occulted out of circulation. Speech in storage, literature disrupts the interchange of flow and influence, producing blockage in the marketplace. To borrow a key term from *Dubliners*, literature is the "paralysis" of language.

By detaining words, literature introduces gaps into the narrative, aporias obstructing the exchange of meaning:

He stood still and gazed up at the sombre porch of the morgue and from that to the dark cobbled laneway at its side. He saw the word *Lotts* on the wall of the lane and breathed slowly the rank heavy air.

A proper name, "*Lotts*" means nothing, but refers to someone or something undisclosed. Opaque, "detained," and paralyzed, the word presents itself in smelling distance of the morgue, evoking for Stephen the rank heavy odor of "horse piss and rotted straw" (*P* 86). This association of letters with odors is significant, because the smelliest of all the vapors that circulate through Stephen's nose are those that emanate from literature. Worse than the smell of speech is the stench of writing – dead speech stored in literature – which creeps into his lungs to splutter from his mouth as liquid speech.

Stephen himself contributes to the stench of literature by writing dirty letters and leaving them to ambush unwary readers:

> The sordid details of his orgies stank under his very nostrils … the foul long letters he had written in the joy of guilty confession and carried secretly for days and days only to throw them under cover of night among the grass in the corner of a field or beneath some hingeless door or in some niche in the hedges where a girl might come upon them as she walked by and read them secretly. (*P* 115–16)

The repetition of the term "secretly" reminds us that these letters are the secrets secreted out of Stephen's solitary orgies. Like Odysseus's scar, these letters take deferred effect: they await a younger Irish Eurycleia to read them and release their coffined fumes. If these letters reek of sex, the legends in shop windows stink of mortality:

> diffusing in the air around him [was] a tenuous and deadly exhalation and he found himself glancing from one word to another on his right or left in stolid wonder that they had been so silently emptied of instantaneous sense until every mean shop legend bound his mind like the words of a spell and his soul shriveled up, sighing with age as he walked on in a lane among heaps of dead language. His own consciousness of language was ebbing from his brain and trickling into the very words themselves which set to band and disband themselves in wayward rhythms:

> > *The ivy whines upon the wall*
> > *And whines and twines upon the wall*
> > *The ivy whines upon the wall*
> > *The yellow ivy on the wall*
> > *Ivy, ivy up the wall.*

> Did anyone ever hear such drivel? Lord Almighty! Who ever heard of ivy whining on a wall? (*P* 178–79)

This "tenuous and deadly exhalation" arises from "dead language," in which words have been withdrawn from circulation, heaped up in "mean" shop legends and detained in the miserly economy of literature. Stephen cannot help but inhale these noxious vapors and pass them out again as "drivel." This passage therefore demonstrates the three economies completing a transaction: the economy of *literature* releases deadly exhalations that *influence* the artist's lungs and issue in the *flow* of poetaster's drivel.

Of all the words "detained" in literature, the most mysterious is the inscription *Fœtus*. This word appears at the climax of the trip to Cork in Chapter 2, when Simon Dedalus, having returned to his birthplace with his son, goes to look for his initials, engraved into a desk in the anatomy theatre. But this self-affirmation is belied by the financial motive of this journey, for the bankrupt father is returning to his origins only to auction his possessions, a last resort to stall his family's steep decline to destitution. The rediscovery of his initials is preceded by Stephen's confrontation with the word *Fœtus*:

They passed into the anatomy theatre where Mr. Dedalus, the porter aiding him, searched the desks for his initials. Stephen remained in the background, depressed more than ever by the darkness and silence of the theatre and by the air it wore of jaded and formal study. On the desk before him he read the word *Fœtus* cut several times into the dark stained wood. The sudden legend startled his blood: he seemed to feel the absent students of the college about him and to shrink from their company. A vision of their life, which his father's words had been powerless to evoke, sprang up before him out of the word cut in the desk. A broadshouldered student with a moustache was cutting in the letters with a jackknife, seriously. Other students stood or sat near him laughing at his handiwork. One jogged his elbow. The big student turned on him, frowning. He was dressed in loose grey clothes and had tan boots.

Stephen's name was called. He hurried down the steps of the theatre so as to be as far away from the vision as he could be and, peering closely at his father's initials, hid his flushed face. (*P* 89–90)

This passage, like the graffiti it describes, defies metaphorical interpretation. What is emphasized is not the meaning of the word *Fœtus* but the murderous activity of cutting it: one can almost hear the scraping of the knives. Like Odysseus's scar, this word cuts through the membrane of the present, unleashing a flashback to the past. But the scar needs a reader to release its story, and Stephen *misreads* the incision, performing what Harold Bloom might describe as a "creative misprision" of the trace:[17]

he read the word *Fœtus* cut several times in the dark stained wood. The sudden legend startled his blood … A broadshouldered student was cutting in the letters with a jackknife …

What is puzzling here is the inconsistency of number. "Cut several times," the incision is plural, but among the rascals conjured up in Stephen's vision, only one is credited with authorship. *The* student – singular – who vandalized the desk leaps back into sadistic life, surrounded by his sniggering accomplices. His violent inscription startles Stephen's blood, bringing forth a vision of the broadshouldered moustachioed knife-wielding writer flanked by his lieutenants – a fantasy that causes Stephen to hide his "flushed face."[18]

In at least four ways, the "word cut in the desk" challenges the father's authority. First it breaks out where the father's name should be. Secondly it lets forth a vision of the past which Simon Dedalus's words have been "powerless to evoke." Thirdly it arouses Stephen's "blood," provoking a homoerotic fantasy of writing – a "monstrous reverie" – that flushes his face with guilty excitement. Finally, the plurality of the inscription belies the notion of a singular paternity, "from only begetter to only begotten." How can a mark "cut several times" be pinned down to a single author? But it is crucial that the initials pre-empted by *Fœtus* stand not only for the name of the father but for that of *Stephen Dedalus*.

In a psychoanalytic frame of reference, it is not surprising that the father's name should be associated with an act of violence. In *Moses and Monotheism*, Freud associates the patronymic with circumcision, and Lacan uses the term "nom-du-père" as a synonym for castration. But this does not explain why another cut precedes the father's initials in the *Portrait*, or why this cut spells *Fœtus*. This cut, I would argue, corresponds to the navel, which separates the foetus from the mother. A wounding anterior to naming, the navel testifies to the facticity of motherhood, as opposed to the mystery of paternity. Horrified by the "monstrous reveries" that issue from these scar-letters, Stephen conjures up the broadshouldered student to defend himself against the threat of merger in the mother. Only when his father calls his name is he rescued from the abyss of the unnameable. If the "sudden legend" startles his blood, it is because the phallus has been ambushed by the omphalos.

We have already seen how Joyce associates the omphalos with home: both Bloom and Stephen live in omphalos-symbols, and in the "Proteus" episode of *Ulysses*, Stephen imagines the "navelcord" as a vast telephonic network extending back to the home of humanity in the Garden of Eden (3:37–40). Yet the navel also signifies the exile of the newborn child from its original home in the uterus. The navel separates the child from the mother's body but also testifies to their original connectedness: "the cords of all link back, standentwining cable of all flesh" (*U* 3:37–40). More terrifying than these tangled navelcords, however, is the danger that the navel may reopen, pouring out the contents of the self. This threat materializes in Joyce's epiphany about the death of his brother Georgie, also quoted above in Chapter 1:

[DUBLIN: in the house in
GLENGARIFF PARADE: evening]
MRS. JOYCE – (crimson, trembling, appears at the parlour door) … Jim!
JOYCE – (at the piano) … Yes?
MRS. JOYCE – Do you know anything about the body? … What ought I do?
   … There's some matter coming away from the hole in Georgie's stomach
   … Did you ever hear of that happening?
JOYCE – (surprised) … I don't know …
MRS. JOYCE – Ought I send for the doctor, do you think?
JOYCE – I don't know … What hole?
MRS. JOYCE – (impatient) … The hole we all have … here (points)
JOYCE – (stands up)[19]

In a few brisk strokes, this scene stages the collapse of symbolization. First the mother looms up at the parlor-door, bursting through the membrane of Joyce's artistic self-absorption. She hails him – "Jim!" – demanding that he answer to his name: "the name that we are told is ours," in Stephen Dedalus's words. To name is to subject, but Joyce's epiphany dramatizes the failure of this mechanism, since the act of naming fails to ward off the irruption of the unrepresentable.[20] What the mother has witnessed, beyond the frail enclosure of the mise-en-scène, is something literally unspeakable – a monstrous inversion of the process of gestation, the body vomiting its "matter" out of the same "hole" through which the foetus fed upon the mother's matter in the womb.

Mrs. Joyce, choking on her own euphemisms, finally resorts to pointing, as if her index finger – like the proverbial finger in the dyke – could stave off the breakdown of the indexical function of language. But what is she pointing at? Only the speaking, pointing body can provide the "here" with a location; in writing, the deictic "here" floats free of space or time. For this reason, as Luke Thurston has argued, the "hole … here" refers not only to the mother's unseen navel, but to "the invisible and traumatic centre" of the text itself, the hole through which symbolic meaning disappears. The mention of this "hole," this "here," opens up a hole in language that sucks out signification, like "the umbilical vanishing-point of the Freudian dream."[21] In this epiphany the navel, which testifies to the literality of motherhood, as opposed to the symbolic nature of paternity, also marks the limits of language, the failure of the sign to represent the real.

The *Portrait* is riddled with these navels of literality. In particular, Joyce's epiphanies operate like navels, mining the narrative with gaps where metaphor dissolves into facticity. In *Stephen Hero* Joyce defines epiphany as "a sudden spiritual manifestation, whether in the vulgarity of speech or of gesture or in a memorable phase of the mind itself."[22] This exalted rhetoric contradicts the effect of the epiphanies themselves, however, whose triviality often "borders on nonsense," as Catherine Millot has observed. Metonymic as opposed to metaphoric, these epiphanies present themselves as cinders: "obscure remainders of a silent conflagration … blind and useless witnesses of the inexpressible."[23] In this sense they resemble the Freudian conception of trauma, in which fragments of the real, lodged within the psyche, obstruct the curative effects of metaphor with stubborn literalism.[24] Joyce's epiphanies, including the traumatic scene of Georgie's hemorrhage, scar the narrative with fragments of the real, in much the same way that the navel scars the skin with the literality of motherhood.

In "Proteus," Stephen attempts to erase the navel by imagining Eve's "belly without blemish, bulging big, a buckler of taut vellum," her skin as smooth as an unwritten page (*U* 3:42). In this fantasy, the mother is depicted as a blank page to be written on – "taut vellum" – rather than the author of the navel written on the flesh (*P* 171). Erasing the navel is Stephen's way of saying "Woman, what have I to do with thee?" It is also his way of denying the past, for Stephen associates the navel with the nightmare of history from which he is trying to awake. This birthscar reminds him that he is "made not begotten," unlike Adam who was begotten not made (*U* 3:45). But Stephen wishes to be self-begotten, to break free of the Daedalean nets of navelcords extending from his belly to prehistory: "the cords of all link back, strandentwining cable of all flesh."

Nonetheless the insistence of the navel in Joyce's fiction indicates that mothers cannot be so easily forgotten. In the "Hades" episode of *Ulysses*, Bloom links the "coffinband" with the "navelcord," implying that the life-giving umbilical cord also represents the noose of death. In *Finnegans Wake*, where every death implies a resurrection, the "neverstop navelcord" (*FW* 475:14) represents a world without end, which is also a world without beginning. Never stopping, never starting, the *Wake* begins in the middle of its final sentence, thus evoking the unbroken circularity of the umbilical cord. In the *Wake* as in the Freudian dream, there are no "definite endings," since every pun links back to former words (SE 5:525), branching out into the intricate network of the already written. The psychoanalyst Michèle Montrelay describes the fantasy of uterine existence as "a time when nothing was thinkable: then, the body and the world were confounded in one chaotic intimacy which was too present, too immediate – one continuous expanse of proximity or unbearable plenitude. What was lacking was lack."²⁵ In the "allwombing" world of *Finnegans Wake*, what is lacking is a birth-scar that could separate the corpus of a text from its progenitors – instead, all merge in one chaotic intimacy (*U* 3:402).

The *Portrait*, on the other hand, compulsively returns to the severance of the umbilical cord. If the *Wake* is a "commodius vicus of recirculation," with neither an end nor a beginning, the *Portrait* is a series of false starts and dead ends (*FW* 3:2). Several Stephens are engendered in the novel, but none of them is self-contained. The moment of birth is constantly revisited: in Stephen's visions of transcendence of his origins; in his fantasies of flying by the "nets" of nationality, language, and religion; in his cycles of unrest and weariness, punctuated by his verbal and seminal "ejaculations"; in his ambition to give birth to the "soaring impalpable imperishable being" of his art: "O! In the virgin womb of the imagination the word was made flesh" (*P* 203, 169, 217). Both the *Portrait* and the *Wake* could be described as omphalocentripetal, but the navel represents a point of rupture in the *Portrait*, while it represents a point of coalescence in the *Wake*. If the *Portrait* associates memory with "disremembering," the *Wake* presents memory as mammary: an endless process of "recirculation" through the navelcords of intertextuality.

CHAPTER 7

Skinscapes in Ulysses

Joyce once remarked that "modern man has an epidermis rather than a soul."[1] It is therefore appropriate that *Ulysses*, the story of a day in the life of modern man, puts the epidermis in the foreground. Joyce described *Ulysses* as the "epic of the human body," and assigned a body organ to each episode, specifying "skin" as the organ of the "Lotus-Eaters" episode.[2] Accordingly "Lotus-Eaters" abounds with references to skin, the action of the chapter interspersed with snapshots of epidermal suffering. The prose itself, speckled with images of boils, pimples, warts, bunions, flakes, and pustules, seems to be afflicted with a rash of epidermal metaphors. These images of diseased and tormented skin may be understood as symptoms of modernist anxiety about the boundaries of the human body. From a psychoanalytic perspective, such images reveal archaic fears about the fragility of the bodily envelope, fears – I would argue – that precede the Freudian castration complex. To investigate these epidermal complexities, the present chapter focuses on "Lotus-Eaters," while branching out into the pimpled, scarred, and pockmarked skinscapes of modernity.

Despite the prevalence of skin in "Lotus-Eaters," this organ was an afterthought in Joyce's plans for his epic of the human body. The first of his schemata for *Ulysses*, known as the Linati schema (1920), designates "genitals" as the organ for "Lotus-Eaters," while the second, known as the Gilbert/Gorman schema (1921), replaces genitals with "skin."[3] Yet most of the references to skin were interpolated in the page proofs of the chapter in 1921.[4] The fact that skin was added on after the body of the episode had been completed casts doubt on the authority of Joyce's schemata, with their elaborate inventories of organs, arts, technics, symbols, and correspondences. Is this bric-à-brac intrinsic to the text, its bone structure, we wonder? Or do these charts create an exoskeleton, a carapace, a defensive second skin imposed upon a writing forever threatening to overflow its bounds – the bounds of time, place, language, gender, authorship, and copyright, not to mention those of taste and self-control? Whatever the status of the schemata, it seems appropriate that Joyce's references to skin, belatedly inserted in the proofs, hover between the inside and the outside of the text, dismantling this very binarism. For skin itself is simultaneously hidden and exposed, profound and superficial; it is associated both with the deceptive surface and with the shivering, defenceless nakedness of truth.

In Homer's *Odyssey*, Odysseus's men partake of the lotus-flower and forget the way home, preferring to remain in drugged euphoria than to face the dangers of return to Ithaca. This myth renews itself in many forms; in the television series *Star Trek*, for example, the officers of the Starship Enterprise beam down to a laid-back planet, not dissimilar to California, where even the robotic Mr. Spock, under the influence of a narcotic flower, falls idiotically in love. The implication is that lotus-eating is the archetypal cop-out; time and again our cultural heroes have to teach us to renounce such blissed-out holidays in favor of the strenuous rewards of work and family.

In Joyce's version of "Lotus-Eaters," Leopold Bloom forgets his latch-key, which is one way of forgetting home. He also forgets the recipe for "skinfood" (*U* 69:497) – his wife's skin-lotion – and forgets to collect the preparation from the chemist later in the day, when he gets distracted by Gertie MacDowell's "undies" (*U* 288:171). He forgets names, forgets words, forgets physics, forgets the libretto of *Don Giovanni*, forgets to fasten the lower buttons of his waistcoat, and forgets his previous identity – his name, his wife, and his address. Instead he adopts the pseudonym of Henry Flower to engage in a clandestine correspondence with his erotic penpal, Martha Clifford. The name Flower, a synonym for Bloom, aligns the hero with the Lotus-Flower, and suggests that Henry Flower is himself the foreign substance, the forgetful drug, that circulates around the postal and commercial arteries of Dublin.

So Bloom presents himself in this chapter as a wanderer, straying from his home, his marriage, his identity: he assumes the role of rootless city stroller or flâneur. In the urban world that he inhabits, life is no longer to be described in terms of essences but phenomenologically, in terms of brief encounters, fleeting moments, unstable, shifting impressions. The substance of experience has migrated to the surface of things. This is one reason why skin is so important: Bloom takes careful note of the complexions of the faces that he meets, mapping out a skinscape of the city. (I borrow the term skinscape from Dennis Potter's *The Singing Detective* [1986], where Skinscape's is the name of the pub frequented by the psoriasis-afflicted hero.) "Lotus-Eaters" opens with a reference to skin disease, the "scars of eczema" disfiguring an urchin's face (*U* 58:6); later pages refer to smallpox, dandruff, freckles, warts, bunions, pimples, barber's itch, and worst of all to the unfortunate Lord Ardilaun, who was forced to change his shirt four times a day because his skin reputedly bred lice and vermin.

Bloom's mission in "Lotus Eaters" (which he notably fails to accomplish) is to combat skin disease by purchasing "Skinfood" for Molly at the chemist's. Here his thoughts turn to Prince Leopold, one of the sons of Queen Victoria, who suffered from hemophilia, an affliction attributed by popular belief to having "only one skin": "Three we have," Bloom reassures himself (*U* 69:498–99). Throughout the chapter, Bloom ruminates about the depth, both metaphorical and literal, of skin. When he visits the church, he imagines women revealing their "lovely shame" to their confessors, and reflects that their repentance is only "skindeep" (*U* 68:430–31). How deep is skin? Paul Valéry once wrote, "Ce qu'il y a de plus profond dans l'homme, c'est la peau."[5] To understand the rampancy of skin disease in "Lotus-Eaters," it is necessary to explore the profundities of skin.

Touchy feely

What is skin? This organ, which covers the entire surface of the body, constituting 17.8% of its weight, and giving rise to all its sense organs, is often overlooked, as if its sheer ubiquity had rendered it invisible. Yet of all the sense organs, skin is the most vital: we can live without sight, hearing, taste, or smell, but we die if the greater portion of our skin is not intact. And skin is more than just a sense organ: it breathes, perspires, absorbs, expels, and also stimulates the respiration, circulation, and digestion. Sex is basically the meeting of two skins, or more. Many metaphors in English reveal the centrality of skin to our ideas of self and other: we speak of being "in touch" or "in contact" with our friends; of "rubbing" people the wrong way, or "handling" them with kid gloves. If we are "thick-skinned," insults bounce off us; if we are "touchy," they "get under our skin."[6] Social groups are differentiated by the texture, age, and pigmentation of their skin, some of the most terrible atrocities of history having been perpetrated in the name of skin-color. We recognize our intimates by the odor of their skin, which can be enhanced by perfume, one of many the flower-products prevalent in "Lotus-Eaters." In the "Nausicaa" episode, Bloom imagines perfume as a second skin woven over women's bodies: "It's like a fine fine veil or web they have all over the skin, fine like what do you call it gossamer, and they're always spinning it out of them, fine as anything, like rainbow colours without knowing it. Clings to everything she takes off" (*U* 307:1019–22).

In spite of the importance of skin, Western culture traditionally privileges depth at the expense of surface. We tend to overlook the outside for the inside, the container for that which is contained. Value is attributed only to profundity: to be described as "superficial" is an insult; as "deep," a tribute. From this prejudice arises our inveterate distrust of make-up, which adds a further surface to the surface, a second skin supposedly more specious than the first. The beautification of the body, undertaken to enhance the self, paradoxically erases individuality; the person, as we say, becomes a "sex-object," emptied of personhood.[7] Thus cosmetics, which adorn the surface of the body, are condemned for belying its interior. Valéry, however, mocks this prejudice, proposing instead that the inner depths are merely phantoms created by the surface. "Marrow, brain, all those things we require in order to feel, to suffer, to think … are inventions of the skin; we burrow down in vain, doctor; we are ectoderm."[8]

There is some biological evidence for Valéry's assertion that the inside is the invention of the outside, since the cortex of the brain is formed by the introversion and reticulation of the surface of the embryo. Didier Anzieu, in a psychoanalytic study of the "skin ego," observes that the internal organs develop *in utero* through a folding-up process technically known as "invagination," which creates the endlessly complicated array of folds, creases, envelopes, tubes, caps, fans, and pockets of which the body is composed.[9] In other words, the inside of our bodies is composed of skin turned outside in: the core is created by the husk, the kernel by the shell.

Anzieu's central insight is that skin is a double-sided entity: one side faces inwards, enveloping the contents of the body, and registering its sensations, needs, and drives; the other faces outwards, shielding the interior but also filtering exchange between the body and the world. This traffic, mediated by the skin, forms the basis of the ego, which is itself a kind of envelope designed to mediate between the psyche and the stimuli impinging on it from without and from within. A similar traffic occurs in Bloom's interior monologue, which registers impressions from the outside world while embedding each new message into the connective tissue of his memory. This monologue implies that thinking consists of the continuation of the operations of the skin.

Anzieu's conception of the ego was anticipated by Freud, who argued in 1923 that the "ego is first and foremost a bodily ego; it is not merely a surface entity, but is itself the projection of a surface" (SE 19:26). A later footnote in the English translation adds that "the ego is ultimately derived from bodily sensations, chiefly those springing from the surface of the body" (SE 19:26n1). In other words, the ego develops out of the surface of the body as the phantasmatic counterpart of skin, containing mental life in the same way that the skin contains the entrails. Having been formed by the sensations of the skin, the ego represents a monument to early cutaneous experience: its well-being depends upon the way in which the infant's skin is held, which has the effect of delimiting the boundaries of the body. Ashley Montagu, in a study of touching, shows how new-born bears are literally "licked into shape" by their mother's tongues, which outline every curve and crevice of their bodies, nudging their internal organs into action. In human beings, he argues, this licking is replaced by the prolonged contractions of human labor (a questionable advance of evolution), which provide the newborn baby with an all-over body massage, stimulating respiratory and digestive functions. In any case, the body simply does not work unless the skin is touched: we must be licked or squeezed or tickled into life. In the same way, consciousness is called into existence by the touch of others: a dramatic instance is Helen Keller, whose mind was literally created by the stimulation of her skin.[10]

The Kleinian psychoanalyst Esther Bick, in an influential essay on the experience of skin in early infancy, postulates that the parts of the personality, in its most primitive form, are felt to have no binding force among themselves and therefore depend on an external object for their integration.[11] This object – usually the mother's nipple, voice, or smell – must be "introjected" or internalized in order for the ego to experience itself as self-contained. If this introjection fails, the infant takes refuge in fantasies of omnipotence that avoid the need for passive submission to an object. These fantasies produce what Bick describes as "second-skin," a pseudo-independence often leading to the precocious development of speech or strength, whereby the infant uses the sound of its own voice, or the rigidity of its musculature, to hold the fragments of its personality together. Without this carapace, the ego leaks into infinite space, in a collapse of boundaries experienced as an explosion, annihilation, or catastrophe.

Explosion is the image used by Frantz Fanon to describe the trauma of discovering his blackness in a world controlled by those with paler skin. Having internalized the white man's gaze, Fanon recalls: "I took myself far off from my own presence, far indeed, and made myself an object. What else could it be for me but an amputation, an excision, a hemorrhage that spattered my whole body with black blood?"[12] Paradoxically, Fanon's awakening to skin takes the form of an unskinning, a flaying, in which his body is turned inside out. "My body was given back to me sprawled out, distorted, recolored, clad in mourning in that white winter day," he writes. White eyes "cut away slices of my reality," "burning" the surface of his flesh. "I burst apart. Now the fragments have been put together again by another self" – crushed into a skin reorganized by the racist gaze.[13]

Thus Fanon implies that victims of racism suffer from violent alienation from their skin. Yet it is questionable whether self and "epidermal schema" ever fully coincide. Anorexics who perceive themselves as fat, or amputees who suffer pain in phantom limbs, reveal that the mental image of the body often differs drastically from its physical reality. Even in "normal" circumstances (whatever they may be), it is unlikely that proprioception corresponds to the exact dimensions of the skin. This is because the body's envelope is moulded by the touch of others: an enclosing sac and a protective shield, the skin is also a receptive surface on which the marks of others are inscribed. "Their smiles catch into my skin, little smiling hooks," writes Sylvia Plath, in a macabre image of this process of inscription.[14] To take another example, Beckett's strange work *How It Is* (1961/1964) presents a world of nameless beings crawling in primeval slime, each compelled to torture other beings into speech by cutting questions on their skin. The implication is that speech and consciousness begin with the branding of the other on the skin, a mutilation that establishes the social order.[15] A similar mutilation takes place in Kafka's story "The Penal Colony" (1914), where the sentences of the condemned are stabbed into their skin by the needles of a monstrous typewriter. These parables imply that the subject is created by the symbols tattooed upon the skin, signifying the subordination of the body to the social contract.

Anzieu postulates that the infant originally shares its mother's skin, which is imagined as a single indivisible integument. The emergence of the ego, however, necessitates the rupture of this membrane. There are many ways in which this separation may be thwarted: sometimes the skin becomes too tight and suffocates the ego, an experience reflected in mythology by tales of poisoned garments. The shirt of Nessus, given by Deianeira as an aphrodisiac to Heracles, consumes the hero's flesh, driving him to flay himself alive; a poisoned veil destroys Medea's rival, Glauca. Similarly, Balzac's novel *La Peau de Chagrin* (1830) recounts how the hero Raphael acquires a magic ass's skin that grants him everything he desires, but shrinks with every wish that it fulfills. As the ass's skin contracts, the hero's body wastes away, as if its substance had been squeezed out by the pelt at one remove.

In Balzac's novel skin becomes too tight, but skin may also prove too porous, allowing the contents of the self to leak away. In a case discussed by Anzieu, a little girl suffers from amnesia because she envisages her head as full of holes; in another case, an anorexic patient dreams that her skin has turned into a sieve through which her entrails seep into the outer darkness.[16] Sylvia Plath's poetry vacillates between these terrors; at times the speaker feels suffocated by her skin, at other times excoriated by it. "Skin doesn't have any roots," she writes, "it peels away easy as paper."[17]

Psychoanalytic studies of the skin tend to focus on its meanings for the individual, whereas anthropological studies emphasize its social implications. For skin functions as a boundary between the subject and the social order, marking both their cooperation and their antagonism. In certain parts of Polynesia, the entire surface of the body is covered in tattoos, signifying the initiation of the body into the symbolic order. According to the anthropologist Alfred Gell, Polynesian society makes no distinction between self and skin, between the inner soul and its decorated epidermis. Gell explains:

This reasoning runs: the skin is on the outside of the body – the outside of the body is that part which is public and which comes into contact with other people – people are the sum total of their relations with other people – the person is his/her skin.[18]

The reason that shame traditionally appears upon the skin, whether in the form of blushes (in Western culture) or hot sweats (in Papua New Guinea), is that shame is social: it is experienced when other people see us, find us out; as opposed to guilt, which gnaws at us invisibly.[19] In the myth of Genesis, shame originates in the recognition of the skin, the nakedness of skin, and its exposure to the gaze of others; and it is shame that produces the compulsion to clothe or decorate the body, which is shared by all human communities. "Society," Thomas Carlyle once wrote, "is founded upon cloth"; man is "bound by invisible bonds" to all other men, and his clothes are "the visible emblems of that fact."[20] Shame, however, harks back to a more primitive relation to other beings, because shame finds expression in the unclothed face, in the blushes that reveal a nakedness beyond the nakedness of skin, the nakedness of capillaries, muscles, viscera.

Emmanuel Levinas has argued that "the skin of the face is that which stays most naked, most destitute; there is an essential poverty in the face; the proof of this is that one tries to mask this poverty by putting on poses, by taking on a countenance." It is through the skin, Levinas contends, that we experience the other in "proximity," prior to rational cognition. In this form of apprehension:

> skin is neither a container nor the protection of an organism, nor purely and simply the surface of a being, but nudity, presence abandoned by a departure, exposed to everyone and then too unfaithful to itself, insolvent, yet also delivered over to the things, contaminated, profaned, persecuted, in fault and in distress.[21]

According to Levinas, the primary relation to other beings consists of neither mastery nor Hegelian recognition, but rather of exposedness and passivity. The skin, naked and vulnerable to wounds and outrage, but also to caresses and eroticism, embodies this essential passivity or "passion" of being.[22]

THE EPIDERMISTS

Why is skin disease so rife in "Lotus Eaters"? The simplest explanation is historical: in 1904, Dublin was riddled with diseases, many of whose symptoms manifested themselves on the skin. Stories in the *Lancet* at the turn of the century speak of the "barbaric uncleanliness" of the city, citing among other horrors an ill-regulated private slaughterhouse in Townsend Street, where hundreds of children at a local school were forced to breathe "the effluvia wafted to them from the hideous quagmire of blood and offal."[23] It was only in 1906 that the main drainage system began to deposit city sewage out beyond the harbor. Oliver St. John Gogarty, when he escaped execution during the Civil War by swimming across the Liffey, described the escapade (mindful of the sewage bobbing around his head) as "going through the motions."[24]

In 1899 the death rate in Dublin was higher than in any big city in Europe or America, the figures swollen by a fierce onslaught of measles which caused nearly 650 deaths in the city alone. The 1904 smallpox scare in Belfast, mentioned by Bloom ("I hope that smallpox up there doesn't get worse" [*U* 62:188–89]), was preceded by an outbreak in Dublin in 1903, in which 34 out of more than 250 cases resulted in death. Tuberculosis, known in this period as "the Irish disease," peaked in 1902, attacking not only lungs, intestines, spine, and bones, but also skin, in which it took the form of lupus. Syphilis, which darkened the skin, was also epidemic, especially among the British army stationed in Dublin, which Arthur Griffith condemned as the most immoral army in Europe, and Bloom describes in "Lotus Eaters" as "an army rotten with venereal disease" (*U* 59:72). In the "Circe" episode, Bloom himself is accused of being "bronzed with infamy" (*U* 401:1757), a reference to a syphilitic rash. A "*dark mercurialised face*" (*U* 372:748), which features among the hallucinations of this episode, reveals the cutaneous effects of mercury, the kill-or-cure remedy for syphilis.

Joyce's inventory of skin diseases in "Lotus-Eaters" could be compared to the cabinet of cutaneous horrors in the Hôpital Saint-Louis in Paris, which contains lifelike simulacra of every form of skin disease encountered on the European urban street in the early twentieth century. These surgical casts, designed by Jules-Pierre-François Baretta (1834–1923) between 1867 and 1914, reveal the evolution and often fatal course of infantile syphilis, scarlatina, measles, mumps, leprosy, scurvy, scrofula, lupus, smallpox, ringworm, and impetigo, along with countless and nameless disfiguring spots, ulcerated scabs, fungous infections, and running sores. Before the widespread use of X-ray, ultrasound, SPECT, and other imaging techniques, many diseases could be diagnosed only through eruptions on the skin: smallpox, tuberculosis, and typhus, for instance, were identified by peculiar sores and blisters on the skin.[25]

Theorists of degeneration in the nineteenth century, such as Cesare Lombroso and B. A. Morel, regarded skin deformities as the stigmata of moral and physical decline. Even tattoos, according to Lombroso, were evidence of atavism, the traces of a "primitive" language disfiguring the bodies of the "lower orders." In literature, Lombroso argued, degeneration manifested itself in such idiosyncracies (dear to readers of Joyce) as "a tendency to puns and plays on words," "an excessive fondness of systems," "an exaggerated minuteness of detail," and "an extreme predilection for the rhythm and assonances of verse in prose writing."[26] If the race is to regenerate itself, Lombroso intimated, the blemished page, like the disfigured skin, must be scrubbed clean of the marks of its polluted heritage. Similarly, Max Nordau, author of *Degeneration* (1892/1895), fulminated that the "outer crust" of humanity was cracking into "cold, vitrified scoria." Turning his ire to the arts, Nordau accused "impressionists," "stipplers," "mosaists," "pappilloteurs," "quiverers," and "roaring" colorists of degrading literature and painting into crazed dermatologies of spots and blotches.[27]

Joyce's personal sensitivity to skin disease may be attributed in part to his short-lived training as a doctor, although he abandoned his degree in medicine in 1904, like his father before him (a decision that "saved many lives," as Joyce's brother Stanislaus commented about their father).[28] Nonetheless Bloom reads the lineaments of disease on the bodies of the crowd with the discernment of a medical student. Like the speaker in Blake's poem "London," he roams the streets of Dublin seeing "marks of weakness, marks of woe" inscribed on the faces he encounters. Blakean, too, is Bloom's interest in blemishes, for Blake defended such "Peculiar marks" against Joshua Reynolds's neo-classical distaste for them. Where Reynolds wrote that "Peculiarities in the work of art, are like those in the human figure … They are always so many blemishes," Blake retorted angrily: "Infernal Falsehood! Peculiar marks are the only merit."[29]

Stephen Dedalus also champions peculiar marks: in "Scylla and Charybdis" he instances his mole as evidence of his unique and continuous identity. Although his "molecules all change," his mole regenerates itself incessantly: "the mole on my right breast is where it was when I was born, though all my body has been woven of new stuff time after time" (*U* 159–60:378–80). According to Barbara Maria Stafford, this obsession with a "quirky and thus personalised integument and with a broken or suffering veneer" belongs to a Romantic outlook. She argues that the science of dermatology, invented by Jean-Louis Alibert (1766–1837) in the early nineteenth century, resembles divisionist chiaroscuro in painting insofar as both express a Romantic fascination with the "externalisation of idiosyncracy."[30]

If the interest in spots is distinctively Romantic, the interest in skin is associated with the realist novelists. In fact some fin-de-siècle critics attack the realists not only for describing skin disease but for propagating it in literary form. Barbey D'Aurevilly accuses Balzac of turning description into "a skin-disease of the realists."[31] In 1894 the American critic William Thayer, vilifying the "new Realists," including such novelists as James and Zola, dubs them the "Epidermists":

The camera sees only the outside; the Realist sees no more, and so it would be more appropriate to call him "Epidermist," one who investigates only the surface, the cuticle of life, – usually with a preference for very dirty skin …

Thayer goes on to argue that the "heaping up of minute details," characteristic of these Epidermists, has been smuggled into literature from the sciences. No one could be fonder of heaping up details than Joyce, nor more aware of the cloacal pleasures of the exercise. For Thayer, however, such heaps are nothing but the "dirty skin," the carbuncular exterior, concealing the profundities of life.[32] His tirade against realism resembles Nordau's attack on Impressionism, a movement that Nordau accuses of reducing painting to excremental splotches in defiance of a classical conception of the whole.

In different ways, both naturalism and aestheticism attempt to revalorize the surface, so long disparaged in favor of the depths. Joyce's writing shows allegiances to both these schools. The naturalist Zola, through the minute registration of empirica, asserts the importance of the external forces in determining the character of individuals. In his novels, the surface of the body, rather than expressing individuality, provides a written record of the cruel impingements of the outer world. In *Germinal* (1885), Maheu's skin is "white as that of an anaemic girl," but "tattooed with scratches and grazes made by the coal – grafts, the miners called them." His daughter Catherine's complexion has also been "ruined" by her labor in the mine, and Etienne, watching her undress, is disturbed by the contrast between "the pale whiteness" of her hidden flesh and "the ravaged skin of her hands and face."[33] For Zola, who believed the individual to be determined by hereditary factors on the one hand, and environmental factors on the other, the miners' skin reveals the influence of both determinisms, its pallor signifying the degeneration of their race, its scars the imprint of their merciless environment.

In the same period, aestheticists from Baudelaire to Beerbohm defend the artificiality of surfaces against the Romantic preference for the depths. In his famous defence of make-up (1863), Baudelaire argues that "the use of rice-powder, so stupidly anathematized by our Arcadian philosophers, is successfully designed to rid the complexion of those blemishes that Nature has outrageously strewn there …"[34] Similarly, Max Beerbohm, in his "Defence of Cosmetics" of 1894, contends that we have grown suspicious of the surface because we have reduced it to a token of the depths. "Too long has the face been degraded from its rank as a thing of beauty to a mere vulgar index of character or emotion." With the full renascence of cosmetics, "surface will finally be severed from soul," and a woman's face will no longer be read as a "barometer" of character, but admired as an artifact, "beautiful and without meaning."[35]

In *Finnegans Wake*, Shem the Penman writes on his own skin with his own excretions, literally expressing himself, or pressing himself out, into a writing that confounds the distinction between surface and depth, or inside and outside (*FW* 185.27–186.8). While *Finnegans Wake* revels in writing on the skin, "Lotus-Eaters" is preoccupied with reading epidermal signatures. Bloom, for instance, ponders the melodrama *Leah, the Forsaken* (1862), performed in Dublin on June 16th 1904, which climaxes in a scene of skin-reading. Here the blind patriarch Abraham unmasks the villain Nathan, an apostate Jew masquerading as an anti-Semite, by touching his face: "With my fingers I read thy dead father's face, for with my fingers I closed his eyes, and nailed down his coffin! Thou art a Jew!"[36] This scene, in which Abraham reads the father in the features of the son, harks back to the biblical story in which the blind patriarch Isaac mistakes his "smooth" son Jacob for his "hairy" son Esau, Jacob having disguised his hands in goatskin in order to usurp his brother's blessing (Genesis 27). What these scenes of recognition and misrecognition have in common is that the son's skin functions as a text in which the father's legacy is enigmatically inscribed.[37]

If skin stands for a modernist celebration of the surface, as opposed to a Romantic obsession with the depths, the images of skin-disease in "Lotus-Eaters" undermine this opposition. For the boils, pustules, warts, and pimples of the episode represent the depths erupting on the surface – the inside on the outside of the flesh – thus violating the interiority of subjectivity. Similarly, in F. Scott Fitzgerald's novel *Tender is the Night* (1934), a minor character dies of eczema, her illness attributed to her refusal to divulge her "secret."[38] Since she does not know her secret she can only show it in the pustulous abrasions of her skin: her secret secretes, her inner self "breaks out" into a rash that devours the surface of her flesh.

In "Lotus-Eaters," however, skin disease expresses neither personality, as in the Romantics; nor the ravages of labor, as in Zola; nor degeneration, as in Nordau; nor hysteria, as in Fitzgerald. Bloom's sensitivity to skin disease is one symptom of a far-reaching anxiety about the security of the bodily envelope. This anxiety is largely projected onto women, whose outer coverings of clothes and skin are perceived by Bloom as dangerously detachable. A salient example is the scene where Bloom is watching women praying and confessing in the church, and discovers that his waistcoat is unbuttoned. He imagines the women gloating over his embarrassment: "Women enjoy it. Never tell you." Then he takes revenge on these imaginary women, punishing them for their castrating gaze, by imagining their skirts unfastened, "placket unhooked," exposing "glimpses of the moon" (*U* 68:452–55). Thus Bloom, disconcerted by his own unbuttoning, projects his shame onto the "plackets" of the other sex.

This pattern of projection recurs throughout the episode. When Bloom is "fingering" Martha Clifford's letter, with its innuendoes of castration ("Remember … I will punish you … you naughty boy" [*U* 63–64:251–52]), he draws a pin out of the pocket in which it is concealed:

Fingering still the letter in his pocket he drew the pin out of it. Common pin, eh? He threw it on the road. Out of her clothes somewhere: pinned together. Queer the number of pins they always have. No roses without thorns. (*U* 64:275–78)

Thus Bloom responds to the threat of castration, implicit in the letter's message as well as in the pin, by imagining the female body as a garment loosely "pinned together" and about to split apart. By fetishistic logic, he transfers his own anxiety about dismemberment onto women's detachable parts, especially their underclothes, which are neither clothes nor skin but represent the ambiguity between these coverings. Bloom's next association is to undergarments, the subject of a ditty sung by two prostitutes he met in the Coombe:

> *O, Mairy lost the pin of her drawers.*
> *She didn't know what to do*
> *To keep it up,*
> *To keep it up.*

> It? Them.
>
> (*U* 64:281–84)

In this song, the woman Mairy, having lost her "pin," has also been divested of her "drawers" or her second skin: only the pin can "keep it up." The job of a prostitute is "to keep it up," but Bloom, somewhat naively, misses this innuendo. He is puzzled by the pronoun "it," since "drawers" are plural: "It? Them," he thinks, as if anticipating Luce Irigaray's conception of femininity as "the sex that is not one." His next gesture is to tear up Martha's envelope – a kind of voodoo substitute for tearing off her clothes or skin.

This chain of thought suggests that Bloom's castration-fears serve as a decoy, deflecting his (and our) attention from a vast unnameable anxiety extending over the entire surface of his flesh. In his imagination, the penis, like the pin, is that which "keeps it up," prevents the skin from falling off. Molly describes the penis as a "button" in "Penelope": "I made him blush a little when I got over him that way when I unbuttoned him and took his out and drew back the skin it had a kind of eye in it theyre all Buttons men down the middle on the wrong side of them" (*U* 626:814–17). The fantasy that men's bodies, like their feelings, are "buttoned up," whereas women are forever "unbuttoning" themselves, exposing both their feelings and their flesh, is widespread in our culture. For Bloom, the penis is the button that keeps his skin securely fastened to his flesh; women, on the contrary, must substitute the "pin," which is forever dropping off, leaving them unhooked, unpeeled, unskinned.

In "Hades," Bloom remembers the day when Molly, wearing a cream gown "with the rip she never stitched," and aroused by the sight of two dogs copulating, begged him for "a touch": "Give us a touch, Poldy. God,

I'm dying for it." It was from this touch that Rudy was conceived: "How life begins" (*U* 73–74:78–81). The ripped gown, "never stitched," represents the female body, torn asunder, breeding death-in-life and life-in-death – for the "rip" is the vagina, where "life begins," but also represents the grave where Rudy lies (R.I.P.). Back in the present, Bloom reflects that Molly's body is "getting a bit softy," and wonders if "the skin can't contract quickly enough when the flesh falls off" (*U* 76:204–06). Once again, the female skin is imagined as a loose and flimsy garment liable to detach itself and drop away. The only man (apart from himself) whom Bloom imagines "unpinned" is a priest:

He saw the priest stow the communion cup away, well in, and kneel an instant before it, showing a large grey bootsole from under the lace affair he had on. Suppose he lost the pin of his. He wouldn't know what to do to. Bald spot behind. Letters on his back: I.N.R.I.? No: I.H.S. Molly told me one time I asked her. I have sinned: or no: I have suffered, it is. And the other one? Iron nails ran in. (*U* 66:369–74)

According to Ernest Jones, the function of the Catholic priest is to symbolize castration: "the effeminate costume of the priests, their compulsory celibacy, shaven head, and so on, plainly signify deprivation of masculine attributes, being thus equivalent to a symbolic self-castration."[39] The priest in "Lotus-Eaters" also represents imperiled masculinity: like a woman, he is "pinned together," revealing a "bald spot behind" where his hair or his genitals should be. His large grey bootsole is absurdly masculine, peeking out from underneath his campy "lace affair." His robes are inscribed with the initials "I.H.S.," misread by Bloom as "I.N.R.I.," both of which are acronyms for Christ. But Bloom, following Molly, misinterprets them hilariously, reading I.H.S. as "I have suffered," and I.N.R.I. as "Iron nails ran in." It is significant that both misreadings emphasize the sado-masochistic side of Christianity. The letters themselves – which are notably described as "on his back," not on his clothes – evoke the wounds inflicted on the flesh of Christ. In this way, the priest's back is pictured as a surface for punishing inscriptions nailed into his skin, like the sentences of the condemned in Kafka's penal colony.

These episodes suggest that Bloom conceives of skin as a thin and fragile membrane, liable to be stretched, loosened, ripped, peeled, flayed, nailed, scarified, and crucified. Surrounded by these threats to skin, Bloom shrinks from any form of penetration of the body's surface. "Much better to close up all the orifices … Seal up all," he meditates about the corpse in "Hades," fearful that its innards might spill out of its skin

(*U* 81:425–26). Molly says that Bloom "knows a lot of mixedup things especially about the body and the inside" (*U* 612:179–80), but he prefers to fantasize about the inner organs than to break the skin, welcoming the X-ray, invented by Wilhelm Roentgen in 1895, as a preferable diagnostic method. The polysyllabic narrator of "Ithaca" explains that Bloom's hand possesses the "operative surgical quality," but that he is "reluctant to shed human blood even when the end justified the means, preferring, in their natural order, heliotherapy, psychophysicotherapeutics, osteopathic surgery" (*U* 551:293–95). With Roentgen rays, Bloom speculates, one could watch the metamorphoses of food as it journeyed through the alimentary canal. Similarly, if a fellow were to "swallow a pin" (that pin again!), one could trace its odyssey through all the body's secret passageways. Sometimes such objects "come out of the ribs years after, tour around the body changing biliary duct spleen squirting liver gastric juice coils of intestines like pipes. But the poor buffer would have to stand all the time with his insides entrails on show. Science" (*U* 147:1047–50). It is his reluctance to break skin that inhibits Bloom from sexual intercourse, because he fears the act of penetration as a rupture of the bodily envelope. Andrea Dworkin might applaud his squeamishness, but in the context of *Ulysses*, the dread of penetration represents a torturing anxiety about the continence of skin.

Bloom's task in "Lotus-Eaters" is to save his skin, threatened by wounding from without, by leakage from within, as well as by the skin diseases that confound this very distinction. Images of skin disease, epidemic in "Lotus-Eaters," may be understood as a symptom of contemporary fears about degeneration; but they also bring to light the existential insecurity of skin, its susceptibility to wounding, penetration, desquamation. The only remedy for this anxiety is to be merged again in the maternal envelope. Hence Bloom is overcome by the desire for a bath, a "womb of warmth" in which he will immerse his skin to make it whole again, after its exposure to the broken skins of Dublin: "This is my body" (*U* 71:566–67), he declares, quoting the Communion service. He ends the chapter proleptically admiring his penis in the bath: "limp father of thousands" (*U* 71:571).

Yet other flowers float in these imaginary waters, competing with the penis for priority. In particular, Bloom contemplates "his navel, bud of flesh," which is the sign of his maternal, rather than paternal, origin (*U* 71:570). Even Bloom's penis is rendered sexually ambiguous by the term "limp father of thousands," which alludes to "mother of thousands," the common name of *Saxifraga stolonifera*, a flower that spreads through rhizomatic runners, like the telephonic navelcord of "Proteus" (*U* 32:37–40).

As we have seen, Stephen Dedalus argues that the navelcords "of all link back" to an intricate network of foremothers. Yet the navel also marks the point of rupture with the original maternal skin in which Bloom longs to be re-enveloped. Both wound and seam, the navel confirms identity by buttoning the body in its private skin, yet always threatens to reopen "the hole we all have – here," as Joyce's mother stammers in Epiphany 19. What is clear is that the psychoanalytic concept of castration fails to account for primal fears encapsulated in the navel, fears of both connectedness and separation. In Joyce's works, the law of the phallus, associated with the name of the father, is constantly subverted by the nameless omphalos.

Afterword

What is the omphalos? Previous chapters of this book have shown how the omphalos in Joyce signifies both separation and connectedness, specifically connectedness to the dead (or undead) mother. In the "Proteus" episode of *Ulysses*, Stephen envisages an incestuous merger with the mother via the rhizomatic networks of the umbilical cord. He also associates these networks with the cables of the telephone. This humble instrument, as David Trotter has observed, transformed social relations in the twentieth century, establishing "new forms of remote contact, of intimacy at a distance."[1] Like Stephen's navelcord, the telephone connects users across time and space yet also marks their separation from each other, enforcing solitude and interconnectivity at once. The "cords of all" that link the modern subject back to matrilineal prehistory also inosculate this subject in a networked world, creating uncontrollable dependencies and interfusions.

This book has traced some of the ways that this networked world has been reimagined in modernist fiction. In *The Ambassadors*, networks of representatives branch out from the absent mother, Mrs. Newsome; in Joyce's *Dubliners*, the absence of the father gives rise to networks of substitution and exchange. Woolf's *To the Lighthouse*, on the other hand, is dominated by the motif of the scar, rather than the networks of umbilical connectedness. Yet the navel in both its guises – scar and cable, hole and knot – serves to undermine the notion of the autonomous subject. Instead, the subject in these works is established by a primal scar, and linked through "successive anastomosis" into the labyrinths of intersubjectivity. Self and other interpenetrate, as exemplified in the telepathic transference of thoughts in James's works, the intermingling of voices in *Ulysses*, or the chameleon transformations of Woolf's narrative voice as it flits from consciousness to consciousness.

Yet the navel represents only one filament in the entangled themes of modernist fiction. None of these themes could be exhausted in a single monograph, but I hope my contributions will encourage further explorations. One such theme is the relation between trauma and visualization, which emerges out of the comparison between Freud's Wolf Man and Virginia Woolf in Chapter 4. Does trauma inhere in a primordial vision, or in the imposition of a scene or theater in the mind? Is this imposition traumatic in itself, regardless of the contents of the primal scene? Such questions also pertain to the Lambinet episode of *The Ambassadors*, where Strether's confrontation with the scene of the lovers in "a boat of their own" shatters his repressed or scotomized conception of reality. Meanwhile the recurrent theme of blindness in the modernist short story, particularly in Joyce's *Dubliners*, intimates that seeing depends on not seeing the blindness constitutive of vision.

Another recurrent theme in modernist writing is the changing relation between the human and the animal, which I have touched upon in my discussions of the modernist rat in Chapter 1, and the canine avatars of Woolf and the Wolf Man in Chapter 4. Modernism, apparently immured against the animal world, nonetheless retains a loophole for pets and vermin, creatures that have adapted to the conditions of urban existence. For this reason, these creatures unsettle the distinction between human and inhuman life. Pets, for instance, are given human names, human food, and human dwelling-places, as Woolf points out in her obituary of Shag, the Stephens' family dog (discussed above in Chapter 4). Vermin, by contrast, are eternal strangers in the human home, abject reminders of its porous boundaries. Nonetheless the distinction between pets and vermin is often blurred: dogs and cats may be demoted into vermin, rats and mice promoted into pets. The *heimlich* pet is readily transformed into the *unheimlich* pest, because the difference lies only in the laws of property; a mouse with an owner is a pet, whereas a dog without an owner is a verminous parasite.

According to Marc Shell, the family pet is a sentimental phantom of the totem animal, whose purpose is to enforce the taboo against incest. "In psychoanalytic and anthropological terms," Shell argues, "ontogenetically the pet is a transitional object, and phylogenetically it is a totem."[2] Installed within the family to restrain familiarity between familiars, the pet marks the limits of endogamy, by deflecting incestuous desire into harmless cuddling, but also marks the limits of exogamy, by defusing sexual desire between species. Yet if pets are too remote from us to be seduced, they are nonetheless too close to be eaten. The pet is the only animal that Western Christians forbid themselves to eat, not because of a religious injunction – since Christianity is fundamentally omnivorous – but because pet-eating would be tantamount to cannibalism. The weaker taboo against eating vermin, such as rats, may derive from the same uncomfortable sense of consanguinity. Like pets, vermin have evolved in tandem with the human species, and partake of the same metaplasm.

It will be clear from this brief preview that the question of the animal in modernism provides enough material for many books, some of which have already been written.[3] The burgeoning field of animal studies, which encompasses biology, anthropology, history, and literary and cultural studies, opens up exciting prospects of interdisciplinary research, while also reflecting a renewed ethical commitment to animal – and planetary – welfare. In some ways animal studies may seem far afield from the omphalocentric concerns of the present book. But Stephen Dedalus's notion of the "strandentwining cable of all flesh" is partially indebted to Darwin's notion of the webs that implicate the human in the animal. "All nature," Darwin declared, "is bound together by an inextricable web of relations …"[4] In Darwinian terms, the navelcord does not terminate in Eve's "belly without blemish," but interweaves the whole organic world. In this sense the networks of modernity, such as Stephen's imaginary telephone, reproduce at a technological level the webs of interdependency constitutive of organic life. Seemingly at odds with nature, the nets of commerce, communication, and utilities mirror Darwin's notion of the "tangled bank" of life, and reaffirm its ecological imperative. In technological modernity, as in the natural world, "relations stop nowhere."

The importance of the metaphor of webs in Darwin indicates that this motif does not originate in modernism. On the contrary, imagery of nets and webs occurs frequently in Victorian fiction, most famously in George Eliot's *Middlemarch* (1871). What is peculiar, though not unique to modernism, is the association of these nets with the violation of individual autonomy. The notion that the self, in Stephen Dedalus's words, is linked through "successive anastomosis" to vast networks of unknown beings induces paranoia about vampirism and telepathy, fantasies implying the invasion of the body and the mind. The bites, wounds, scars, and cuts discussed in the present study reveal anxieties about the fragility of the bodily envelope and, by analogy, about the porous boundaries of the self. The navel in Joyce, the "cut" in the Lambinet episode of *The Ambassadors*, the sensory scar on James's leg in *To the Lighthouse*, as well as the bites in the phantasmatics of the Wolf Man and the Rat Man, testify in different ways to the trauma of intersubjectivity. These wounds represent the apertures through which the subject is "anastomosed" into the networks of the modern world.

"Intervamp.com," the name of a popular website for today's vampire-fans, encapsulates the fears – as well as the surreptitious pleasures – arising from these rhizomatic networks. Almost a century before the worldwide web, modernism had already foreseen what James described as the "exposed and entangled state" of the subject in a networked world. There is no flying by such nets.

Notes

1 INTRODUCTION: WHAT HOLE?

1 James, Preface to the New York Edition of *Roderick Hudson* (1907), ed. Geoffrey Moore (London: Penguin, 1986), p. 37.

2 "He comes, pale vampire, through storm his eyes, his bat sails bloodying the sea, mouth to her mouth's kiss" (*U* 40:407–08). See Christine Froula's insightful discussion of this passage in *Modernism's Body: Sex, Culture, and Joyce* (New York: Columbia, 1996), pp. 95–105, where she argues that Stephen's vampire poem, itself vamped or plagiarized from a poem by Douglas Hyde, "symbolically feeds on female bodies to bring the artist–son's female voice to life" (p. 105).

3 See Andreas Huyssen, *After the Great Divide: Modernism, Mass Culture, Postmodernism* (Bloomington: Indiana University Press, 1986), who uses the term "the great divide" to designate the gulf between high modernism and mass culture dating back to Baudelaire's Paris.

4 For vampirism and technology, see Friedrich Kittler, *Discourse Networks*, trans. Michael Metteer and Chris Cullens (Stanford University Press, 1992), pp. 353–56; Laurence A. Rickels, *The Vampire Lectures* (Minneapolis: University of Minnesota Press, 1999), pp. 40–48; Jennifer Wicke, "Vampiric Typewriting: *Dracula* and its Media," *English Literary History* 59 (1992), 467–93; and my introduction to Bram Stoker, *Dracula* (Oxford University Press, 1996), pp. i–xxviii. For the general studies of the influence of technological networks on modernism, see *inter alia* Armand Mattelart, *Networking the World: 1794–2000*, trans. Liz Carey-Libbrecht and James A. Cohen (Minneapolis: University of Minnesota Press, 2000); Nicholas Daly, *Literature, Technology, and Modernity, 1860–2000* (Cambridge University Press, 2004); Tim Armstrong, *Modernism, Technology, and the Body* (Cambridge University Press, 1998).

5 As Robert Millward writes, "The growth of the urban infrastructure was the most dynamic element in the British economy from the 1870s to the 1930s … the investment in public health, urban transport, policing, water, electricity and gas was accounting, by the early 1900s, for one quarter of all capital formation in Britain …" See Millward, "The Political Economy of Urban Utilities," in Martin Daunton, ed., *The Cambridge Urban History*

of Britain (Cambridge University Press, 2001), vol. III, p. 315. For a general history of utilities in the United States, see Ruth Schwartz Cowan, *A Social History of American Technology* (Oxford University Press, 1997), esp. ch. 7, pp. 149–72. For the history of electricity in Britain, see I. R. C. Byatt, *The British Electrical Industry, 1875–1914* (Oxford: Clarendon Press, 1979); Thomas P. Hughes, *Networks of Power: Electrification in Western Society 1880–1930* (Baltimore, MD, and London: Johns Hopkins University Press, 1983), esp. ch. 9, pp. 227–61; in America, see David E. Nye, *Electrifying America: Social Meanings of a New Technology, 1880–1940* (Cambridge, MA: MIT Press, 1992); and Ronald C. Tobey, *Technology as Freedom: The New Deal and the Electrical Modernization of the American Home* (Berkeley: University of California Press, 1997), pp. 10–39. For the history of gas, see Malcolm W. H. Peebles, *Evolution of the Gas Industry* (New York University Press, 1980), esp. pp. 11–24, 51–60; for the history of gas in British households, see Anne Clendinning, *Demons and Domesticity: Women and the British Gas Industry, 1889–1939* (Aldershot, Hants.: Ashgate, 2004), esp. pp. 131–41. See also Laura Otis, *Networking: Communicating with Bodies and Machines in the Nineteenth Century* (Ann Arbor: University of Michigan Press, 2001), which demonstrates that networks are much older than modernism, but that they come to be associated in the late nineteenth century with fears about the penetrability of selves; for the history of these fears, see also Otis's *Membranes: Metaphors of Invasion in Nineteenth-Century Literature, Science, and Politics* (Baltimore, MD: Johns Hopkins University Press, 1999).

6 For an influential discussion of the uncanny effects of the telephone, see Avital Ronell, *The Telephone Book: Technology, Schizophrenia, Electric Speech* (Lincoln, NE: University of Nebraska Press, 1991); see also Nicholas Royle, *Telepathy and Literature* (Oxford: Blackwell, 1990). For telephony and other forms of communication at a distance in *Ulysses*, see Jacques Derrida, "Ulysses Gramophone: Hear Say Yes in Joyce," in *Acts of Literature*, ed. Derek Attridge (London: Routledge, 1992), pp. 253–309; and David Trotter, "e-Modernism: Telephony in British Fiction 1925–1940," *Critical Quarterly* 51:1 (2009), 1–32.

7 According to Wolfgang Schivelbusch, this dependence on a centralized supply accounts for the reluctance of the nineteenth-century European bourgeoisie to install gas and electric lighting. "By keeping their independent lights," Schivelbusch argues, "people symbolically distanced themselves from a centralized supply. The traditional oil-lamp or candle in a living-room expressed both a reluctance to be connected to the gas mains and the need for a light that fed on some visible fuel." Hence "the unease about gas and electric light in the nineteenth century can now take its place in a larger setting. Like daylight, this sort of light had an outside source. Ostensibly burning in the middle of the room in the lamp, its real origin was in the gasworks or in the central electric supply station, that is in 'big industry,' from which the bourgeois psyche tried to separate itself as it did from the public sphere. Just as the public sphere gained access to the home with daylight, so

big industry forced its way in with the light of the gas flame and the electric bulb." Schivelbusch, *Disenchanted Night: The Industrialization of Light in the Nineteenth Century* (Berkeley: University of California Press, 1995), pp. 162, 186.

8 Michel Foucault, *Discipline and Punish: The Birth of the Prison*, trans. Alan Sheridan (New York: Vintage–Random House, 1979), p. 217.

9 As Ariela Freedman has observed, this passage shows that "Water does not merely flow from a tap; it comes through pipes and tanks, a subterranean system of delivery that creates the illusion of water appearing from nothing." It is worth noting that this "system of delivery" bears a strong resemblance to the strandentwining cable of the navelcord that challenges the myth of creation from nothing in the "Proteus" episode. Freedman also points out that Joyce "subtly changes the terminus of the water supply, ending the tanks at the city boundary instead of in central Dublin, where they ended according to the Dublin directory." In this way "he cuts off a system of pipes at the edge of the city, leaving their ghostly, actual counterparts to meander to the city's centre." See Ariela Freedman, "Did it Flow?: Bridging Aesthetics and History in Joyce's *Ulysses*," *Modernism/Modernity* 13:1 (2006), 854, 859. See also Robert Adams Day, "Joyce's AquaCities," in Morris Beja and David Norris, eds., *Joyce and the Hibernian Metropolis* (Columbus: Ohio State University Press, 1996), pp. 3–20.

10 See Elizabeth Bronfen, *The Knotted Subject: Hysteria and its Discontents* (Princeton University Press, 1998), pp. 18–19.

11 James Joyce, "Epiphany 19" (March 1902) in *The Workshop of Dedalus: James Joyce and the Raw Materials for "A Portrait of the Artist as a Young Man,"* ed. Robert Scholes and Richard M. Kain (Evanston, IL: Northwestern University Press, 1965), p. 29. This epiphany is discussed in greater detail in Chapter 5.

12 Derrida, *Of Grammatology* (1967), trans. Gayatri Chakravorty Spivak, rev. ed. (Baltimore, MD: Johns Hopkins, 1997), pp. 65–73.

13 As Fritz Senn remarks in "Gnomon Inverted" (in *ReJoycing: New Readings of "Dubliners,"* ed. Rosa Maria Bosinelli Bollettieri and Harold Mosher [Lexington, KY: University of Kentucky Press, 1980], p. 249): "Few of Joyce's own embedded cues have been as provocative as the triad of strange words that trouble the young boy in "The Sisters": *paralysis, gnomon, simony.* In their privileged position, closing the initial paragraph … They have been amply commented on and their alleged directions have been avidly followed." Among these ample commentators are Gerhard Friedrich, "The Gnomonic Clue to James Joyce's Dubliners," *Modern Language Notes* 72:6 (1957), 421–24; J. Martin, "Paralysis Simony Gnomon and James Joyce: Conditions of the Representation of Desire in *Dubliners*," *Cahiers victoriens et edouardiens* 14 (1981), 29–37; Bernard Benstock, "The Gnomonics of *Dubliners*," *Modern Fiction Studies* 34 (1988), 519–39; David Weir, "Gnomon is an Island: Euclid and Bruno in Joyce's Narrative Practice," *James Joyce Quarterly* 29 (1991), 343–60; John Gordon, "*Dubliners* and the Art of Losing," *Studies in Short*

Fiction 32:3 (1995), 343–52. For further discussion of this triad of strange terms, see below, Chapter 5.

14 Fred Botting, *Sex, Machines and Navels: Fiction, Fantasy and History in the Future Present* (Manchester University Press, 1999), p. 1.

15 Sir Thomas Browne, *Pseudodoxia Epidemica* (1646) in *The Works of Sir Thomas Browne*, ed. G Keynes (London: Faber and Faber, 1964), vol. 11, pp. 345–47.

16 Philip Henry Gosse, *Omphalos: An Attempt to Untie the Geological Knot* (London: John Van Voorst, 1857), p. 349.

17 Edmund Gosse, *Father And Son: A Study of Two Temperaments* (1907; Harmondsworth: Penguin, 1989), p. 104.

18 Jorge Luis Borges, *Other Inquisitions, 1937–1952*, trans. Ruth L. C. Simms (Austin: University of Texas Press, 1964), p. 24; Jean Baudrillard, *The Perfect Crime*, trans. C. Turner (London: Verso, 1996), p. 21. The old chestnut of Adam's navel enjoyed a brief revival in 1944, when a pamphlet called *The Races of Mankind*, designed to be distributed to US soldiers, included a cartoon of Adam and Eve with little black dots on their abdomens. Officials objected to the cartoon on the grounds that these dots would offend fundamentalists among the troops. But later commentators, reading between the lines, have surmised that the controversy was sparked off, not by these navels, but by the pamphlet's evidence that northern blacks scored higher than southern whites in Air Force intelligence tests. See Martin Gardner, "Did Adam and Eve Have Navels?" in *Did Adam and Eve Have Navels? Discourses on Reflexology, Numerology, Urine Therapy, and Other Dubious Subjects* (New York: Norton, 2000), p. 8.

19 Freud observes, however, that his grandson stages the sado-masochistic "first act, that of departure," more frequently than the reassuring drama of return. This "compulsive repetition" reveals an addictive, "demonic" element in the child's ritual that overrides the pleasure principle. On this basis Freud hypothesizes the existence of a death-drive, a "power in mental life which we call the instinct of aggression or of destruction according to its aims, and which we trace back to the original death instinct of living matter" (SE 18:243). The extraordinary speculative chapters of *Beyond the Pleasure Principle* hypothesize that "*the aim of all life is death*," and that instincts are the urges "*inherent in organic life to restore an earlier state of things*," the earliest of which is death itself (SE 18:38, 36). Thus the pleasure principle, which aims for "constancy" or equilibrium within the organism, is co-opted by the instincts of destruction, which crave the ultimate constancy of death, the stillness of inorganic matter. Freud's first statement of the "principle of constancy" appears in *Studies on Hysteria* (1893–95), SE 2:197. See Jean Laplanche, *Life and Death in Psychoanalysis*, trans. Jeffrey Mehlman (Baltimore, MD: Johns Hopkins University Press, 1976); Jacques Derrida, "To Speculate – on Freud" in *The Post Card: From Socrates to Freud and Beyond*, trans. Alan Bass (Chicago: University of Chicago Press, 1987), pp. 257–409; and Peter Brooks, "Freud's Masterplot," in *Reading for*

the Plot: Design and Intention in Narrative (New York: Vintage, 1985), pp. 90–112, for influential re-interpretations of *Beyond the Pleasure Principle*.

20 Walt Whitman, "A Noiseless Patient Spider," in *Leaves of Grass* (1891–92), in *Complete Poetry and Collected Prose*, ed. Justin Kaplan (New York: Library of America, 1982), p. 564.

21 Deleuze and Guattari, *A Thousand Plateaus: Capitalism and Schizophrenia*, trans. Brian Massumi (Minneapolis: University of Minnesota Press, 1987), pp. 19, 21.

22 Vicki Mahaffey, *States of Desire: Wilde, Yeats, Joyce and the Irish Experiment* (Oxford University Press, 1998), p. 26.

23 See Panthea Reid Broughton, "'Virginia is Anal': Speculations on Virginia Woolf's Writing *Roger Fry* and Reading Sigmund Freud," *Journal of Modern Literature* 14 (1987), 151–57.

24 See Fred Kaplan, *Henry James: The Imagination of Genius* (London: Hodder and Stoughton, 1992), p. 532.

25 See Daniel Ferrer, "The Freudful Couchmare of LAMBDAd: Joyce's Notes on Freud and the Composition of Chapter XVI of *Finnegans Wake*," *James Joyce Quarterly* 22 (1985), 367–82.

26 Shoshana Felman, *Jacques Lacan, the Adventure of Insight: Psychoanalysis and Contemporary Culture* (Cambridge, MA: Harvard University Press, 1987), p. 75.

27 *Oxford Literary Review* 26 (2004), *The Blind Short Story*, ed. Nicholas Royle.

2 THE MODERNIST RAT

1 Steve Baker, *The Postmodern Animal* (London: Reaktion Books, 2000), pp. 20–21.

2 Margot Norris, *Beasts of the Modern Imagination* (Baltimore, MD: Johns Hopkins University Press, 1985), p. 6.

3 Julia Kristeva, *Powers of Horror: An Essay on Abjection*, trans. Leon Roudiez (New York: Columbia, 1982), p. 56.

4 Georges Bataille, "L'abjection et les formes misérables," *Oeuvres complètes*, vol. II (Paris: Gallimard, 1970), p. 219.

5 See Derrida, *Of Grammatology*, trans. Gayatri Spivak (Baltimore, MD: Johns Hopkins University Press, 1997), pp. 141–64.

6 "Droll rat, they would shoot you if they knew / Your cosmopolitan sympathies" (Isaac Rosenberg, "Break of Day in the Trenches").

7 Hans Zinsser, *Rats, Lice, and History* (London: George Routledge and Sons, 1935), p. 208.

8 Günter Grass, *The Rat*, trans. Ralph Manheim (London: Picador, 1988), p. 5.

9 Georges Bataille, *The Accursed Share: An Essay on General Economy*, vol. I: *Consumption*, trans. Robert Hurley (New York: Zone Books, 1988), p. 21.

10 This finding has recently been challenged by a new hypothesis that the plague was air-borne or water-borne. For a history of the outbreak at the turn of the century, see Myron Echenberg, *Plague Ports: The Global Urban Impact of Bubonic Plague, 1894–1901* (New York University Press, 2007).

11 See Peter Stallybrass and Allon White, *The Politics and Poetics of Transgression* (Ithaca, NY: Cornell University Press, 1986), pp. 143–47.

12 Christopher Herbert, "Rat Worship and Taboo in Mayhew's London," *Representations* 23 (1988), 14.

13 See Stephen Smith, *Underground London: Travels Beneath the City Streets* (London: Little, Brown, 2004), pp. 50–52.

14 The SPCA had been founded in Britain in 1924, and became the RSPCA when it received its Royal charter in 1940. See Robert Sullivan, *Rats: Observations on the History and Habitat of the City's Most Unwanted Inhabitants* (New York: Bloomsbury, 2004), pp. 76–79.

15 See Henry Mayhew, *London Labour and the London Poor*, ed. John D. Rosenberg (London: Griffin, Bone and Co., 1861), vol. III, pp. 1–21, which includes brief portraits of Jack Black the Rat-Catcher and Jimmy Shaw the rat-fight entrepreneur.

16 See Charles Golding, *Rats: The New Plague* (London: Weidenfeld and Nicolson, 1990), pp. 30–32.

17 The dedication reads: "IN REMEMBRANCE OF 'SAMMY,' THE INTELLIGENT PINK-EYED REPRESENTATIVE OF A PERSECUTED (BUT IRREPRESSIBLE) RACE. AN AFFECTIONATE LITTLE FRIEND. AND MOST ACCOMPLISHED THIEF!" Beatrix Potter, *The Roly-Poly Pudding* [*The Tale of Samuel Whiskers*] (New York: Frederick Warne and Co., 1908).

18 See Harriet Ritvo, *The Animal Estate: The English and Other Creatures in the Victorian Age* (Cambridge, MA: Harvard University Press, 1987), pp. 82–121.

19 See Robert V. Guthrie, *Even the Rat Was White: A Historical View of Psychology* (New York: Harper and Row, 1976).

20 Bram Stoker, *Dracula*, p. 252.

21 His "big child-brain" was reputedly arrested at the battle of Mohács (1526). See Stoker, *Dracula*, p. 302; see also Friedrich A. Kittler, *Discourse Networks 1800/1900* (1985), trans. Michael Metteer with Chris Cullens (Stanford University Press, 1992), p. 356.

22 Stoker, *Dracula*, p. 306. Marx, in a famous metaphor, described capitalism as vampirism, sucking the lifeblood out of the bodies of the workers. Revisiting this metaphor, Franco Moretti aligns Stoker's Dracula specifically with monopoly capitalism and its destruction of all forms of economic independence. See Karl Marx, *Capital: A Critique of Political Economy*, vol. I, trans. Ben Fowkes (Harmondsworth: Penguin, 1976), p. 342; Franco Moretti, *Signs Taken for Wonders*, trans. Susan Fischer *et al.* (1983; London: Verso, 1988), pp. 91–93.

23 Max Horkheimer and Theodor W. Adorno, *Dialectic of Enlightenment*, trans. John Cumming (New York: Continuum, 2002), p. 36.

24 See Jennifer Wicke, "Vampiric Typewriting," p. 475.

25 W. F. Barrett, F. W. H. Myers *et al.*, "Report of the Literary Committee," *Proceedings of the Society for Psychical Research* 1:2 (1882), 147: "we venture to introduce the words *Telaesthesia* and *Telepathy* to cover all cases of impression

received at a distance without the normal operation of the recognized sense organs." See also Pamela Thurschwell, *Literature, Technology and Magical Thinking, 1880–1920* (Cambridge University Press, 2001), esp. pp. 20–32.

26 See Kittler, *Discourse Networks*, pp. 353–56.

27 Similarly, the Rat Man once spotted a rat sneaking across his father's grave, a detail Freud footnotes with the observation that "in legends generally the rat appears not so much as a disgusting creature but as something uncanny – as a chthonic animal … used to represent the souls of the dead" (SE 10:215n2).

28 *U* 94:974–75; *Hamlet* Act 1, Scene v. Freud also comments, in a curiously confident correction of the Rat Man's account, that the so-called rat was undoubtedly a weasel (SE 10:215n3).

29 The first known experiments on rats date back to 1856, but the cradle of the modern laboratory is thought to be the Wistar Institute in Philadelphia, where wild rats were replaced by albino rats, possibly descended from Jack Black's fancy rats, in 1895. See Birgitta Edelman, "'Rats are people, too!' Rat–Human Relations Re-Rated," *Anthropology Today* 18:3 (2002), 5.

30 Sullivan, *Rats*, p. 12; see also John B. Watson, "Kinaesthetic and Organic Sensations; Their Role in the Reactions of the White Rat," *Psychological Review Monograph*, 8:33 (1907), 96; and Golding, *Rats*, pp. 3, 52.

31 Watson, *ibid*., pp. 1–2.

32 These questions are proposed as alternatives to those of the behaviorist scientists by J. M. Coetzee in *Elizabeth Costello* (London: Secker and Warburg, 2003), p. 72.

33 Edward Chase Tolman, "Cognitive Maps in Rats and Men" (1948), in *Collected Papers in Psychology* (Berkeley: University of California Press, 1951), pp. 250, 253, 260.

34 Watson, "Kinaesthetic and Organic Sensations," pp. 98–99. Watson seems to anticipate humane objections when he reports that the mutilated rat made a full recovery, once its curiosity about the maze had been revived, and was still alive a year later at the time of writing.

35 Tolman, "Determiners of Behaviour at a Choice Point" (1938), in *Collected Papers in Psychology*, p. 172.

36 Coetzee, *Elizabeth Costello*, p. 105.

37 Tolman, "Cognitive Maps," pp. 242–43.

38 Henry H. Donaldson, *The Rat: Data and Reference Tables for the Albino Rat (Mus norvegicus albinus) and the Norway Rat (Mus norvegicus)* (1915; rev. 1924); quoted in J. Russell Lindsey, "Historical Foundations," in *The Laboratory Rat*, 2 vols., ed. Henry J. Baker, J. Russell Lindsey, and Steven H. Weisbroth (New York: Academic Press/Harcourt Brace Jovanovich, 1979), vol. 1, p. 5.

39 Golding, *Rats*, p. 54.

40 See www.nobel.se/literature/laureates/1999/lecture-e.html

41 Grass, *The Rat*, p. 136.

42 Hugh Sykes Davies, *The Papers of Andrew Melmoth* (London: Methuen and Co., 1960).

43 Grass, *The Rat*, p. 5. See also Robert Hendrickson, *More Cunning than Man: A Complete History of the Rat and its Role in Human Civilization* (New York: Kensington, 1983), which begins with an account of Engebi Island, a Western Pacific atoll where the United States tested its nuclear arsenal. When scientists visited the island in 1950, they found that all animal and plant life was radioactive, yet the island abounded with rats, which had not only survived but prospered (pp. 1–2).

44 Octave Mirbeau, *The Torture Garden* (1899), trans. Michael Richardson (Sawtry: Dedalus, 1995), pp. 155–58. The Wolf Man reports that Freud held a very unfavourable opinion of Mirbeau; see Gardiner, p. 146.

45 Freud, "On Transformations of Instinct as Exemplified in Anal Erotism" (1917), SE 7:131.

46 See note 28 above.

47 Corpses are "devoured by scuttling plump-bellied rats" (as Joyce puts it in *A Portrait of the Artist* [*P* 120]), SE 10:213–16. For a more detailed discussion of the relation between rats and cannibalism, see Leonard Shengold, "More on Rats and Rat People," in *Freud and his Patients*, ed. Mark Kanzer and Jules Glenn (New York: Jason Aronson, 1980), pp. 183–84, 192–96.

48 Curiously, such reversals of above and below recur in other literary rat-attacks; in George Orwell's *Nineteen Eighty-Four* (1949), Winston Smith is haunted by the fear of rats boring through his upper rather than his lower "cheeks," devouring his face rather than his buttocks, in a phobia that turns the Mirbeau fable downside-up. Threatened with this facial rat-torture in "Room 101," Smith collapses under interrogation and betrays his lover. In this novel the threat of rat-penetration could also be interpreted as homosexual seduction, since it causes Smith to ditch his girlfriend and transfer his allegiance to his torturer-confessor. According to Bakhtin, such carnivalesque inversions of face and buttocks, mouth and anus, signify the overturning of social hierarchies: the higher regions of the body represent the upper classes that oppress the "downtrodden."

49 SE 10:216n1, 183, 180, 207n, 214n1, 215n2, 241n2.

50 SE 10:216n1; Goethe, *Faust*, trans. and ed. Stuart Atkins (1984), Princeton University Press, 1994), Part I, "Faust's Study II: Easter Night," p. 40, lines 1512–24.

51 See Jacques Berchtold, *Des rats et des ratières: Anamorphoses d'un champ métaphorique de Saint Augustin à Jean Racine* (Geneva: Librairie Droz, 1992), pp. 11–19.

52 François Rabelais, *The Histories of Gargantua and Pantagruel*, trans. J. M. Cohen (London: Penguin, 1955), p. 42.

53 Lettre "à mon fils," 4 October 1692, in Jean Racine, *Oeuvres complètes* (Paris: Gallimard, 1960), vol. II, p. 524; quoted in Berchtold, *Des rats et des ratières*, p. 12.

54 See Berchtold, *Des rats et des ratières*, pp. 12–13.

55 A priest is driven to a similar extremity in Thomas Pynchon's *V* (1961), published three years after Hugh Sykes Davies's novel. During the depression of

the 1930s, Father Fairing becomes convinced that human civilization is dying out, and that rats will inherit the earth. For this reason he descends into the New York sewers, equipped with his catechism and breviary, in an attempt to convert the rats to Catholicism. Yet although he is supposedly striving for the salvation of his rat-congregation, he survives in the sewers by eating them at the rate of three per day (Thomas Pynchon, *V.* [New York: HarperCollins, 1999], pp. 120–22). See also M. Keith Booker, "The Rats of God: Pynchon, Joyce, Beckett, and the Carnivalization of Religion," *Pynchon Notes*, 24–25 (1989), 21–30:22.

56 Davies, *The Papers of Andrew Melmoth*, 21. According to Derrida, Antonin Artaud also plays on the anagram of rat and art, which involves a further pun on the first syllable of his surname. Derrida argues that the syllable "RA," a homonym of rat and a palindrome of "AR," which is a homonym of art, disseminates itself throughout Artaud's writing – "RA, the grammar of the future"; see *The Secret Art of Antonin Artaud*, ed. Jacques Derrida and Paule Thévenin, trans. Mary Ann Caws (1986; Cambridge, MA: MIT Press, 1998), p. 128. See also Berchtold, *Des rats et des ratières*, p. 14n14.

57 This process could be compared to the simultaneous creation and decreation of the author by the text, as described by Roland Barthes, who uses the image of the spider rather than the rat: "lost in this tissue – this texture – the subject unmakes himself, like a spider dissolving in the constructive secretions of its web." Roland Barthes, *The Pleasure of the Text*, trans. Richard Miller (New York: Hill and Wang, 1975), p. 64.

58 See Walter Pater, *The Renaissance: Studies in Art and Poetry: The 1893 Text*, ed. Donald Hill (Berkeley: University of California Press, 1981), pp. 186–88; see also Vicki Mahaffey, *Reauthorizing Joyce* (Cambridge University Press, 1988), pp. 145–46.

59 Beckett, letter in German to Martin Esslin, 9 July 1937, quoted in Leo Bersani and Ulysse Dutoit, *Arts of Impoverishment: Beckett, Rothko, Resnais* (Cambridge, MA: Harvard University Press, 1993), p. 22.

60 Jean-Michel Rabaté, "Watt/Sade: Beckett et l'humain à l'envers," in *L'Inhumain*, ed. Marie-Christine Lemardeley-Cunci, Carle Bonnafous-Murat and André Topia (Paris: Presses Sorbonne Nouvelles, 2004), p. 78.

61 This letter, famous for its lurid expression of modernist linguistic angst, was recently revisited by J. M. Coetzee in *Elizabeth Costello: Eight Lessons* (London: Secker and Warburg, 2003), which concludes with a postscript to the Chandos letter, supposedly written by Chandos's wife Elizabeth. (In the same way, Elizabeth Costello supposedly composed a postscript to *Ulysses*, rewriting Joyce's novel from the wife's perspective.) In Coetzee's letter as in Hofmannsthal's, language is overrun by vermin: "Words no longer reach [my husband]," Elizabeth Chandos laments; "they shiver and shatter" on contact with his "shield of crystal," and only fleas, rats, and beetles can penetrate this carapace (pp. 229–30).

62 Hugo von Hofmannsthal, *The Lord Chandos Letter and Other Writings*, trans. Joel Rotenberg (New York: New York Review of Books, 2005), pp. 121–24.

63 *Ibid.*, p. 124.

64 *Ibid.*

65 James Knowlson, *Damned to Fame* (New York: Simon and Schuster, 1996), p. 307.

66 See also Mary Bryden, "Rats in and around Beckett," in Marius Buning *et al.*, eds., *Beckett versus Beckett* (Amsterdam: Rodopi, 1998), pp. 317–29.

67 Beckett, *Watt* (1953/1963; London: Calder, 1998), pp. 79–82.

68 Here it is worth noting that the word "rodent" derives from either the Latin *radere*, which means "to scratch," or the Latin *rodere*, which means "to gnaw"; either the scratching or the gnawing could produce a "rattle." Meanwhile, a "rattle" can also mean a kind of fishing-net, otherwise known as a "rattle-net" or a "wolf-net": the "rattle" therefore connects the rat with the net, while also intertwining rat(tle) and wolf(net), the two principal Freudian animals.

69 T. S. Eliot, *The Waste Land*, lines 185–95.

70 Wyndham Lewis, *The Apes of God* (London: Nash and Grayson, 1930), pp. 145, 154, 155.

71 Eliot, *The Waste Land*, line 22.

72 Admittedly Eliot made this remark in 1951, long after writing "Burbank," but he must have been aware of this meaning of "piles" and the possibility of double entendre in the line. See Peter Ackroyd, *T. S. Eliot* (Harmondsworth: Penguin, 1984), p. 303.

73 See www.holocaust-history.org/der-ewige-jude/stills.shtml. See also Boria Sax, *Animals in the Third Reich: Pets, Scapegoats, and the Holocaust* (New York: Continuum, 2000), p. 159.

3 STRANDENTWINING CABLES: HENRY JAMES'S
THE AMBASSADORS

1 Henry James, *The Complete Notebooks*, ed. Leon Edel and Lyall H. Powers (Oxford University Press, 1987), p. 88.

2 James, *The Sacred Fount*, ed. John Lyon (1901; London: Penguin, 1994), p. 187.

3 See Rebecca West, *Henry James* (New York: Henry Holt & Co., 1916), pp. 107–08, where she complains that *The Sacred Fount* "records how a week-end visitor spends more intellectual force than Kant can have used on *The Critique of Pure Reason* in an unsuccessful attempt to discover whether there exists between certain of his fellow-guests a relationship not more interesting among these vacuous people than it is among sparrows."

4 In a Notebook entry of 15 February 1899 (*Notebooks*, p. 176), James reminds himself: "Don't lose sight of the little *concetto* … that begins with fancy of the young man who marries an old woman and becomes old while she becomes young. Keep my play on idea: the *liaison* that betrays itself by the *transfer* of qualities … from one to the other of the parties to it. They *exchange*. I see 2 couples. One is married – this is the *old–young* pair. I watch *their* process, and it gives me my light for the spectacle of the other (covert, obscure, unavowed) pair who are *not* married."

5 See Sharon Cameron, *Thinking in Henry James* (Chicago: University of Chicago Press, 1986), pp. 31–32, 41.

6 James, *The Turn of the Screw*, ed. Deborah Esch and Jonathan Warren (New York: Norton, 1999), p. 85.

7 James, *Notebooks*, 12 January 1895, p. 178.

8 Stéphane Mallarmé, letter to Maurice Guillemot, quoted by Jacques Derrida, "The Double Session," in *Dissemination*, trans. Barbara Johnson (London: Continuum, 2000), p. 194.

9 Virginia Woolf, *A Room of One's Own*, ed. Susan Gubar (1929; Orlando, FL: Harcourt Inc., 2005), p. 26.

10 Another example of the taboo imposed upon the father's name occurs when Maggie announces to her husband Prince Amerigo that she knows about his "two relations" with Charlotte, and he wonders if "anyone else" knows. "It was as near as he could come to naming her father, and [Maggie] kept him at that distance" (*GB* 447).

11 Cornelia Atwood Pratt commented in a witty review of 1901 that *The Sacred Fount* "is sublimated gossip. The experienced reader does not need to be told that gossip plus Henry James changes its substance and becomes incorporeal, dazzling, and, to the vulgar, impossible … " (Roger Gard, ed., *Henry James: The Critical Heritage* [London: Routledge and Kegan Paul, 1968], p. 307).

12 Peter Brooks, *Henry James Goes to Paris* (Princeton University Press, 2007), p. 44.

13 Frank Moore Colby, "In Darkest James," in *The Question of Henry James*, ed. F. W. Dupee, ed. (New York: Henry Holt and Co., 1945), p. 22; and Ludwig Lewisohn, *Expression in America* (1932), quoted by Philip Rahv, "Attitudes Toward Henry James" (1943), in Dupee, *ibid.*, p. 274.

14 Mikkel Borch-Jacobsen (*The Freudian Subject* [1982], tr. Catherine Porter [Stanford University Press, 1988], p. 26), argues that "desire is mimetic before it is anything else": it is the desire to desire the desire of the other.

15 One of the best discussions of the entanglement of knowledge and inter-subjective desire is Leo Bersani's chapter "The Jamesian Lie" in *A Future for Astyanax* (New York: Columbia, 1984), pp. 128–55.

16 A remarkable example of the use of the term "interest" may be found in *The Wings of the Dove* (1902; London: Penguin, 2003), in the scene in Maud Lowder's drawing-room where Lord Mark is introduced to his rival Merton Densher. "'Oh!' said the other party while Densher said nothing – occupied as he mainly was on the spot with weighing the sound in question … It wasn't … he knew, the 'Oh!' of the idiot, however great the superficial resemblance … it was the very speciality of the speaker, and a deal of expensive training and experience had gone to producing it. Densher felt somehow that, as a thing of value accidentally picked up, it would retain an interest of curiosity" (*Wings* 282). J. Hillis Miller has remarked on how *The Wings of the Dove* is punctuated with such "Oh!'s," which tend to surface at moments of potential melodrama. In this case Densher understands the "Oh!" as a "object of value accidentally picked up," a kind of conversational *objet trouvé*, likely to retain its "interest" in the future, where

"interest" could be understood as the dividends of "curiosity." This use of "Oh!" may also allude to the Fool's joke in *King Lear* (Act 1, Scene iv) that the sovereign is "an O without a figure." In the case of *The Wings of the Dove* it is Lord Mark who provides the cipher – the "mark" – that confers "value" or cultural capital upon the "Oh!" As Adrian Poole has pointed out, *The Wings of the Dove* is full of "marks," in addition to those recurrent "Oh!'s" spotted by Miller. In the scene in Aunt Maud's drawing room, it is the mark (Lord Mark) that endows the "Oh!" with "value" and "interest." See J. Hillis Miller, *Literature as Conduct: Speech Acts in Henry James* (New York: Fordham University Press, 2005), pp. 178; 199–202; and Adrian Poole, *Henry James* (New York: St. Martin's Press, 1991), pp. 115–17. For general discussions of James's economic metaphors, see Laurence Holland, *The Expense of Vision* (1964; Baltimore, MD: Johns Hopkins University Press, 1982); Jan Dietrichson, *The Image of Money in the American Novel of the Gilded Age* (Oslo, Norway: University of Oslo American Institute Publications, 1969); Donald L. Mull, *Henry James's "Sublime Economy"* (Middletown, CT: Wesleyan University Press, 1973); Daniel J. Schneider, *The Crystal Cage: Adventures of the Imagination in the Fiction of Henry James* (Lawrence: Regents Press of Kansas, 1978).

17 Note, for instance, the veritable orgy of financial puns at the end of *The Golden Bowl*, where Maggie:

> had an instant of terror that … always precedes, on the part of the creature to be paid, the certification of the amount … Amerigo knew it, the amount; he still held it, and the delay in his return, making her heart beat too fast to go on, was like a sudden blinding light on a wild speculation. She had thrown the dice, but his hand was over her cast.
>
> He opened the door, however, at last – he hadn't been away ten minutes; and then, with her sight of him renewed to intensity, she seemed to have a view of the number.

In this passage the "wild speculation" means either a conjecture or a gamble, the latter connotation reinforced by the metaphor of casting the dice, while Amerigo's "return," in this context, suggests a financial dividend as well as a homecoming. The specular dimension of speculation is accentuated by the references to light and sight, culminating in the Prince's closing line: "I see nothing but you" (*GB* 566–67).

18 One of the first and best comparisons of James's late fiction to Foucault's conception of the *pouvoir–savoir* network in modern society may be found in Leo Bersani, "The Subject of Power," *Diacritics* 7 (1977), 2–21. See also my "'The Intimate Difference': Power and Representation in *The Ambassadors*" (1984), a revised version of which is published in the Norton Critical Edition of Henry James's *The Ambassadors*, ed. S. P. Rosenbaum (New York: Norton, 1994), pp. 501–14; and Mark Seltzer's *Henry James and the Art of Power* (Ithaca, NY: Cornell University Press, 1984).

19 Paul G. Beidler, in *Frames in James: "The Tragic Muse," "The Turn of the Screw," "What Maisie Knew," and "The Ambassadors"* (Victoria, BC: University of

Victoria Press, 1993), p. 90: "The Lambinet chapters form a frame because they contain the truth and the action that must be excluded from the text."

20 Quoted as appendix to Jerome McGann, "Revision, Rewriting, Rereading; or, 'An Error [Not] in *The Ambassadors*,'" *American Literature* 64:1 (1992), 108.

21 See my "'The Intimate Difference,'" and Julie Rivkin, *False Positions: The Representational Logics of Henry James's Fiction* (Stanford University Press, 1996), ch. 2, pp. 57–81, who makes a similar argument about *The Ambassadors*.

22 James plays on the double meaning of representation, political and aesthetic, in *The Tragic Muse* ([1890], in James, *Novels 1886–1890* [New York: Library of America, 1989], p. 759), in which Nick Dormer, imagining his future as a member of parliament, thinks that his studio would be "an absurd place to see his constituents, unless he wanted to paint their portraits, a kind of representation with which they scarcely would have been satisfied."

23 Gustave Flaubert, letter to Louise Colet, 9 December 1852, in *Correspondance*, 9 vols. (Paris: Conard, 1926–33), vol. III, p. 62. In his Preface to *The Golden Bowl*, James speaks of "the impersonal author's concrete deputy or delegate, a convenient substitute or apologist for the creative power otherwise so veiled and disembodied," terms that could apply to Strether as the representative either of James or of the veiled and disembodied Mrs. Newsome (*GB* xli).

24 Jennifer Wicke, in *Advertising Fictions: Literature, Advertisement, and Social Reading* (New York: Columbia University Press, 1988), p. 104, makes the intriguing suggestion that the "article" remains unnamed because it has yet to be distinguished from its rivals by advertisement, which is the magic that Chad is destined to perform.

25 See David Lodge, *Author, Author* (London: Secker and Warburg, 2004), for a highly entertaining novelistic account of the relationship between James, George du Maurier, and *Trilby*.

26 See also Posnock, *The Trial of Curiosity: Henry James, William James, and the Challenge of Modernity* (Oxford University Press, 1991), p. 240.

27 For a useful summary of debates about James's putative homosexuality, see Wendy Graham, *Henry James's Thwarted Sexuality* (Stanford University Press), pp. 8–51. See also Eric L. Haralson, *Henry James and Queer Modernity* (Cambridge University Press, 2003), p. 104, for the argument that *The Ambassadors* "attempts an evacuation of sexual discourse as such," diffusing libidinal activity into a variety of "queer" motivations.

28 Laurence Holland, in *The Expense of Vision*, p. 251, argues that Strether is "making up late for what he didn't have early," but only "by living vicariously through the experience of younger people." Carren Kaston, in *Imagination and Desire in the Novels of Henry James* (New Brunswick, NJ: Rutgers University Press, 1984), p. 69, views Strether's experience as a perversion of Emersonian transcendentalist vision, arguing that James has "socialised or domesticated Emerson's visionary eyeball self. Being visionary now meant floating out over other characters' consciousness, becoming a medium of

reception capable of registering what it is like to be them, at the risk, as with Emerson, of making the personal self tenuous." *The Ambassadors* is "a study of substitutive or second-hand agency, a type of unoriginal relation to the world in which Strether's absence from himself inevitably traps him" (pp. 82–83). Neither Holland nor Kaston considers whether James is trying to debunk the very notion of firsthand experience; from a psychoanalytic perspective, desire is necessarily vicarious, and *The Ambassadors* seems to endorse this viewpoint.

29 Wicke points out that James said that Strether was based on Howells, but that James decided not to make Strether a straightforward author in case the parallel was too close. But Strether is, as Wicke points out, an "author man-qué" (*Advertising Fictions*, p. 106).

30 James, *Letters*, ed. Leon Edel, 4 vols. (Cambridge: Belknap Press, 1974–78, 4:111.

31 McGann, "Revision, Rewriting, Rereading," p. 95. Theodora Bosanquet also makes this point about James's conception of revision in *Henry James at Work*, ed. Lyall H. Powers (Ann Arbor: University of Michigan Press, 2006), p. 42.

32 Jonathan Freedman, in *Professions of Taste: Henry James, British Aestheticism, and Commodity Culture* (Stanford University Press, 1990), p. 197, under-stands this image as "a revised but nevertheless recognizable redaction of Pater's hard, flamelike gem," and reads the passage as part of a coded debate with aestheticism.

33 Adrian Poole makes a similar point in *Henry James*, pp. 50–51.

34 Ian Watt, "The First Paragraph of *The Ambassadors*: An Explication," *Essays in Criticism* 10 (1960), 250–74; an abridged version is reprinted in *A* 442–55.

35 Roland Barthes, *Image – Music – Text*, ed. Stephen Heath (Glasgow: Fontana, 1977), p. 158.

36 Letter to the Duchess of Sutherland, 23 December 1903, in James, *Letters* 4:302–03; *A* 408–09.

37 F. R. Leavis, *The Great Tradition* (New York University Press, 1963), p. 161, rpt. *A* 439; for Arnold Bennett, see *Henry James: The Critical Heritage*, ed. Roger Gard (London: Routledge and Kegan Paul; New York: Barnes and Noble, 1968), p. 373.

38 Barthes, *Image – Music – Text*, p. 159.

39 The title of Ross Posnock's masterly study of the James brothers.

40 James, *The American* (1877), ed. James W. Tuttleton (New York: Norton, 1978), p. 50. As Thomas Sergeant Perry has argued, James's early fiction is highly melodramatic, his "sophisticated heroines … seem to have read all Balzac in the cradle and to be positively dripping with lurid crimes." Quoted in Peter Brooks, *The Melodramatic Imagination: Balzac, Henry James, Melodrama, and the Mode of Excess* (1976; New Haven, CT: Yale University Press, 1995), p. 153. Christopher Newman, on the other hand, has "never read a novel!" (*The American*, p. 37).

41 See also James's 1914 note in his pocket diary about this "mere germ" of inspiration in James, *Letters* 4:3.

42 See Foucault, *The History of Sexuality: An Introduction*, trans. Robert Hurley (London: Allen Lane, 1978), especially pp. 88–98.

43 As Marianna Torgovnick points out, the first American edition of *The Ambassadors* intensifies Strether's sense of loss by describing the Lambinet as "the material acquisition that, in all his time, he had most sharply failed of": see Torgovnick, *The Visual Arts, Pictorialism, and the Novel* (Princeton University Press, 1985), p. 181.

44 See Mary Ann Caws's useful diagram of the frames within frames involved in this scene in *Reading Frames in Modern Fiction* (Princeton University Press, 1985), p. 157.

45 Here James anticipates Derrida's critique of Kant's trivialization of *staffage*; see *La vérité en peinture* (Paris: Flammarion, 1978), especially ch. 2. See also my "'The Intimate Difference'" (*A* 511) and Beider, *Frames in James*, pp. 86–87.

46 Kaja Silverman, "Too Early/Too Late: Subjectivity and the Primal Scene in Henry James," *Novel: A Forum on Fiction* 21:2/3 (1988), 159–61; Henry James, *The Portrait of a Lady* (1881), ed. Geoffrey Moore (London: Penguin, 2003), p. 484. Peter Brooks traces what James calls his "scenic method" to his early enthusiasm for Balzac, whose novels regularly work "toward the scenic 'show-down,' the *scène à faire*" (*Henry James Goes to Paris*, pp. 159–60). See also James's *Notebook* entry of December 21, 1896: "I realize – none too soon – that the *scenic* method is my absolute, my imperative, my *only* salvation" (p. 167).

47 Jennifer Wicke makes the interesting point that "Chad's ability to 'assault' Strether's eyes, to force Strether to be a voyeur at a framed scene of sexuality, is similar in kind to the energy released by an advertisement, in which all consumers become hapless, voyeuristic readers" (*Advertising Fictions*, p. 112).

48 Henry James, *Autobiography*, ed. F. W. Dupee (New York: Criterion, 1956), p. 150; quoted by Posnock, *Trial of Curiosity*, p. 173.

49 Posnock, *ibid.*, p. 235.

50 *Ibid.*

51 Mary F. S. Hervey, *Holbein's "Ambassadors": The Picture and the Men* (London: George Bell and Sons, 1900).

52 Adeline R. Tintner, *Henry James and the Lust of the Eyes: Thirteen Artists in his Work* (Baton Rouge: Louisiana State University Press, 1993), pp. 87–94.

53 See David Hockney, *Secret Knowledge: Rediscovering the Lost Techniques of the Old Masters* (New York: Viking Studio, 2001), pp. 56–57, which shows the death's head with its perspective "corrected" by a computer.

54 Jacques Lacan, *The Four Fundamental Concepts of Psycho-Analysis* (1973), ed. Jacques–Alain Miller, trans. Alan Sheridan (New York: Norton, 1998), p. 88.

55 See Posnock, *Trial of Curiosity*, pp. 231–34.

56 Leslie Fiedler, for example, sees Strether as "the most maidenly of all James's men" (*Love and Death in the American Novel* [New York: Dell, 1969], p. 241). Carolyn Porter describes Strether as "James's most intense perceiver … but

the condition of his seeing is his impotence..." (*in Seeing and Being: The Plight of the Participant Observer in Emerson, James, Adams, and Faulkner* (Middletown, CT: Wesleyan University Press, 1981), p. 126.

57 James, Preface to *The Princess Casamassima* (1886; Harmondsworth: Penguin, 1977), pp. 11–12; also in James, *Literary Criticism: French Writers; Other European Writers; The Prefaces to the New York Edition* (New York: Library of America, 1984), vol. II, p. 1091.

58 Mark Goble, "Wired Love: Pleasure at a Distance in Henry James and Others," *English Literary History* 74 (2007), 413. For the question of telegraphy in *In the Cage*, see *inter alia* John Carlos Rowe, *The Other Henry James* (Durham, NC: Duke University Press, 1998), ch. 6, pp. 155–80; Jennifer Wicke, "Henry James's Second Wave," *The Henry James Review* 10:2 (1989), 146–51; Pamela Thurschwell, *Literature, Technology and Magical Thinking*, pp. 87–89, 93–100; Richard Menke, "'Framed and Wired': Teaching *In the Cage* at the Intersection of Literature and Media," *The Henry James Review* 25 (2004), 33–43.

59 Goble, "Wired Love," p. 415.

60 Posnock, *Trial of Curiosity*, p. vii.

4 THE WOOLF WOMAN

1 The authors of this argument are the psychoanalytic writers Nicholas Abraham and Maria Torok, whose views are discussed later in this chapter.

2 Freud's writings were much discussed in Woolf's social circle, and the Hogarth Press, which she founded with Leonard Woolf, published the first translations of Freud in Britain, as well as the Standard Edition of Freud's *Complete Psychological Works*, ed. James Strachey, from 1953–1974. See Leonard Woolf's autobiography, particularly the fourth volume, *Downhill All the Way: An Autobiography of the Years 1919–1939* (London: Hogarth Press, 1967), pp. 163–68, and the fifth volume, *The Journey Not the Arrival Matters: An Autobiography of the Years 1939–1969* (London: Hogarth Press, 1969), pp. 117–18. See also Rachel Bowlby, *Feminist Destinations and Further Essays on Virginia Woolf* (Edinburgh University Press, 1997), p. 57.

3 See Hermione Lee, *Virginia Woolf* (London: Chatto and Windus, 1996), ch. 10, pp. 175–200. See also Nicole Ward Jouve, "Virginia Woolf and Psychoanalysis," in Sue Roe and Susan Sellers, eds., *The Cambridge Companion to Virginia Woolf* (Cambridge University Press, 2000), p. 248.

4 As Charlotte F. Otten has pointed out, lycanthropy was "a baffling metaphysical question" in the Middle Ages, the metamorphosis attributed by some to demonic possession, by others to an excess of black bile, the humour responsible for melancholia. See Charlotte F. Otten, ed., *A Lycanthropy Reader: Werewolves in Western Culture* (Syracuse University Press, 1986), p. 10.

5 Robert Burton, *Anatomy of Melancholy*, ed. Floyd Dell and Paul Jordan-Smith (New York: Tudor Press, 1948), pp. 122–23.

6   Diane Antonio, "Of Wolves and Women," in *Animals and Women: Feminist Theoretical Explorations*, ed. Carol J. Adams and Josephine Donovan (Durham, NC: Duke University Press), pp. 224–25.

7   Otten points out that lycanthropy, which was blamed on demons in antiquity, was also attributed to cuckoldry in the Middle Ages, with the implication that the wolfish husband was "unmanned" and denatured by his faithless wife (Otten, Introduction to *A Lycanthropy Reader*, p. 7).

8   T. S. Eliot, *The Waste Land* (1922), ed. Michael North (New York: Norton, 2001), lines 74–75; John Webster, *The White Devil* (1612), in *The Duchess of Malfi and Other Plays*, ed. René Weis (New York: Oxford University Press, 1996), Act v, Scene iv, lines 99–100, p. 89.

9   Note that in French '*entre chien et loup*' means twilight.

10 I borrow the subtitle "Wolf-Gathering" from Robert Manson Myers's hilarious *From Beowulf to Virginia Woolf: An Outstanding and Wholly Unauthorized History of English Literature* (1951; Chicago: University of Illinois Press, 1984), p. 21.

11 Jacques Lacan describes the Wolf Man as "one of Freud's great psychoanalytic cases, the greatest of all, the most sensational," in *The Four Fundamental Concepts of Psychoanalysis*, p. 251.

12 See, *inter alia*, Mary Jacobus, "'The Third Stroke': Reading Woolf with Freud," in Rachel Bowlby, ed., *Virginia Woolf* (London: Longman, 1992) pp. 102–20. For further references see Elizabeth Abel, *Virginia Woolf and the Fictions of Psychoanalysis* (Chicago: University of Chicago Press, 1989), p. 132n6.

13 Pankejeff was born on 25 December 1886 according to the Julian calendar then in use in Russia, and on 6 January 1887 according to the Gregorian calendar: see Peter Brooks, "Fictions of the Wolf Man," in *Reading for the Plot: Design and Intention in Narrative* (New York: A. A. Knopf, 1984), p. 265.

14 Pankejeff later wrote to Freud that "The Wolves sitting on the tree were in fact not wolves at all but white Spitz dogs with pointed ears [in German, *spitzen Ohren*] and bushy tails": Wolf-Man, "Letters pertaining to Freud's 'History of an Infantile Neurosis,'" *Psychoanalytic Quarterly* 26 (1957), 449–50.

15 See Patrick J. Mahony, *Cries of the Wolf Man* (New York: International Universities Press, 1984), p. 146; Obholzer, p. 4.

16 See James Strachey's "Editor's Note" to *From the History of an Infantile Neurosis*, SE 17:5–6. For a list of Freud's works influenced by the Wolf Man's case, see Whitney Davis, *Drawing the Dream of the Wolves: Homosexuality, Interpretation, and Freud's "Wolf Man"* (Bloomington, IN: Indiana University Press, 1995), p. 3.

17 See Lawrence Johnson, *The Wolf Man's Burden* (Ithaca, NY: Cornell University Press, 2001), p. 6, which argues that the case history "bears testimony to Freud's powers of improvization in that it transforms a situation in which all seems to have been gambled and lost into a vehicle for securing Freud's personal legacy and the perpetuation of his metapsychology into the future."

18 F. W. Maitland, *The Life and Letters of Leslie Stephen* (London: Duckworth, 1906), p. 364; quoted by Alison Light, *Mrs. Woolf and the Servants: The Hidden Heart of Domestic Service* (London: Fig Tree, 2006), p. 50.

19 *Diary* 4:153; Virginia Woolf, *Flush* (1933), ed. Kate Flint (Oxford University Press, 1998).

20 Pamela L. Caughie, however, argues that *Flush* can be read as a satire of canonicity, which challenges "distinctions between genres, or between popular and highbrow, mutt and pure-bred": see Caughie, "*Flush* and the Literary Canon: Oh Where Oh Where Has That Little Dog Gone?" *Tulsa Studies in Women's Literature* 10:1 (1991), 62.

21 Virginia Woolf, *Letters* 5:161–62; see also *Letters* 5:169, where she expresses her amazement to Vita Sackville-West that "an American Adams wants to buy the MS. of Flush – that foolish witless joke with which I solaced myself when I was all of a gasp having done The Waves."

22 See Woolf, *Letters* 5:219.

23 Virginia Woolf, *A Room of One's Own* (1929), ed. Susan Gubar (New York: Harcourt, 2005), p. 85.

24 Kate Flint, Introduction to Woolf, *Flush*, p. xvii.

25 See Harriet Ritvo, *The Animal Estate: The English and Other Creatures in the Nineteenth Century* (Cambridge, MA: Harvard University Press, 1987), esp. ch. 2, pp. 82–121.

26 Curiously the Wolf Man's nose also plays a prominent role in his case history, but his nasal obsession is purely visual. Shiny, pimpled, scarred, or wart-infested, his nose magnetizes both his fetishism and his hypochondria. As a young man he feels ashamed of his snub, foreshortened "Russian" nose, but he learns to appreciate its shortness when the Nazis come to power and denounce long noses as Jewish. According to Brunswick, the Wolf Man's father (who was not Jewish) was once called a *sale juif*: see Gardiner, p. 286. Freud's essay on "Fetishism" (1927) takes as its main example the Wolf Man's fetish for a "shine on the nose," interpreted by Freud as a bilingual pun on "Glanz," meaning "shine" in German, but also a homonym of the "glance" in English, which was the language of the Wolf Man's childhood governess (SE 21:152–53). See below Chapter 5 for a fuller discussion of Freud's essay.

27 Charles Darwin, *The Descent of Man* (London: John Murray, 1871), pp. 17–18; Freud, *Civilization and its Discontents* (1930), SE 21:99n1.

28 Freud also proposes that this process of repression and defense "is repeated on another level when the gods of a superseded period of civilization turn into demons" (SE 21:99n1). The example he probably has in mind is the Furies, relics of a prior matriarchal order suppressed by the cult of Apollo. This suppression laid the foundations of monotheism, a development attributed by Freud in *Moses and Monotheism* to the rise of imperialism in the ancient world, which established the hierarchy of oneness over multiplicity by banishing the plural spirits of the pagan universe. This argument, extended over two astonishing footnotes to *Civilization and its Discontents* (1930), implies a chain of equivalences whereby standing upright = vision =

patriarchy = monotheism = oneness = separation = homogeneity, as opposed to the subordinate chain in which four-footedness = smell = matriarchy = polytheism = multiplicity = merger = heterogeneity.

29 See Susan M. Squier, *Virginia Woolf and London: The Sexual Politics of the City* (Chapel Hill and London: University of North Carolina Press, 1985), ch. 6: "Flush's Journey from Imprisonment to Freedom," pp. 125–37, where Squier develops the comparison between women and dogs as fellow victims of "marginalization and oppression" (p. 125). Yet as Caughie ("*Flush* and the Literary Canon," p. 60) points out, Flush bears less resemblance to Barrett than to her maid Lily Wilson, to whom Woolf devotes a six-page footnote, describing the servant's mind as more impenetrable than the animal's: "for [Wilson] was typical of the great army of her kind – the inscrutable, the all-but-silent, the all-but-invisible servant maids of history" (*Flush* 113). Alison Light, in her fascinating study *Mrs. Woolf and the Servants* (p. 50), points out that dogs often stand for "that other dogsbody, the servant" in Woolf's writing. If dogs represented the play side of life for Woolf, they also represented "the Victorian past with their ready capacity to obey authority and respond to discipline."

30 Woolf made this remark just after discovering the death of Pinka (or Pinker), the Woolfs' dog who provided the model for Flush: letter to Ethel Smyth, 2 June 1935 (*Letters* 5:396).

31 Quentin Bell, *Virginia Woolf: A Biography*, 2 vols. (London: Hogarth Press, 1972), vol. ii, p. 175.

32 "On a Faithful Friend" (1905), *Essays* 1:12.

33 Bell, *Virginia Woolf*, vol. i, p. 90.

34 *MB* 69. See also Woolf, *The Voyage Out* (1915), ed. Lorna Sage (Oxford University Press, 2002), p. 81, where Rachel Vinrace, after being kissed, dreams that she is walking down a long tunnel, at the end of which "a little deformed man … squatted on the floor gibbering, with long nails. His face was pitted and like the face of an animal."

35 Roger Poole, *The Unknown Virginia Woolf* (Brighton: Harvester, 1982), pp. 25ff. For Woolf's curiously telescoped accounts of the Duckworths' assaults, see *MB* 69, 177. Louise DeSalvo has explored some of the implications of these seductions in *Virginia Woolf: The Impact of Childhood Sexual Abuse on her Life and Work* (London: Women's Press, 1989).

36 Woolf's feelings towards pug-dogs seem ambivalent; in her first feminist manifesto, which was also a defense of the Plumage Bill, a parliamentary motion to outlaw the millinery use of feathers on the grounds of cruelty to birds, she imagines a lady of fashion gazing at egret plumes in a shop window with "the greedy petulance of a pug-dog's face at tea-time" (*Essays* 3:242). On the other hand Woolf also wrote, only half in jest: "I expect I shall leave all my fortune to a home for stray pug-dogs, having become entirely maudlin in my old age" (*Letters* 1:364). See Reginald Abbott, "Birds Don't Sing in Greek: Virginia Woolf and 'The Plumage Bill,'" in Adams and Donovan, eds., *Animals and Women*, pp. 263–89.

37 Virginia Woolf, *The Voyage Out*, p. 29.

38 Leonard Woolf also anticipated Orwell's *Animal Farm* of 1945 with his 1925 pamphlet, "Fear and Politics: A Debate at the Zoo" (1925), a political satire in which animals are the debaters; see *In Savage Times: Leonard Woolf on Peace and War*, intro. Stephen J. Stearns (New York: Garland Publishing Inc., 1973), pp. 4–24.

39 Leonard Woolf, letter to Virginia Stephen, 29 April 1912, cited in Lyndall Gordon, *Virginia Woolf: A Writer's Life* (New York: Norton, 1984), p. 142. For examples of the Mongoose and Mandrill correspondence, see Virginia Woolf's letters to Leonard Woolf in *Letters* 2:32–44. In Leonard Woolf's "Fear and Politics," p. 15, the Mandril is a Bolshevik.

40 Virginia Woolf's short story "Lappin and Lapinova" (1939; reprinted [slightly revised] in *A Haunted House and Other Short Stories* [London: Hogarth Press, 1943]), is about honeymooners who concoct a rabbit language, which the husband eventually rejects, causing the failure of their marriage. See also Lyndall Gordon, *Virginia Woolf*, pp. 133–35, 141, 142, 143n, 249; and Hermione Lee, *Virginia Woolf*, pp. 111–12.

41 Here it is worth noting that errors in translation crop up throughout the Wolf Man's case, producing much of his psychic iconography. One such error was embedded in his famous fetish for a "shine on the nose": see note 26 above.

42 Nicolas Abraham and Maria Torok, in *The Wolf Man's Magic Word: A Cryptonomy*, trans. Nicholas Rand (Minneapolis: University of Minnesota Press, 1986), p. 17.

43 Freud's gift to Anna of the dog Wolf coincided with the announcement by Anna's former suitor, Hans Lampl, of his engagement to Jeanne de Groot: "Lampl got his Jeanne and Anna got her Wolf," a Viennese gossip columnist joked; see Johnson, *The Wolf Man's Burden*, p. 165n19.

44 Letter from Freud to Ferenczi, 13 February 1910, quoted in Davis, *Drawing the Dream of the Wolves*, p. 24. In a curious (Freudian?) slip, Stanley Fish reverses the roles of violator and violated in his account of the Wolf Man's fantasy, misreporting that the Wolf Man thought Freud "wants to use me from behind and shit on my head." Fish goes on to argue that "the Wolf Man got it right" – but Fish got it wrong. See Stanley Fish, "Withholding the Missing Portion: Power, Meaning, and Persuasion in Freud's 'The Wolf-Man,'" *Times Literary Supplement* 4352 (8 August 1986), 935; see also Robert Winer, "Echoes of the Wolf Men: Reverberations of Psychic Reality," in Joseph H. Smith and Humphrey Morris, eds., *Telling Facts: History and Narration in Psychoanalysis* (Baltimore, MD: Johns Hopkins University Press, 1992), pp. 148–49.

45 Ernest Jones, *The Life and Works of Sigmund Freud*, 3 vols. (New York: Basic Books, 1953–57), vol. I, p. 4.

46 Carlo Ginzburg, "Freud, the Wolf-Man, and the Werewolves," in *Myths, Emblems, Clues*, trans. John and Anne C. Tedeschi (London: Hutchinson, 1990), pp. 146–55.

47 See Mahony, *Cries of the Wolf Man*, p. 46n26; Davis, *Drawing the Dream of the Wolves*, p. 26.

48 A variation on Peter Brooks's variation on Villiers de l'Isle-Adam's *Axël*, famous for his decadent slogan: "Live? Our servants will do that for us." See Brooks, *Reading for the Plot*, p. 267.

49 Gardiner, p. 138; Obholzer, p. 30.

50 For Deutsch's reactions, which included her first episode of depression, see her *Confrontations with Myself* (New York: Norton, 1973), p. 133.

51 Mahony, in his intriguing speculations on Brunswick's countertransference, points out that Freud ceased to collect money for the Wolf Man in 1927, having possibly received a tip-off from Brunswick about the Wolf Man's concealment of the jewels (*Cries of the Wolf Man*, p. 145). In her "Supplement," Brunswick claims the secret jewels were worthless, but Pankejeff claimed that they were neither worthless nor secret, and that he had used the proceeds from the sale of a necklace to buy an apartment. See Gardiner, p. 267; Obholzer, p. 61.

52 See Mahony, *Cries of the Wolf Man*, p. 140.

53 Gardiner, pp. 278, 301, 271, 264; see also Obholzer, p. 54.

54 Frank Cioffi, *Freud and the Question of Pseudoscience* (Chicago: Open Court, 1998), p. 110. See Mahony (*Cries of the Wolf Man*, p. 138) for Otto Rank's interpretation of the Wolf dream as the product of the current transferential scene, with the child's bed standing for the analytic couch, and the six or seven wolves for Freud's six children (with the patient as the seventh), as well as for the photographs of Freud's six disciples displayed in the consulting room.

55 See Mahony, *Cries of the Wolf Man*, p. 144.

56 *Ibid.*, p. 151.

57 See Anna Freud, Foreword to Gardiner, p. xi.

58 SE 17:32; Wolf-Man, "Letters pertaining to Freud's 'History of an Infantile Neurosis,'" p. 449.

59 SE 17:43n2; in this long footnote Freud also drops the hint, "later on we shall see that the white clothes are also an allusion to death," but never develops this intriguing point. A "high tree," he argues, is a symbol "of observing, of scopophilia," while the "strained attention" of the wolves results from "an interchange of subject and object, of activity and passivity: being looked at instead of looking" (SE 17:43n2, 35). In his conversations with Karin Obholzer, the Wolf Man finds Freud's observations about nightclothes particularly "farfetched" (Obholzer, p. 35).

60 SE 17:42; see also Brooks, *Reading for the Plot*, p. 275.

61 In a footnote (SE 17:87n2), Freud attributes the Wolf Man's "grotesque" obsession with tailors to the castration-phobia induced or exacerbated by this fairy-tale; Brunswick points out that the Wolf Man later transferred his tailor-mania to his wolfish dentists (Gardiner, p. 298).

62 In a footnote added later, Freud suggests: "perhaps what the child observed was not copulation between his parents but copulation between animals,

which he then displaced on to his parents, as though he had inferred that his parents did things in the same way" (SE 17:57n1).

63 Lacan, *The Four Fundamental Concepts of Psychoanalysis*, ed. Jacques-Alain Miller, trans. Alan Sheridan (New York: Norton, 1988), p. 251.

64 Mahony, *Cries of the Wolf Man*, p. 103; Mark Kanzer, Review of Muriel Gardiner, ed., *The Wolf-Man by the Wolf-Man*, *International Journal of Psycho-Analysis* 53 (1972), 422.

65 For Freud's "chronic constipation," see Ernest Jones, *The Life and Work of Sigmund Freud*, 3 vols. (New York: Basic Books, 1955), p. 391. In 1911 Freud wrote to his wife, "The emptiness of life devoted to the care of a full bowel is becoming unbearable" (*ibid.*, p. 90). Todd Dufresne, in *Tales from the Freudian Crypt: The Death Drive in Text and Context* (Stanford University Press, 1999), p. 201n14, points out that Freud was reluctant to consider constipation as a psychosomatic disorder.

66 "We were obliged," Freud announces grandly, to translate the dreamer's fear of being eaten by the wolves into a fear "of being copulated with by his father," the accomplishment of which would entail the child's castration (SE 17:106). See Melanie Klein, *The Psychoanalysis of Children* (London: Hogarth Press, 1975–), p. 223; discussed in Ricardo E. Bernardi, "The Role of Paradigmatic Determinants in Psychoanalytic Understanding," *International Journal of Psycho-Analysis* 70 (1989), 346.

67 Bernardi does not specify these implications, but the image suggests that the analysand, identified with the kid in the clock-face, is yearning for extra time to bleat (Bernardi, "The Role of Paradigmatic Determinants," p. 346; see also Johnson, *The Wolf Man's Burden*, p. 8).

68 SE 17:5, 17:53–54; Johnson, *The Wolf Man's Burden*, pp. 28–29; Mahony, *Cries of the Wolf Man,* p. 9; Davis, *Drawing the Dream of the Wolves*, pp. 27–28.

69 Nicolas Abraham and Maria Torok, *The Shell and the Kernel* (1978), ed. and trans. Nicholas T. Rand (Chicago: University of Chicago Press, 1994).

70 *Ibid.*, pp. 132, 105n, 159.

71 Johnson, *The Wolf Man's Burden*, p. 16.

72 Paul C. Vitz, in *Sigmund Freud's Christian Unconscious* (New York: Guilford Press, 1988), pp. 2, 139–40, offers the intriguing speculation that Freud acquired from his first nanny, a Czeck Catholic called Resi (short for Theresa, the name of the Wolf Man's wife), a strong unconscious attraction to Christianity, despite his vociferous atheism. For this reason he either recognized in or projected onto the Wolf Man his own identification with Christ.

73 Bernardi, "The Role of Paradigmatic Determinants," p. 351.

74 Abraham and Torok connect these wolves to the patient's verbal and bowel inhibitions: "The 'wolves' of his desire crowd to his lips (like a diarrhoea that comes 'wolfing' out); the words are ready to cross the limiting wall … they throng in a rush to break the obstacle, the anal hymen that can hardly contain them" (*The Wolf Man's Magic Word*, p. 12).

75 Woolf, *To the Lighthouse: The Original Holograph Draft*, ed. Susan Dick (London: Hogarth Press, 1983), Appendix A, p. 48.

76 The phrase comes from the passage where Mrs. Ramsay conceals the boar's skull in the children's bedroom with her shawl: "the ruin was veiled" (*TL* 28).

77 Lacan uses the term "phallic ghost" with reference to the death's head in Holbein's painting *The Ambassadors*, which is discussed below in Chapter 4. See Jacques Lacan, *The Four Fundamental Concepts*, p. 88.

78 Melanie Klein introduces the concept of "projective identification" in "Notes on some schizoid mechanisms," *International Journal of Psychoanalysis* 27 (1946), 99–110. See also Hannah Segal, *An Introduction to the Work of Melanie Klein* (New York, Basic Books, 1974), pp. 27–28.

79 These and other references to sandwiches provide a comic counterpoint to the narrative structure, in which two scenes are sandwiched around a central gap, like an old-fashioned British sandwich with the stingiest of fillings in the middle. Many further sandwiches are crossed out in the manuscript: see Dick, ed., *To the Lighthouse: The Original Holograph Draft*, pp. 358–59.

80 Here it is worth noting that the harpies of Greek mythology are female creatures, notorious for stealing food, whose name means "that which snatches." The harpies have often been confused with the Sirens, the birdwomen whose enchanting song entices sailors to destruction in the *Odyssey*.

81 In her diary Woolf wonders, "Could I do it in a parenthesis? so that one had the sense of reading the two things at the same time?" (*Diary* 3:106)

82 Christine Froula, in *Virginia Woolf and the Bloomsbury Avant-Garde* (New York: Columbia, 2005), p. 139, points out that Lily's moving of the tree to the middle of the canvas corresponds to Woolf's moving of Lily to the center of the book's design: "Lily sidles belatedly into the draft as 'Miss Sophie Briscoe,'" but gradually "morphs into the aspiring painter."

83 Laura Marcus, *Virginia Woolf* (1997; Tavistock: Northcote House, 2004), p. 105.

84 Douglas Mao, in *Solid Objects: Modernism and the Test of Production* (Princeton University Press, 1998), p. 59, points out that Woolf in "Time Passes" has to reverse "the habit, common to both novelists and novel readers, of referring descriptions of the nonhuman world either to characters' psychology or to what Barthes would term *l'effet du réel* …"

85 Daniel Ferrer, *Virginia Woolf and the Madness of Language*, trans. Geoffrey Bennington and Rachel Bowlby (London: Routledge, 1990), p. 53.

86 The term "stroke" associates Mrs. Ramsay's third stroke of the Lighthouse beam with the "stroke" of the clock (*TL* 123), the "quick decisive stroke" of Lily's paintbrush" (*TL* 130), the image of Mr. Ramsay as a fierce sudden black-winged harpy "that struck and struck at you" (*TL* 151), and the sudden death (by stroke?) of Mrs. Ramsay. Mary Jacobus ("'The Third Stroke': Reading Woolf with Freud," in Rachel Bowlby, ed., *Virginia Woolf* [London: Longman, 1992], p. 118), argues that Lily "abjects" the mother-figure in order to establish subjectivity and signification. See also Lois Cucullu, *Expert Modernists, Matricide, and Modern Culture* (Basingstoke: Palgrave Macmillan, 2004), pp. 86–90.

87 Abraham and Torok (pp. 49–54 and *passim*) argue that the Wolf Man's analyses involve a kind of dance between three positions, designated as father,
"Tierka," and "Stanko," of which the latter two are "cryptonyms" of brother
and sister respectively. None of these roles is identical to the historical
Pankejeff, who alternates between these three positions.

88 See Freud, "Character and Anal Eroticm" (1908), SE 9:167–76; and "On
Transformations of Instinct as Exemplified in Anal Eroticism" (1917), SE
17:125–34.

89 Here is the full text of the dream: "The patient's father, in the dream a professor, resembling, however, a begging musician known to the patient, sits
at a table and warns the others present not to talk about financial matters
before the patient, because of his tendency to speculate. His father's nose is
long and hooked, causing the patient to wonder at its change" (Gardiner,
286). In this dream the patient's father is conflated with Freud the "professor." Yet this professor's resemblance to a "begging musician" suggests that
he represents a projection of the dreamer's own indebtedness to Freud.

90 Mahony, *Cries of the Wolf Man*, p. 65.

91 *MB* 79; see letter to Ethel Smyth, 16 October 1930, *Letters* 4:231.

92 "The wordless are the happy," Woolf writes wistfully in a late diary entry
(5 September 1940), a sentiment that recalls her envy of the wordlessness of
animals in *Flush*: "Not a single one of [Flush's] myriad sensations ever sub-
mitted itself to the deformity of words" (*Diary* 5:315; *Flush*, p. 87).

93 In "The Mark on the Wall" the mark takes the place of characters' life-
stories. Similarly, the marks imprinted by the primal scene give rise to the
Wolf Man's dreams and paintings. One such mark is the wolf; another is
the V, interpreted by Freud as a reversal of the mother's posture in the primal scene, which also accounts for the Wolf Man's censorship of the W in
"Espe." By a curious coincidence V and W are the initials of Virginia Woolf,
and the V in *To the Lighthouse* also provides the "mark" of Mrs. Ramsay: the
"wedge-shaped core of darkness" associated with her inner life, the triangu-
lar shadow that she casts over the threshold, and the purple triangle with
which she is portrayed in Lily's painting (*TL* 52, 164).

94 "*La troisième ne dit rien*," Freud quotes from Offenbach's operetta *La belle
Hélène* (SE 12:294–95); the third woman who says nothing, in mythology
and literature, represents the death-drive, which Freud defines as the "power
in mental life which we call the instinct of aggression or of destruction
according to its aims, and which we trace back to the original death instinct
of living matter" (SE 23:243).

5 THE DARKENED BLIND: JOYCE, GIDE, LARSEN,
AND THE MODERNIST SHORT STORY

1 James Elkins, *The Object Stares Back* (San Diego: Harcourt, Inc., 1996), pp.
201–05.

2 Roy Gottfried, *Joyce's Iritis and the Irritated Text: The Dis-Lexic "Ulysses"* (Gainesville: University of Florida Press, 1995).

3 Jorge Luis Borges, "Blindness" (1977) in *Selected Non-Fictions*, ed. Eliot Weinberger, trans. Esther Allen, Suzanne Jill Levine, and Eliot Weinberger (New York: Viking, 1999), p. 481. See also Borges's story "His End and his Beginning" (*In Praise of Darkness*, trans. Norman Thomas di Giovanni [New York: E. P. Dutton and Co., 1974], pp. 116–19), in which the nameless protagonist wakes up from a long sleep after death to discover that the world has dimmed: "Letters swarmed and throbbed, faces – familiar faces – began to blur, and men and objects kept drifting away from him … Even the fingers of his own hands were shadows … He belonged to another world now … Gradually, this world came to enclose him." At first he is terrified of his nightmares, devoid of "shapes or sounds or colours," until he realizes that these are not his dreams but his reality: "a reality beyond silence or sight and so, beyond memory." In the end he overcomes his fear of shadows, understanding that their "horror lay in their utter newness and splendour. He had attained grace; from the moment of his death he had been in heaven." This parable implies that the artist is an Orpheus who must consent to blindness, to the death of "all his perceptions, memories, and hopes," in order to find grace in the darkness.

4 Elizabeth Bowen, Vassar College notebooks, [Notes for lectures at Vassar College on the short story], Bowen Collection, Harry Ransom Humanities Research Center, University of Texas at Austin.

5 Bowen, "Truth and Fiction" (1956), in *Afterthought: Pieces about Writing* (London: Longmans, Green, 1962), p. 134.

6 Elizabeth Bowen, *The Mulberry Tree: Writings of Elizabeth Bowen*, ed. Hermione Lee (London: Virago, 1986), p. 276.

7 Sean O'Faolain, "The Secret of the Short Story," *United Nations World* 3 (March 1949), 37–38; quoted in Charles E. May, ed., *Short Story Theories* (Columbus: Ohio University Press, 1976), p. 245.

8 Frank O'Connor, "The Lonely Voice," rpt. in Charles E. May, ed., *Short Story Theories*, pp. 85–87.

9 See Oscar Wilde, "The Sphinx Without a Secret: An Etching" (1891), in *The Complete Works of Oscar Wilde* (London: Collins, 1966), p. 217. Like Poe's "The Purloined Letter" (1845), "The Sphinx without a Secret" could be understood as an allegory of reading the short story, and it is telling that both these stories concern failures of vision, specifically the inability to see the obvious. In Wilde's story, Lord Murchison has tried to read too much into the "darkened blind" presented by his fiancée, "a woman with a mania for mystery," "a passion for secrecy," who was prone to disappear for no good reason. After her death, Murchison attempts to penetrate the secret of her furtive habits, luring the reader up the same blind alley, since Wilde's title has already announced the secret that there is no secret to reveal.

10 Edgar Allan Poe, review of *Twice-Told Tales*, in May, *Short Story Theories*, p. 47.

11 In "Howe's Masquerade," for example, the double is "cloaked," as in Poe's own story "William Wilson" – a coincidence that Poe regards as evidence of plagiarism (whether intentional or blind), thereby implying that Hawthorne's story is the cloaked double of his own. *Ibid.*, p. 50. The full text of Poe's review is available at http://xroads.virginia.edu/~HYPER/poe/hawthorne.html

12 Diego Gambetta, *The Sicilian Mafia* (Cambridge, MA: Harvard University Press, 1993), p. 134.

13 Edith Wharton, *The Writing of Fiction* (London: Charles Scribner's Sons, 1925), p. 47.

14 Dominic Head, *The Modernist Short Story: A Study of Theory and Practice* (Cambridge University Press, 1992), p. 1.

15 Elizabeth Bowen, Vassar College notebooks.

16 Bowen reworks this Flaubertian theme in her story "The Parrot" (1925).

17 Arthur Schnitzler, "Blind Geronimo and his Brother," in *Night Games and Other Stories and Novellas*, trans. Margret Schaefer (Chicago: Ivan R. Dee, 2002), pp. 101–24.

18 Joseph Conrad, *The End of the Tether*, in *Tales of Land and Sea*, intro. William McFee (Garden City, NY: Hanover House, 1953), pp. 610, 607.

19 In an astute discussion of "The End of the Tether," Andrew Bennett argues that "Conrad's writing seeks to reveal the experience of losing sight," an experience that caused the author to give up seafaring. Thus Conrad's career as a writer was launched by his inability to see the sea (Andrew Bennett, "Conrad's Blindness and the Long Short Story," *Oxford Literary Review* 26 [2004] 94). Although Conrad famously declared that the purpose of literature was "to make you *see*," his fiction constantly grapples with the threat of blindness (Conrad, Preface to *The Nigger of the "Narcissus,"* ed. Robert Kimbrough (New York: Norton, 1979), p. 147). "Do you see the story? Do you see anything?" Marlow demands of his listeners in *Heart of Darkness* (1899). "Of course," he adds, "you fellows see more than I could then. You see me …" So he says, but the external narrator recalls that "it had become so pitch black that we listeners could hardly see each other." Nor can they see Marlow: "for a long time he, sitting apart, had been no more to us than a voice" (Joseph Conrad, *Heart of Darkness*, ed. Robert Kimbrough [New York: Norton, 1988], p. 30).

20 Herman Melville, *Billy Budd* (written between 1888 and 1891; published posthumously 1924), in *Tales, Poems, and Other Writings*, ed. John Bryant (New York: Random House, 2002), p. 485; *Benito Cereno* (1856), *ibid.*, pp. 252, 256. At the end of the novel, Delano, "more and more astonished and pained" by Cereno's deathly melancholy, cries:
"You are saved … you are saved; what has cast such a shadow upon you?"
"The negro."
There was silence, while the moody man sat, slowly and unconsciously gathering his mantle about him, as if it were a pall. (p. 256)
A few months later, Cereno dies, unable to recover from the "shadow."

21 Oliver Sacks, "To See and Not See," in *An Anthropologist on Mars* (New York: Knopf, 1995), pp. 108–52. An inferior film based on this case-history, *At First Sight*, starring Val Kilmer and Mira Sorvino, directed by Irwin Winkler, was released in 1999. See also Wilkie Collins, *Poor Miss Finch* (1872), ed. Catherine Peters (Oxford University Press, 2000), pp. 105ff.

22 Étienne Bonnet de Condillac, *Traité des sensations* (1754). See also Marjolein Degenaar, *Molyneux's Problem: Three Centuries of Discussion on the Perception of Forms*, trans. Michael J. Collins (Dordrecht: Kluwer Academic Publishers, 1996).

23 Denis Diderot, "Letter on the Blind for the Use of Those who See," in *Diderot's Early Philosophical Works*, ed. Margaret Jourdain (Chicago: Open Court, 1916), p. 77.

24 William R. Paulson, *Enlightenment, Romanticism, and the Blind in France* (Princeton University Press, 1987), p. 5. See also Moshe Barasch, *Blindness: The History of a Mental Image in Western Thought* (London: Routledge, 2001), p. 12: "Other maimed people were sometimes also believed to be guilty of a crime, but only the guilt of the blind is derived from an encounter with the divine."

25 My translation: the original gives "un être incertain," "une masse involuntaire," "ce paquet de chair sans âme." André Gide, *La symphonie pastorale* (1919; Paris: Gallimard, 1925), pp. 15, 18. See also Gide, "The Pastoral Symphony," in *Two Symphonies: Isabelle and The Pastoral Symphony*, trans. Dorothy Bussy (1931; New York: Random House, 1977), pp. 144, 146. Henceforth all quotations from this work are cited by the page number of the French edition followed by the English translation.

26 My translation: the original gives "mensonge que l'art de Dickens s'évertue à faire passer pour pieux, mais dont, Dieux merci! je n'aurai pas user avec Gertrude." For Gide's interest in Dickens's account of Laura Bridgeman, see Alan Sheridan, *André Gide: A Life in the Present* (London: Penguin, 1998), p. 332; see also Elizabeth Gitter, *The Imprisoned Guest: Samuel Howe and Laura Bridgeman, the Original Deaf–Blind Girl* (New York: Farrar Strauss Giroux, 2001).

27 In the original: "On ne m'a pas été donné d'être aveugle."

28 In Bussy's translation, "I would have wept, but I felt my heart more arid than the desert."

29 In Bussy's translation: "I will take advantage of the leisure this enforced confinement affords me …"

30 "La neige qui n'a pas cessé de tomber depuis trois jours, bloque les routes."

31 See *The Journals of André Gide*, trans. Justin O'Brien, vol. II (London: Secker and Warburg, 1948), pp. 224, 235.

32 Jacques Derrida, *Memoirs of the Blind: The Self-Portrait and Other Ruins* (1990), trans. Pascale-Anne Brault and Michael Naas (Chicago: University of Chicago Press, 1993), p. 44.

33 See Naomi Segal, *André Gide: Pederasty and Pedagogy* (Oxford: Clarendon Press, 1998), esp. pp. 326–31.

34 Maurice Blanchot, *The Space of Literature*, trans. Ann Smock (Lincoln: University of Nebraska Press, 1982); quoted in Alessandro Carrera, "Blanchot's Gaze and Orpheus's Singing: Seeing and Listening in Poetic Inspiration," in Wilhelm S. Wurzer, ed., *Panorama: Philosophies of the Visible* (London: Continuum, 1992), p. 45.

35 Elizabeth Bowen, Vassar College Notebooks. Poe sets up a similar structure in "The House of Usher" and other tales to implicate the act of reading in the violation of the house.

36 Simon Stevenson, "The Anorthoscopic Short Story," *Oxford Literary Review* 26 (2004), 84.

37 *Ibid.*

38 See also Margot Norris, "Narration under a Blindfold: Reading the 'Patch' of 'Clay,'" in *Joyce's Web: The Social Unraveling of Modernism* (Austin: University of Texas Press, 1992), pp. 113–98, for an extended discussion of the reader's infection by the blindness of the story.

39 Jean-Michel Rabaté, "Silence in *Dubliners*," in *James Joyce: New Perspectives*, ed. Colin MacCabe (Brighton: Harvester, 1982), p. 53. My reading of *Dubliners* is indebted to Rabaté's groundbreaking essay.

40 Letter to Grant Richards, 5 May 1906: *SL* 83.

41 Freud rejects the neologism "scotomization" for this process, preferring his own coinage "disavowal" (*Verleugnung*), but this term fails to capture the ocularity of fetishism. The term "scotoma," meaning a blind spot in the field of vision, comes closer to describing the selective blindness constitutive of fetishism. See Freud, "Fetishism" (1927), SE 21:153.

42 Margot Norris, "Gambling With Gambles in 'Two Gallants,'" in *Suspicious Readings of Joyce's Dubliners* (Philadelphia: University of Philadelphia Press, 2003), p. 82.

43 See, *inter alia*, Trevor L. Williams, "No cheer for the 'gratefully oppressed' in Joyce's *Dubliners*," *Style* 25:30 (1991), 416–39, which argues that Corley's relationship vis-à-vis the slavey is "precisely analogous to the political relation between imperialist power and colonial dependency … so that 'Two Gallants' reproduces at a deeply internalized level the relationship between Britain and Ireland."

44 See Primo Levi, *If This is a Man* (1947/1958), trans. Stuart Woolf (London: Vintage, 1996).

45 Norris, *Suspicious Readings*, pp. 89–90 and *passim*.

46 In this letter to Grant Richards, Joyce goes on to recommend that the printer read the passage in Gugliamo Ferrero's *Il Militarismo* (1898) which "examines the moral code of the soldier and (incidentally) of the gallant. But it would be useless for I am sure that in his heart of hearts he is a militarist." Giorgio Melchiori translates this passage from Ferrero as follows: "these officers, being short of money to pay for the dissolute lives they were leading, tried, nearly all of them, to become the lovers of rich middle-class ladies, getting money out of them as a recompense for the honour conferred upon those ladies by condescending to make them their mistresses": see Giorgio

Melchiori, "The Genesis of *Ulysses*," in Mechiori, ed., *Joyce in Rome: The Genesis of "Ulysses"* (Roma: Bulzoni Editore, 1984), p. 42, where Melchiori also points out the striking physical resemblance between Joyce and Ferrero. In a letter to Stanislaus Joyce of 11 February 1907, Joyce acknowledges that Ferrero "gave" him "Two Gallants" (*L* 2:212). Robert Spoo has written on this connection in "'Una Piccola Nuvoletta': Ferrero's *Young Europe* and Joyce's Mature *Dubliners* Stories," *James Joyce Quarterly* 24:4 (1987), 401–11. See also Dominic Manganiello, *Joyce's Politics* (London: Routledge & Kegan Paul, 1980), pp. 43–66.

47 Donald Gifford, *Joyce Annotated: Notes for "Dubliners" and "A Portrait of the Artist as a Young Man"* (Berkeley, CA: University of California Press, 1982), p. 62.

48 Freud SE 21:153; Marx, "The Fetishism of the Commodity and its Secret," in *Capital*, vol. i, p. 165.

49 Marilyn Reizbaum points out that Joyce's narrator indulges in an act of simony, trafficking in the language of sacred things, in the mock-apocalyse in which the gold coin is revealed. The words "disciple" and "gold coin," presented in tandem, allude to the parable in Luke 19, where Jesus tells the story of the rich man who entrusts his ten servants with ten gold coins. Those who invest their respective coins for interest are rewarded, but the servant who has kept his coin "laid up in a napkin" is forced to relinquish it to "him that hath ten pounds." In this parable, prudence is presented as sinful because the cautious servant is sticking to the status quo (i.e. the Pharisees), resisting the new religion that will take possession through dissemination. Instead, the prophet and the profit motive must be served by multiplying the gold coins that represent the word or gospel. In Corley's case, as in the cagey servant's, it is clear that the gold coin will have no issue – the buck stops here.

50 Jean Baudrillard, *For a Critique of the Economy of the Sign*, trans. Charles Levin (St. Lewis: Telos Press, 1981), p. 92.

51 Adam Phillips, *Monogamy* (London: Faber, 1996), p. 94.

52 Nathaniel Small makes this point in "The Ineluctable Modality of the Triangle: Shaping Desire in Joyce," an unpublished paper written for my course on Irish Modernism at Northwestern University in 2006. See also Mikkel Borch-Jacobsen, *The Freudian Subject*, trans. Catherine Porter (Stanford University Press, 1982), in which he argues that there is no "essential bond between desire and its object," and that "the desire for an object is a desire-effect; it is *induced*, or at least secondary, with respect to the imitation – the mimesis – of the desire of others. In other words, desire is mimetic before it is anything else" (p. 26 and *passim*).

53 See René Girard, *Deceit, Desire and the Novel: Self and Other in Literary Structure* (1961), trans. Yvonne Freccero (1965; Baltimore, MD: Johns Hopkins University Press, 1976).

54 Joyce, *Poems and "Exiles,"* ed. J.C.C. Mays (London: Penguin Books, 1992), p. 200.

55 For this discussion of "smut" see Freud, *Jokes and Their Relation to the Unconscious* (1905), SE 7:97–102.

56 Garry M. Leonard, *Reading "Dubliners" Again: A Lacanian Perspective* (Syracuse University Press, 1993), p. 130.

57 Mladen Dolar, *A Voice and Nothing More* (Cambridge, MA: MIT Press, 2006), p. 69.

58 This is the first sentence of *The Pastoral Symphony*. The snow in *Dubliners* is also reminiscent of the white-out at the end of Poe's *The Narrative of Arthur Gordon Pym*, as John Limon pointed out to me. I am very grateful to Limon for his astute criticisms of this chapter; his contributions are too numerous to itemize.

59 Samuel Beckett, "A Wet Night" in *More Pricks than Kicks* (1934; New York: Grove Press, 1972), pp. 82–83.

60 Maurice Merleau-Ponty, *The Visible and the Invisible*, trans. Alphonso Lingis, ed. Claude Lefort (Evanston, IL: Northwestern University Press, 1968), p. 247.

61 Derrida, *Memoirs of the Blind*, pp. 41–45.

62 Aristotle, *On Sense and the Sensible*, trans. J. I. Beare, Section 1, Part 3: http://classics.mit.edu/Aristotle/sense.1.1.html

63 Draft of the "Proteus" episode of *Ulysses* (1917), ed. Jorn Barger, www.robotwisdom.com/jaj/ulysses/proteus0.html

64 Aristotle, *On Sense and the Sensible*, Section 1, Part 1.

65 Joyce Carol Oates explores a similar conundrum in her story "Blind," in which the heroine searches vainly for a light, mistaking her own blindness for a power failure. See Joyce Carol Oates, "Blind," in *Haunted: Tales of the Grotesque* (New York: Dutton, 1994), pp. 232–46.

66 See Derrida, *The Truth in Painting* (1978), trans. Geoff Bennington and Ian McLeod (Chicago: University of Chicago Press, 1987); Ludwig Nal, "Visibility, 'Bild,' and 'Einbildungskraft': Derrida, Barthes, Levinas," in Wilhelm S. Wurser, ed., *Panorama: Philosophies of the Visible* (New York and London: Continuum, 2002), p. 25.

67 Ralph Ellison, *Invisible Man* (1952; New York: Random House, 1995), p. 3.

68 Charles W. Mills, *Blackness Visible* (Ithaca, NY: Cornell University Press, 1998), p. xiii.

69 See Patricia J. Williams, *Seeing a Color-Blind Future: The Paradox of Race* (New York: Noonday Press, 1998), p. 3.

70 See Judith Butler, "Passing, Queering: Nella Larsen's Psychoanalytic Challenge," in *Bodies that Matter: On the Discursive Limits of Sex* (New York: Routledge, 1993), pp. 167–86.

71 Nella Larsen's "Sanctuary," the letter from Marion Boyd pointing out the story's "striking similarity" to "Mrs. Adis," together with responses from Larsen and her editors, and the text of Sheila Kaye-Smith's "Mrs. Adis," are all collected in *Revolutionary Tales: African American Women's Short Stories, from the First Story to the Present*, ed. Bill Mullen (New York: Dell, 1995), pp. 140–56.

72 *Ibid.*, pp. 148–49.

73 *Ibid.*, p. 141.

74 Emmanuel Levinas, "The Transcendence of Words," in Seán Hand, *The Levinas Reader* (Oxford: Blackwell, 1989), p. 147.

75 See Martin Jay, *Downcast Eyes: The Denigration of Vision in Twentieth-Century French Thought* (Berkeley: University of California Press, 1993).

6 THE NAME AND THE SCAR: IDENTITY IN *THE ODYSSEY*
AND *A PORTRAIT OF THE ARTIST AS A YOUNG MAN*

1   Ezra Pound, *The Cantos* (London: Faber & Faber, 1975), pp. 426–27.

2   See Guy Davenport, "Pound and Frobenius," in *Motive and Method in the Cantos*, ed. Lewis Leary (New York: Columbia University Press, 1954), p. 49.

3   See *FW* 296n4: "Hasitatense?" See also *FW* 97:26, etc. These puns allude to Piggott's forged letter, supposedly written by Parnell, condoning the Phoenix Park murders of 1882; the forger gave himself away by misspelling "hesitancy."

4   Freud, "Family Romances" (1909), SE 9:232.

5   See Freud, *Moses and Monotheism* (1939), SE 23:114.

6   See Richard Lattimore, Introduction to *The Odyssey of Homer*, O 11.

7   The Greek original is less explicit, but the close conjunction of scar and story justifies Lattimore's translation.

8   Erich Auerbach, *Mimesis: The Representation of Reality in Western Literature* (1946), trans. Willard R. Trask (Princeton University Press, 1953), p. 2.

9   In Stephen's words, "to express, to press out again, from the gross earth … an image of the beauty we have come to understand – that is art" (*P* 207).

10 "A Portrait of the Artist" (1904), in Robert Scholes and Richard M. Kain, eds., *The Workshop of Dedalus: James Joyce and the Materials for 'A Portrait of the Artist as a Young Man'* (Evanston, IL: Northwestern University Press, 1965), pp. 60–68; Joyce, *Stephen Hero*, ed. Theodore Spencer, John J. Slocum, and Herbert Cahoon (New York: New Directions, 1963).

11 Gertrude Stein, "What are Master-Pieces and Why are There so Few of Them," in *Look at Me Now and Here I Am*, ed. Patricia Meyerowitz (Harmondsworth: Penguin, 1984), p. 149.

12 Wordsworth, *The Prelude* (1805), Book XI, lines 278–315.

13 Unsigned review of *A Portrait of the Artist as a Young Man*, *New Age* (12 July 1917), Deming 1:110.

14 Joyce told Grant Richards, the publisher of *Dubliners*, that quotation marks were an "eyesore" that gave "an impression of unreality": see *JJ* 353.

15 Stein, "Composition as Explanation," in *Look at Me Now*, p. 23.

16 Freud, *Civilization and its Discontents* (1930), SE 21:99–100n, 106n.

17 Harold Bloom, *A Map of Misreading* (New York: Oxford University Press, 1975).

18 Seamus Deane, Introduction to Joyce, *A Portrait of the Artist as a Young Man* (Harmondsworth: Penguin, 2000), p. xxxviii.

19 Epiphany 19 (1902), in Scholes and Kain, eds., *The Workshop of Dedalus*, p. 29.

20 See Roland Barthes, *S/Z*, trans. Richard Miller (New York: Hill and Wang, 1975), p. 191.

21 Luke Thurston, "Writing the Symptom: Lacan's Joycean Knot," PhD thesis, University of Kent (1997); see also his discussion of the scene in the anatomy theatre in *James Joyce and the Problem of Psychoanalysis* (Cambridge University Press, 2004), pp. 155–57.

22 *Stephen Hero*, p. 211.

23 Catherine Millot, "On Epiphanies," in *James Joyce: The Augmented Ninth*, ed. Bernard Benstock (Syracuse, NY: Syracuse University Press, 1988), pp. 207–08.

24 For the literality of trauma, see Cathy Caruth, ed., *Trauma: Explorations in Memory* (Baltimore, MD: Johns Hopkins University Press, 1995), pp. 3–12.

25 Michèle Montrelay, "Inquiry into Femininity" (1977), trans. Rachel Bowlby, in Dana Breen, ed., *The Gender Conundrum* (London: Routledge, 1993), pp. 145–83; cited in Elizabeth Bronfen, *The Knotted Subject*, pp. 20–21.

7 SKINSCAPES IN *ULYSSES*

1 Joyce, "L'influenza letteraria universale del rinascimento" ("The Universal Literary Influence of the Renaissance"), written 1912 trans. Louis Berrone, in *James Joyce in Padua* (New York: Random House, 1977), p. 15. I am grateful to Steven Connor for alerting me to this text.

2 Frank Budgen, *James Joyce and the Making of "Ulysses"* (Oxford University Press, 1972), p. 21.

3 These schemata are reproduced in Jeri Johnson's edition of *Ulysses* (Oxford University Press, 1993), pp. 734–39.

4 See *"Ulysses": A Facsimile of Placards for Episodes 1–6*, ed. Michael Groden (New York: Garland, 1978), pp. 85, 90, 91, 180, 187, 199.

5 Paul Valéry, *L'idée fixe, ou Deux hommes à la mer* (1932), in *Oeuvres*, Pleiade edition, ed. Jean Hytier (Paris: Gallimard, 1960), 2:215.

6 See Didier Anzieu, *The Skin Ego* (1985), trans. Chris Turner (New Haven: Yale University Press, 1989), pp. 14–15.

7 See Marilyn Strathern, "The Self in Self-Decoration," *Oceania* 49 (1979), 241–57.

8 Valéry, *L'idée fixe*, p. 216.

9 Anzieu, *Skin Ego*, p. 9.

10 See Ashley Montagu, *Touching: The Human Significance of the Skin* (New York: Columbia, 1971), pp. 5–25.

11 See Esther Bick, "The Experience of the Skin in Early Object-Relations" (1967), in *Melanie Klein Today*, vol. 1 (London: Routledge, 1988), pp. 184–87.

12 Frantz Fanon, *Black Skin, White Masks*, trans. Charles Lam Markmann (New York: Grove, 1967), p. 112.

13 *Ibid.*, p. 109.

14 Sylvia Plath, "Tulips," discussed by Barrie M. Biven, "The Role of Skin in Normal and Abnormal Development with a Note on the Poet Sylvia Plath," *International Review of Psychoanalysis* 9 (1982), 217.

15 See Leo Bersani and Ulysse Dutoit's discussion of *How It Is* in *Arts of Impoverishment* (Cambridge, MA: Harvard University Press, 1993), pp. 55–65.

16 Anzieu, *Skin Ego*, pp. 31–46; Victor V. Weizsächer, "Dreams in So-Called Endogenic *Magersucht* (Anorexia)," in *Evolution of Psychoanalytic Concepts: Anorexia Nervosa: A Paradigm*, ed. M. Ralph Kaufman *et al.* (London: Hogarth Press, 1964), pp. 189–90.

17 Plath, "Face Lift," cited by Biven, "The Role of Skin," p. 218.

18 Alfred Gell, *Wrapping in Images: Tattooing in Polynesia* (Oxford: Clarendon Press, 1993), p. 24.

19 See Andrew Strathern, "Why is Shame on the Skin?" *Ethnology* 14 (1975), 347–56.

20 Thomas Carlyle, *Sartor Resartus* (1833–34), ed. Kerry McSweeney and Peter Sabor (Oxford University Press, 1987), p. 48. Recent anthropological research supports Carlyle's insight: Terence Turner, in an essay on "The Social Skin," in *Not Work Alone: A Cross-Cultural View of Activities Superfluous to Survival*, ed. Jeremy Cherfas and Roger Lewin (London: Temple Smith, 1980), pp. 136–37, argues that the "imposition of a standardized symbolic form upon the body, as a symbol or 'objective correlative' of the social self, invariably becomes a serious business for all societies."

21 Emmanuel Levinas, *Ethics and Infinity: Conversations with Philippe Nemo* (1982), trans. Richard A. Cohen (Pittsburgh: Duquesnes University Press, 1985), p. 86; and Levinas, "Language and Proximity," in *Collected Philosophical Papers*, trans. Alphonso Lingis (Dordrecht: Marinus Nijhoff Publishers, 1987), pp. 120–21.

22 Levinas's conception of skin and proximity derives from Merleau-Ponty's conception of the double-sided "flesh" of the world. Merleau-Ponty uses touch – the skin-sense – to rethink the subject's relation to the world as one of touching and being touched at the same time. Vision, on the contrary, is traditionally misconstrued as a relationship of distance rather than proximity, as if the seeing subject were untouched by the world that s/he surveys. In fact, phenomenology could be seen as the philosophy of skin, since its preoccupation with the epidermis goes back at least as far as Nietzsche and persists into deconstruction: see Eve Kosofsky Sedgwick on Nietzsche's "thematics … of the skin," in *Epistemology of the Closet* (Berkeley: University of California Press, 1990), p. 171. Derrida's terminology abounds with images of pellicular surfaces, such as skins, membranes, films, crusts, veils, folds, envelopes, tympanums, parchments, and phylacteries. Some of these terms are adopted from Merleau-Ponty, such as "invagination," which Derrida describes as "the inward refolding of *la gaine* [the sheath, girdle], the inverted reapplication of the outer edge to the inside of a form where the outside then

opens a pocket" ("Living On," trans. James Hulbert, in Harold Bloom *et al.*, eds., *Deconstruction and Criticism* [New York: Continuum, 1979], p. 97). In addition, Derrida conceives of the "hymen" as a skin that functions as both barrier and copula, separation and connection. In an essay on Mallarmé, "The Double Session," Derrida defines the "hymen" as "an operation that *both* sows confusion *between* opposites *and* stands *between* opposites" (*Dissemination*, trans. Barbara Johnson [Chicago: University of Chicago Press, 1983], p. 222). In this sense the Derridaen hymen corresponds to the Joycean navel, since both unite the contradictory ideas of break and bridge.

23 Cited by Joseph O'Brien in *"Dear, Dirty Dublin": A City in Distress, 1899–1916* (Berkeley: University of California Press, 1982), pp. 110–12, 118.

24 Cited by James Delaney, *James Joyce's Odyssey: A Guide to the Dublin of "Ulysses"* (London: Hodder and Stoughton, 1981), p. 50.

25 See Barbara Maria Stafford, *Body Criticism: Imaging the Unseen in Enlightenment Art and Medicine* (Cambridge, MA: MIT Press, 1991), pp. 281–83.

26 See Daniel Pick, *Faces of Degeneration: A European Disorder, c. 1848–1918* (Cambridge University Press, 1989), p. 117.

27 Max Nordau, *Degeneration* (London: Heinemann, 1913), p. 117.

28 J. B. Lyons, *James Joyce and Medicine* (Dublin: Dolmen Press, 1973), p. 29.

29 Joshua Reynolds, *Discourses on Art*, ed. Robert Wark (San Marino, CA: Huntingdon Library, 1959), p. 44; William Blake, *Complete Writings*, ed. Geoffrey Keynes (London: Oxford University Press, 1966), cited by Stafford, *Body Criticism*, p. 318.

30 Stafford, *ibid.*

31 Cited by Harry Levin, *The Gates of Horn: A Study of Five French Realists* (New York: Oxford University Press, 1963), p. 186.

32 William Thayer, "The New Story-Tellers and the Doom of Realism," *Forum* 18 (December 1894), 470–80; reprinted in *Realism and Romanticism in Fiction: An Approach to the Novel*, ed. Eugene Current-García and Walton R. Patrick (Chicago: Scott, Foresman and Co., 1962), pp. 157–58.

33 Emile Zola, *Germinal*, trans. Leonard Tancock (London: Everyman, 1991), pp. 121, 162, 189.

34 Charles Baudelaire, "In Praise of Make-Up" (1863), in *The Painter of Modern Life and Other Essays*, trans. Jonathan Mayne (New York: Da Capo Press, 1964), p. 33.

35 Max Beerbohm, "A Defence of Cosmetics," in *Aesthetes and Decadents of the 1890s: An Anthology of British Poetry and Prose*, ed. Karl Beckson (Chicago: Academy Chicago Publishers, 1981), pp. 52–53.

36 *Leah, the Forsaken*, trans. Augustin Daly, from Salomon Hermann Mosenthal's *Deborah* (1850) (London and New York: Samuel French, n.d.), p. 25.

37 Compare the recognition scene in Homer's *Odyssey*, discussed in the previous chapter, in which Eurycleia recognizes Odysseus's scar with her massaging fingertips, rather than her eyes. In *Leah, the Forsaken*, hearing also

plays a part in the identification, since Abraham recognizes Nathan's father through the voice as well as the facial contours of the son.

38 F. Scott Fitzgerald, *Tender is the Night* (New York: Macmillan, 1982), pp. 183, 240–41.

39 Ernest Jones, "A Psycho-Analytic Study of the Holy Ghost Concept," *Essays in Applied Psychoanalysis*, vol. II: *Essays in Folklore, Anthropology and Religion* (London: Hogarth, 1951), p. 368.

AFTERWORD

1 See Trotter, "e-modernism: Telephony in British Fiction 1925–1940," *Critical Quarterly* 51:1 (2009), 2. It would be misleading to suggest that this technology determined modern culture, without being determined by that culture in turn. Stephen's greeting to the imaginary operator – "Hello, Kinch here. Put me on to Edenville" – reveals that telephony depends on etiquette as much as electronics. In Trotter's words (*ibid.*, p. 2): "Telephony must be understood to include the salutation 'Hello' and the monthly billing cycle, as well as the wires and cables that connect one instrument to another."

2 Marc Shell, "The Family Pet," *Representations* 15 (1986), 124.

3 The best of these books is Margot Norris's *Beasts of the Modern Imagination* (1985), which was touched upon in Chapter 1. More recent contributions to this subject include Philip Armstrong, *What Animals Mean in the Fiction of Modernity* (New York: Routledge, 2008); Carrie Rohman, *Stalking the Subject: Modernism and the Animal* (New York: Columbia, 2009); and Anat Pick, *Creaturely Bodies*, forthcoming from Columbia University Press. For animals in modern theatre, see the special issue of *The Drama Review* 51:1 (2007) on *Animals and Performance*, ed. Una Chaudhuri. My essay "*Ulysses*: Changing into an Animal," *Field Day Review* 2 (2006), 75–93, discusses the role of pets and vermin in Joyce's *Ulysses*.

4 Darwin, *Charles Darwin's Natural Selection: Being the Second Part of his Big Species Book Written from 1856–1858*, ed. R. C. Stauffer (Cambridge University Press, 1987), p. 272. Joyce indirectly acknowledges a debt to Darwin in the Mime of the Mick, Nick and the Maggies section of *Finnegans Wake*, a parody of "naturel rejection" where the "Rainbow girls," devolving into birds, pipe "Charley, you're my darwing!" [*FW* 252:28].) See Paul Bowers, "'Charley, you're my darwing!' Sexual Selection in the Joycean Nursery," *Journal of Modern Literature* 32:4 (2009), 34–42.

Bibliography

Abel, Elizabeth. *Virginia Woolf and the Fictions of Psychoanalysis.* Chicago: University of Chicago Press, 1989.

Abraham, Nicholas, and Maria Torok. *The Shell and the Kernel.* 1978. Ed. and trans. Nicholas T. Rand. Chicago: University of Chicago Press, 1994.

The Wolf Man's Magic Word: A Cryptonomy. 1976. Trans. Nicholas Rand. Minneapolis: University of Minnesota Press, 1986.

Ackerknecht, Erwin H. "The History of the Discovery of the Vegetative (Autonomic) Nervous System." *Medical History* 18 (1974), 1–8.

Ackroyd, Peter. *T. S. Eliot.* Harmondsworth: Penguin, 1984.

Adams, Carole J., and Josephine Donovan, eds. *Animals and Women: Feminist Theoretical Explorations.* Durham, NC: Duke University Press, 1995.

Antonio, Diane. "Of Wolves and Women." In Carol J. Adams and Josephine Donovan, eds. *Animals and Women: Feminist Theoretical Explorations*, pp. 213–30.

Anzieu, Didier. *The Skin Ego.* 1985. Trans. Chris Turner. New Haven, CT: Yale University Press, 1989.

A Skin for Thought: Interviews with Gilbert Tarrab on Psychology and Psychoanalysis. 1986. London: Karnac Books, 1990.

Beckett et le psychanalyste. Paris: Mentha, 1992.

"Beckett and the Psychoanalyst." Trans. Thomas Cousineau. *Journal of Beckett Studies* 4 (1994), 23–34.

Ardis, Ann L. *Modernism and Cultural Conflict, 1880–1922.* Cambridge University Press, 2002.

Ardis, Ann L. and Bonnie Kime Scott, eds. *Virginia Woolf: Turning the Centuries; Selected Papers from the Ninth Annual Conference on Virginia Woolf.* New York: Pace University Press, 2002.

Armstrong, Philip. *What Animals Mean in the Fiction of Modernity.* New York: Routledge, 2008.

Armstrong, Tim. *Modernism, Technology, and the Body: A Cultural History.* Cambridge University Press, 1998.

Modernism: A Cultural History. Cambridge: Polity, 2005.

Attridge, Derek. *Joyce Effects: On Language, Theory, and History.* Cambridge University Press, 2000.

How to Read Joyce. London: Granta, 2007.

Attridge, Derek, ed. *James Joyce's "Ulysses": A Casebook*. Oxford University Press, 2004.

Attridge, Derek, and Daniel Ferrer, eds. *Post-Structuralist Joyce: Essays from the French*. Cambridge University Press, 1984.

Attridge, Derek, and Marjorie Howes, eds. *Semicolonial Joyce*. Cambridge University Press, 2000.

Auerbach, Erich. *Mimesis: The Representation of Reality in Western Literature*. 1946. Trans. Willard R. Trask. Princeton University Press, 1953.

Auerbach, Nina. *Our Vampires, Ourselves*. Chicago: University of Chicago Press, 1995.

Baker, Henry J., J. Russell Lindsey, and Steven H. Weisbroth, eds. *The Laboratory Rat*. 2 vols. American College of Laboratory Animal Medicine. New York: Academic Press, 1979–80.

Baker, Steve. *The Postmodern Animal*. London: Reaktion Books, 2000.

Bakhtin, Mikhail. *Rabelais and His World*. 1965. Trans. Hélène Iswolsky. Bloomington: Indiana University Press, 1984.

Banta, Martha. *Henry James and the Occult: The Great Extension*. Bloomington: Indiana University Press, 1972.

Taylored Lives: Narrative Productions in the Age of Taylor, Veblen, and Ford. Chicago: University of Chicago Press, 1993.

Barasche, Moshe. *Blindness: The History of a Mental Image in Western Thought*. New York: Routledge, 2001.

Barthes, Roland. *S/Z*. 1970. Trans. Richard Miller. New York: Hill and Wang, 1975.

Image – Music – Text. Trans. Stephen Heath. Glasgow: Fontana, 1977.

The Pleasure of the Text. 1973. Trans. Richard Howard. New York. Hill and Wang, 1975.

The Rustle of Language. 1984. Trans. Richard Howard. New York: Hill and Wang, 1986.

Bataille, Georges. *The Accursed Share: An Essay on General Economy*. 1967. Translated by Robert Hurley. 2 vols. New York: Zone Books, 1988–91.

Oeuvres complètes. Vol. 11. *Écrits posthumes, 1922–1940*. Paris: Gallimard, 1970.

Baudelaire, Charles. *The Painter of Modern Life and Other Essays*. Trans. Jonathan Mayne. New York: Da Capo Press, 1964.

Baudrillard, Jean. *For a Critique of the Economy of the Sign*. 1972. Trans. Charles Levin. St. Louis: Telos Press, 1981.

The Perfect Crime. 1995. Trans. Chris Turner. London: Verso, 1996.

Beckett, Samuel. *More Pricks than Kicks*. 1934. New York: Grove Press, 1972.

Watt. 1953. New York: Grove Press, 1959.

How It Is. 1961. Trans. Samuel Beckett. London: John Calder, 1964.

Beckett, Samuel *et al. Our Exagmination round his Factification for Incamination of Work in Progress*. 1929. 2nd edn. New York: New Directions, 1962.

Beer, Gillian. *Arguing with the Past: Essays in Narrative from Woolf to Sidney*. London: Routledge, 1989.

Beerbohm, Max. "A Defence of Cosmetics." First published as "The Pervasion of Rouge." 1894. In Karl Beckson, ed. *Aesthetes and Decadents of the 1890s: An Anthology of British Poetry and Prose*. Chicago: Academy Chicago Publishers, 1981. Also available at Project Gutenberg www.gutenberg.org/files/1859/1859-h/1859-h.htm

Beidler, Paul Gorman. *Frames in James: "The Tragic Muse," "The Turn of the Screw," "What Maisie Knew," and "The Ambassadors."* Victoria, BC: English Literary Studies, University of Victoria, 1993.

Beja, Morris, and David Norris, eds. *Joyce and the Hibernian Metropolis*. Columbus: Ohio State University Press, 1996.

Belford, Barbara. *Bram Stoker: A Biography of the Author of Dracula*. 1996. Cambridge, MA: Da Capo Press, 2002.

Bell, Ian, ed. *Henry James: Fiction as History*. London: Vision; Totowa, New Jersey: Barnes and Noble, 1984.

Bell, Quentin. *Virginia Woolf: A Biography*. 2 vols. London: Hogarth Press, 1972.

Bennett, Andrew. "Conrad's Blindness and the Long Short Story." *Oxford Literary Review* 26 (2004), 79–100.

Benstock, Bernard. "The Gnomonics of *Dubliners*." *Modern Fiction Studies* 34 (1988), 519–39.

Benstock, Bernard, ed. *James Joyce: The Augmented Ninth*. Syracuse University Press, 1988.

Bernardi, Ricardo E. "The Role of Paradigmatic Determinants in Psychoanalytic Understanding." *International Journal of Psychoanalysis* 70 (1989), 341–57.

Bernheimer, Charles, and Claire Kahane, eds. *In Dora's Case: Freud – Hysteria – Feminism*. 2nd edn. New York: Columbia University Press, 1990.

Bersani, Leo. "The Narrator as Center in *The Wings of the Dove*." *Modern Fiction Studies* 6 (1960), 131–44.

"The Subject of Power." *Diacritics* 7 (1977), 2–21.

A Future for Astyanax: Character and Desire in Literature. 1976. New York: Columbia University Press, 1984.

The Freudian Body: Psychoanalysis and Art. New York: Columbia University Press, 1986.

The Culture of Redemption. Cambridge, MA: Harvard University Press, 1990.

Bersani, Leo, and Ulysse Dutoit. *Arts of Impoverishment: Beckett, Rothko, Resnais*. Cambridge, MA: Harvard University Press, 1993.

Berchtold, Jacques. *Des rats et des ratières: anamorphoses d'un champ métaphorique de Saint Augustin à Jean Racine*. Histoire des idées et critique littéraire 311. Genève: Librairie Droz, 1992.

Bevan, David, ed. *Literary Gastronomy*. Amsterdam: Rodopi, 1988.

Bewick, Thomas, and Ralph Beilby. *A General History of Quadrupeds*. Newcastle upon Tyne, 1790. Reprinted as Vol. III of *Thomas Bewick's Works*. London: B. Quaritch, 1885.

Bick, Esther. "The Experience of the Skin in Early Object-Relations." 1967. In Elizabeth Bott Spillius, ed. *Melanie Klein Today*. Vol. 1. *Mainly Theory*. London: Routledge, 1988, pp. 187–91.

Bion, W. R. *Attention and Interpretation: A Scientific Approach to Insight in Psycho-Analysis and Groups*. London: Tavistock Publications, 1970. Reprint, Social Science Paperbacks 136. London: Tavistock Publications, 1975.

Biven, Barrie M. "The Role of Skin in Normal and Abnormal Development with a Note on the Poet Sylvia Plath." *The International Review of Psychoanalysis* 9 (1982), 205–09.

Blake, William. *Complete Writings*. Ed. Geoffrey Keynes. 1966. Oxford University Press, 1979.

Blanchot, Maurice. *The Space of Literature*. 1955. Trans. Anne Smock. Lincoln, NE: University of Nebraska Press, 1982.

Bloom, Harold, *A Map of Misreading*. New York: Oxford University Press, 1975.

Bloom, Harold, ed. *James Joyce's* Dubliners. New York: Chelsea House, 1988.

Bloom, Harold , *et al.*, eds. *Deconstruction and Criticism*. New York: Continuum, 1979.

Boheemen, Christine van. *The Novel as Family Romance: Language, Gender, and Authority from Fielding to Joyce*. Ithaca, NY: Cornell University Press, 1987.

Joyce, Derrida, Lacan, and the Trauma of History: Reading, Narrative and Postcolonialism. Cambridge University Press, 1999.

Bollettieri, Rosa Maria Bosinelli, and Harold Mosher, eds. *ReJoycing: New Readings of "Dubliners."* Lexington, KY: University of Kentucky Press, 1980.

Bonaparte, Marie. *Topsy: The Story of a Golden-Haired Chow*. 1937. Trans. Gary Genosko. New Brunswick, NJ: Transaction Publishers, 1993.

Booker, M. Keith. "The Rats of God: Pynchon, Joyce, Beckett, and the Carnivalization of Religion." *Pynchon Notes* 24–25 (1989), 21–30.

Borch-Jacobsen, Mikkel. *The Freudian Subject*. 1982. Trans. Catherine Porter. Stanford University Press, 1988.

Borges, Jorge Luis. *Other Inquisitions 1937–1952*. Trans. Ruth L. C. Simms. Austin, TX: University of Texas Press, 1964.

In Praise of Darkness. 1969. Trans. Norman Thomas di Giovanni. New York: E. P. Dutton and Co., 1974.

Selected Non-Fictions. Ed. Eliot Weinberger. Trans. Esther Allen, Suzanne Jill Levine, and Eliot Weinberger. New York: Viking, 1999.

Bosanquet, Theodora. *Henry James at Work*. 1924. Ed. Lyall H. Powers. Ann Arbor: University of Michigan Press, 2006.

Botting, Fred. *Sex, Machines and Navels: Fiction, Fantasy and History in the Future Present*. Manchester University Press, 1999.

Boulby, Mark. "Kafka's End: A Reassessment of *The Burrow*." *German Quarterly* 55 (1982), 175–85.

Bowen, Elizabeth. Lecture Notes on the Short Story for Vassar College. 1960. Bowen Collection. Harry Ransom Humanities Research Center. University of Texas at Austin.

Afterthought: Pieces about Writing. London: Longmans. Green, 1962.

The Collected Stories of Elizabeth Bowen. Intro. Angus Wilson. 1980. London: Vintage, 1999.

The Mulberry Tree: Writings of Elizabeth Bowen. Ed. Hermione Lee. London: Virago, 1986.

Bowers, Paul. "'Charley, you're my darwing!' Sexual Selection in the Joycean Nursery." *Journal of Modern Literature* 32:4 (2009), 34–42.

Bowlby, Rachel, ed. *Virginia Woolf*. Longman Critical Reader. London: Longman, 1992.

Still Crazy After All These Years: Women, Writing and Psychoanalysis. London: Routledge, 1992.

Shopping with Freud. London: Routledge, 1993.

Feminist Destinations and Further Essays on Virginia Woolf. Edinburgh University Press, 1997.

Bourdieu, Pierre. *Distinction: A Social Critique of the Judgement of Taste*. 1979. Cambridge, MA: Harvard University Press, 1984.

Brett, Judith. "Hugo von Hofmannsthal: 'Letter of Lord Chandos' – The Writer's Relationship to his Language." *American Imago* 35 (1978), 238–58.

Brooker, Joseph. *Joyce's Critics: Transitions in Reading and Culture*. Madison, WI: University of Wisconsin Press, 2004.

Brooks, Peter. *The Melodramatic Imagination: Balzac, Henry James, Melodrama, and the Mode of Excess*. 1976. New Haven, CT: Yale University Press, 1995.

Reading for the Plot: Design and Intention in Narrative. New York: A. A. Knopf, 1984.

Henry James Goes to Paris. Princeton University Press, 2007.

Bronfen, Elizabeth. *The Knotted Subject: Hysteria and its Discontents*. Princeton University Press, 1998.

Broughton, Panthea Reid. "'Virginia is Anal': Speculations on Virginia Woolf's Writing *Roger Fry* and Reading Sigmund Freud." *Journal of Modern Literature* 14 (1987), 151–57.

Brown, Richard, *James Joyce and Sexuality*. Cambridge University Press, 1985.

Brown, Richard, ed. *Joyce, "Penelope" and the Body*. Amsterdam: Rodopi, 2006.

A Companion to James Joyce. Oxford: Blackwell, 2008.

Browne, Thomas. *Works*. Vol. II. *Pseudodoxia epidemica*. Ed. Geoffrey Keynes. Chicago: University of Chicago Press, 1964.

Bryden, Mary. "Rats in and around Beckett." In Marius Buning, Danièle de Ruyter-Tognotti, Matthijs Engelberts, and Sjef Houppermans, eds. *Beckett versus Beckett*, pp. 317–29.

Budgen, Frank. *James Joyce and the Making of "Ulysses."* Oxford University Press, 1972.

Buning, Marius, Danièle de Ruyter-Tognotti, Matthijs Engelberts, and Sjef Houppermans, eds. *Beckett versus Beckett*. Amsterdam: Rodopi, 1998.

Burton, Robert. *Anatomy of Melancholy*. Ed. Floyd Dell and Paul Jordan-Smith. New York: Tudor Press, 1948.

Butler, Judith. *Bodies that Matter: On the Discursive Limits of Sex*. New York: Routledge, 1993.

Byatt, I. R. C. *The British Electrical Industry, 1875–1914.* Oxford: Clarendon Press, 1979.

Cameron, Sharon. *Thinking in Henry James.* Chicago: University of Chicago Press, 1986.

Carlyle, Thomas. *Sartor Resartus.* 1833–34. Ed. Kerry McSweeney and Peter Sabor. Oxford University Press, 1987.

Caruth, Cathy, ed. *Trauma: Explorations in Memory.* Baltimore, MD: Johns Hopkins University Press, 1995.

Castle, Gregory. *Modernism and the Celtic Revival.* Cambridge University Press, 2001.

Caughie, Pamela L. "Flush and the Literary Canon: Oh Where Oh Where Has That Little Dog Gone?" *Tulsa Studies in Women's Literature* 10 (1991), 47–66.

Caughie, Pamela L., ed. *Virginia Woolf in the Age of Mechanical Reproduction.* New York: Garland Publishing, 2000.

Caws, Mary Ann. *Reading Frames in Modern Fiction.* Princeton University Press, 1985.

Chabot, C. Barry. *Freud on Schreber: Psychoanalytic Theory and the Critical Act.* Amherst: University of Massachusetts Press, 1982.

Chatman, Seymour Benjamin. *The Later Style of Henry James.* Oxford: Blackwell, 1972.

Chaudhuri, Una, ed. *Animals and Performance.* Special issue of *The Drama Review* 51:1 (2007).

Cheng, Vincent J. *Shakespeare and Joyce: A Study of "Finnegans Wake."* University Park: Pennsylvania State University Press, 1984.

   "Stephen Dedalus and the Black Panther Vampire." *James Joyce Quarterly* 24 (1987), 161–76.

   Joyce, Race, and Empire. Cambridge University Press, 1995.

Cherfas, Jeremy and Roger Lewin, eds. *Not Work Alone: A Cross-Cultural View of Activities Superfluous to Survival.* London: Temple Smith, 1980.

Cioffi, Frank. *Freud and the Question of Pseudoscience.* Chicago: Open Court, 1998.

Clendinning, Anne. *Demons and Domesticity: Women and the British Gas Industry, 1889–1939.* Aldershot, Hants.: Ashgate, 2004.

Coetzee, J. M. *Elizabeth Costello*: Eight Lessons. London: Secker and Warburg, 2003.

Colby, Frank Moore. "In Darkest James." 1904. In F. W. Dupee, ed. *The Question of Henry James*, pp. 20–27.

Collins, Wilkie. *Poor Miss Finch.* 1872. Ed. Catherine Peters. Oxford University Press, 2000.

Conrad, Joseph. *The Nigger of the Narcissus.* 1897. Ed. Robert Kimbrough. New York: Norton, 1979.

   Heart of Darkness. 1899. Ed. Robert Kimbrough. New York: Norton, 1988.

   The End of the Tether. 1902. In *Tales of Land and Sea.* Intro. William McFee. Garden City, NY: Hanover House, 1953.

Coulson, Victoria. *Henry James, Women and Realism*. Cambridge University Press, 2007.

Cowan, Ruth Schwartz. *A Social History of American Technology*. Oxford University Press, 1997.

Cucullu, Lois. *Expert Modernists, Matricide, and Modern Culture: Woolf, Forster, Joyce*. Basingstoke, UK: Palgrave Macmillan, 2004.

Current-García, Eugene and Walton R. Patrick, eds. *Realism and Romanticism in Fiction*. Chicago: Scott, Foresman and Co., 1962.

Curtin, Maureen F. *Out of Touch: Skin Tropes and Identities in Woolf, Ellison, Pynchon, and Acker*. New York: Routledge, 2003.

Cutting, Andrew. *Death in Henry James*. Basingstoke, UK: Palgrave Macmillan, 2005.

Daly, Nicholas. *Literature, Technology, and Modernity, 1860–2000*. Cambridge University Press, 2004.

Day, Robert Adams. "Joyce's AquaCities." In Morris Beja and David Norris, eds. *Joyce and the Hibernian Metropolis*, pp. 3–20.

Darwin, Charles. *Charles Darwin's Natural Selection: Being the Second Part of his Big Species Book Written from 1856–1858*. Ed. R. C. Stauffer. Cambridge University Press, 1987.

  The Descent of Man. London: John Murray, 1871.

Daston, Lorraine and Gregg Mitman, eds. *Thinking with Animals: New Perspectives on Anthropomorphism*. New York: Columbia University Press, 2005.

Daunton, Martin, ed. *The Cambridge Urban History of Britain*. Vol. III. Cambridge University Press, 2000.

Davenport, Guy. "Pound and Frobenius." In Lewis Leary, ed. *Motive and Method in the Cantos*. New York: Columbia University Press, 1954, pp. 33–59.

Davies, Hugh Sykes. *The Papers of Andrew Melmoth*. London: Methuen and Co., 1960.

Davis, Lloyd. *Sexuality and Textuality in Henry James: Reading through the Virginal*. New York: P. Lang, 1988.

Davis, Whitney. *Drawing the Dream of the Wolves: Homosexuality, Interpretation, and Freud's "Wolf Man."* Bloomington, IN: Indiana University Press, 1995.

Degenaar, Marjolein. *Molyneux's Problem: Three Centuries of Discussion on the Perception of Forms*. 1992. Trans. Michael J. Collins. Dordrecht: Kluwer Academic Publishers, 1996.

Delaney, James. *James Joyce's Odyssey: A Guide to the Dublin of "Ulysses."* London: Hodder and Stoughton, 1981.

Deleuze, Gilles, and Felix Guattari. *Kafka: Toward a Minor Literature*. 1975. Trans. Dana Polan. Minneapolis: University of Minnesota Press, 1986.

  A Thousand Plateaus: Capitalism and Schizophrenia. 1980. Trans. Brian Massumi. Minneapolis: University of Minnesota Press, 1987.

Deming, Robert H. *James Joyce: The Critical Heritage*. 2 vols. London: Routledge and Kegan Paul, 1970.

Dennison, Michael J. *Vampirism: Literary Tropes of Decadence and Entropy*. New York: P. Lang, 2001.

Derrida, Jacques. *Of Grammatology*. 1967. Trans. Gayatri Spivak. Rev. edn. Baltimore, MD: Johns Hopkins University Press, 1997.

Dissemination. 1972. Trans. Barbara Johnson. London: Continuum, 2000.

The Truth in Painting. 1978. Trans. Geoff Bennington and Ian McLeod. Chicago: University of Chicago Press, 1987.

"Living On." Trans. James Hulbert. In Harold Bloom *et al.*, eds. *Deconstruction and Criticism*, pp. 75–186.

The Post Card: From Socrates to Freud and Beyond. 1980. Trans. Alan Bass. Chicago: University of Chicago Press, 1987.

Memoirs of the Blind: The Self-Portrait and Other Ruins. 1990. Trans. Pascale-Anne Brault and Michael Naas. Chicago: University of Chicago Press, 1993.

Acts of Literature. Ed. Derek Attridge. London: Routledge, 1992.

Derrida, Jacques, and Paule Thévenin. *The Secret Art of Antonin Artaud*. 1986. Abridged trans. Mary Ann Caws. Cambridge, MA: MIT Press, 1998.

DeSalvo, Louise. *Virginia Woolf: The Impact of Childhood Sexual Abuse on her Life and Work*. London: Women's Press, 1989.

Deutsch, Helene. *Confrontations with Myself: An Epilogue*. New York: Norton, 1973.

Dickens, Charles. *A Christmas Carol and Other Christmas Books*. Ed. Robert Douglas-Fairhurst. Oxford University Press, 2006.

Diderot, Denis. *Diderot's Early Philosophical Works*. Ed. Margaret Jourdain. Chicago: Open Court, 1916.

Dietrichson, Jan. *The Image of Money in the American Novel of the Golden Age*. Oslo, Norway: University of Oslo American Institute Publications, 1969.

Dolar, Mladen. *A Voice and Nothing More*. Cambridge, MA: MIT Press, 2006.

Douglas, Mary. *Implicit Meanings: Essays in Anthropology*. London: Routledge and Kegan Paul, 1975.

Dufresne, Todd. *Tales from the Freudian Crypt: The Death Drive in Text and Context*. Stanford University Press, 2000.

Du Maurier, George. *Trilby*. 1894. Intro. Elaine Showalter. Oxford University Press, 1998.

Dupee, F. W., ed. *The Question of Henry James: A Collection of Critical Essays*. New York, H. Holt and Company, 1945.

Echenberg, Myron J. *Plague Ports: The Global Urban Impact of Bubonic Plague, 1894–1901*. New York University Press, 2007.

Edelman, Birgitta. "'Rats are People Too!' Rat–Human Relations Re-Rated." *Anthropology Today* 18:1 (2002), 3–8.

Eisler, Robert. *Man into Wolf: An Anthropological Interpretation of Sadism, Masochism, and Lycanthropy; A Lecture Delivered at a Meeting of the Royal Society of Medicine*. 1949. New York, Greenwood Press, 1969.

Elias, Norbert. *The Civilizing Process*. Vol. 1. *The History of Manners*. 1939. Trans. Edmund Jephcott. New York: Urizen Books, 1978.

Eliot, T. S. *The Waste Land*. 1922. *Authoritative Text, Contexts, Criticism*. Ed. Michael North. Norton Critical Edition. New York: W. W. Norton, 2001.

  After Strange Gods: A Primer of Modern Heresy. London: Faber, 1934.

Elkins, James. *The Object Stares Back*. San Diego: Harcourt, Inc., 1996.

Ellison, Ralph. *Invisible Man*. 1952. New York: Random House, 1995.

Ellmann, Maud. "'The Intimate Difference': Power and Representation in *The Ambassadors*." In *Henry James: Fiction as History*. Ed. Ian Bell. London: Vision; Totowa, New Jersey: Barnes and Noble, 1984, pp. 98–113. Rev. edn. The Norton Critical Edition of Henry James's *The Ambassadors*. 2nd edn. Ed. S. P. Rosenbaum. New York: Norton, 1994, pp. 501–14.

  "The Woolf Woman." *Critical Quarterly* 35:3 (1993), 86–100.

  "Drawing the Blind: Gide, Joyce, Larsen and the Blind Short Story." *Oxford Literary Review* 26 (2004), 30–61.

  "Writing like a Rat." *Critical Quarterly* 46:1 (2004), 59–76.

  "*Ulysses*: Changing into an Animal," *Field Day Review* 2 (2006), 75–93

Ellmann, Maud, and Marilyn Reizbaum. "En-Garde: 'Two Gallants.'" In Vicki Mahaffey, ed. *Collaborative "Dubliners": Joyce in Dialogue*. Syracuse University Press, forthcoming.

Ellmann, Richard. *James Joyce*. 1959. Rev. edn. Oxford University Press, 1982.

  Ulysses on the Liffey. 1972. London: Faber, 1984.

  "Henry James among the Aesthetes." *Proceedings of the British Academy* 69 (1983), 209–28.

Esty, Joshua. *A Shrinking Island: Modernism and National Culture in England*. Princeton University Press, 2004.

Fanon, Frantz. *Black Skin, White Masks*. 1952. Trans. Charles Lam Markmann. New York: Grove Press, 1967.

Feher, Michel, Ramona Naddaff, and Nadia Tazi, eds. *Fragments for a History of the Human Body*. 3 vols. New York: Zone, 1989.

Felman, Shoshana. *Jacques Lacan, the Adventure of Insight: Psychoanalysis and Contemporary Culture*. Cambridge, MA: Harvard University Press, 1987.

Felman, Shoshana, ed. *Literature and Psychoanalysis: The Question of Reading: Otherwise*. 1977. Baltimore, MD: Johns Hopkins University Press, 1982.

Ferrer, Daniel. "The Freudful Couchmare of LAMBDAd: Joyce's Notes on Freud and the Composition of Chapter XVI of *Finnegans Wake*." *James Joyce Quarterly* 22 (1985), 367–82.

  Virginia Woolf and the Madness of Language. 1997. Trans. Geoffrey Bennington and Rachel Bowlby. London: Routledge, 1990.

Fish, Stanley. "Withholding the Missing Portion: Power, Meaning, and Persuasion in Freud's *The Wolf-Man*." *Times Literary Supplement* 4352 (8 August 1986), 935.

Fitzgerald, F. Scott. *Tender is the Night*. 1934. New York: Macmillan, 1982.

Flaubert, Gustave. *Correspondance*. 9 vols. Paris: L. Conard, 1926–33.

Fletcher, John. "The Haunted Closet: Henry James's Queer Spectrality." *Textual Practice* 14 (2000), 53–80.

Fogarty, Anne, and Timothy Martin, eds. *Joyce on the Threshold*. Gainesville, FL: University Press of Florida, 2005.

Fogel, Daniel M. *Covert Relations: James Joyce, Virginia Woolf, and Henry James*. Charlottesville: University Press of Virginia, 1990.

Ford, Ford Madox. *Joseph Conrad: A Personal Remembrance*. London: Duckworth, 1924.

Foucault, Michel. *Discipline and Punish: The Birth of the Prison*. 1975. Trans. Alan Sheridan. New York: Vintage–Random House, 1979.

  The History of Sexuality: An Introduction. 1976. Trans. Robert Hurley. London: Allen Lane, 1978.

Fox, Richard Wightman, and T. J. Jackson Lears, eds. *The Culture of Consumption: Critical Essays in American History, 1880–1980*. New York: Pantheon Books, 1983.

Freedman, Ariela. "Did it Flow?: Bridging Aesthetics and History in Joyce's *Ulysses*." *Modernism/Modernity* 13:1 (2006), 853–68.

Freedman, Jonathan. *Professions of Taste: Henry James, British Aestheticism, and Commodity Culture*. Stanford University Press, 1990.

Friedrich, Gerhard. "The Gnomonic Clue to James Joyce's *Dubliners*." *Modern Language Notes* 72:6 (1957), 421–24.

Freud, Sigmund. *The Complete Psychological Works of Sigmund Freud*. Standard Edition. Trans. James Strachey. 24 vols. London: Hogarth Press, 1953–74.

  The Freud/Jung Letters: The Correspondence between Sigmund Freud and C. G. Jung. Ed. William McGuire. Trans. Ralph Manheim and R. F. C. Hull. Bollingen 94. Princeton University Press, 1974.

  The Complete Letters of Sigmund Freud to Wilhelm Fliess, 1887–1904. Trans. and ed. Jeffrey Moussaieff Masson. Cambridge, MA: Belknap Press of Harvard University Press, 1985.

  The "Wolfman" and Other Cases. Trans. Louise Adey Huish. Intro. Gillian Beer. New York: Penguin Books, 2003.

Froula, Christine. *Modernism's Body: Sex, Culture, and Joyce*. New York: Columbia, 1996.

  Virginia Woolf and the Bloomsbury Avant-Garde: War, Civilization, Modernity. New York: Columbia University Press, 2005.

Fuss, Diana. *The Sense of an Interior: Four Writers and the Rooms That Shaped Them*. New York: Routledge, 2004.

Gallop, Jane. *The Daughter's Seduction: Feminism and Psychoanalysis*. Ithaca, NY: Cornell University Press, 1982.

Gambetta, Diego. *The Sicilian Mafia*. Cambridge, MA: Harvard University Press, 1993.

Gard, Roger. *Henry James: The Critical Heritage*. London: Routledge and Kegan Paul, 1968.

Gardiner, Muriel, ed. *The Wolf Man and Sigmund Freud*. 1971. London: Hogarth, 1972.

Gardner, Martin. *Did Adam and Eve Have Navels? Discourses on Reflexology, Numerology, Urine Therapy, and Other Dubious Subjects.* New York: Norton, 2000.

Gay, Peter. *Freud: A Life for Our Time.* 1988. New York: Anchor Books, 1989.

Geismar, Maxwell David. *Henry James and the Jacobites.* Boston, MA: Houghton Mifflin, 1963.

Gell, Alfred. *Wrapping in Images: Tattooing in Polynesia.* Oxford: Clarendon Press, 1993.

Gibson, Andrew. *Joyce's Revenge: History, Politics, and Aesthetics in* Ulysses. Oxford University Press, 2002.

Gide, André. *La symphonie pastorale.* 1919. Paris: Gallimard, 1925.

"The Pastoral Symphony." In *Two Symphonies: "Isabelle" and "The Pastoral Symphony."* Trans. Dorothy Bussy. 1931. New York: Random House, 1977.

Journals 1889–49. Trans. and ed. Justin O'Brien. Harmondsworth: Penguin, 1967.

Gifford, Don. *Joyce Annotated: Notes for "Dubliners" and "A Portrait of the Artist as a Young Man."* Berkeley, CA: University of California Press, 1982.

Gifford, Don, with Robert J. Seidman. *"Ulysses" Annotated: Notes for Joyce's "Ulysses."* 2nd edn. Berkeley, CA: University of California Press, 2008.

Gigante, Denise. *Taste: A Literary History.* New Haven, CT: Yale University Press, 2005.

Ginzburg, Carlo. *Myths, Emblems, Clues.* 1986. Trans. John and Anne C. Tedeschi. London: Hutchinson Radius, 1990.

Girard, René. *Deceit, Desire and the Novel: Self and Other in Literary Structure.* 1961. Trans. Yvonne Freccero. 1965. Baltimore, MD: Johns Hopkins University Press, 1976.

Gitter, Elizabeth. *The Imprisoned Guest: Samuel Howe and Laura Bridgeman, the Original Deaf–Blind Girl.* New York: Farrar Strauss, 2001.

Glenny, Allie. *Ravenous Identity: Eating and Eating Distress in the Life and Work of Virginia Woolf.* New York: St. Martin's Press, 2000.

Goble, Mark. "Wired Love: Pleasure at a Distance in Henry James and Others." *English Literary History* 74 (2007), 397–427.

Goethe, Johann Wolfgang von. *Faust I and II.* In *Goethe's Collected Works.* Ed. and trans. Stuart Atkins. 1984. Princeton University Press, 1994.

Golding, Charles. *Rats: The New Plague.* London: Weidenfeld and Nicholson, 1990.

Gordon, John. "*Dubliners* and the Art of Losing." *Studies in Short Fiction* 32:3 (1995), 343–52.

Gordon, Lyndall. *Virginia Woolf: A Writer's Life.* New York: Norton; Oxford University Press, 1984.

Gosse, Edmund. *Father and Son: A Study of Two Temperaments.* 1907. Harmondsworth: Penguin, 1989.

Gosse, Philip Henry. *Omphalos: An Attempt to Untie the Geological Knot.* London: Jan Van Voorst, 1987.

Gottfried, Roy. *Joyce's Iritis and the Irritated Text: The Dis-Lexic "Ulysses."* Gainesville, FL: University of Florida Press, 1995.

Graham, Wendy. *Henry James's Thwarted Love.* Stanford University Press, 1999.

Grass, Gunter. *The Rat.* 1986. Trans. Ralph Manheim. London: Picador, 1988. Nobel Prize Acceptance Speech. 1999. www.nobel.se/literature/laureates/1999/lecture-e.html

Greenacre, Phyllis. "The Primal Scene and the Sense of Reality." *Psychoanalytic Quarterly* 42 (1973), 10–41.

Green, André. "An Unexpected Encounter: Henry James and Sigmund Freud." *Revue française de psychanalyse* 59 (1995), 561–64.

Griffin, Susan M. *The Historical Eye: The Texture of the Visual in Late James.* Boston, MA: Northeastern University Press, 1991.

Guest, Kristen, ed. *Eating Their Words: Cannibalism and the Boundaries of Cultural Identity.* Albany, NY: State University of New York Press, 2001.

Gunn, Daniel. *Psychoanalysis and Fiction: An Exploration of Literary and Psychoanalytic Borders.* Cambridge University Press, 1988.

Guthrie, Robert V. *Even the Rat Was White: A Historical View of Psychology.* New York: Harper and Row, 1976.

Hall, Roberta L., and Henry S. Sharp, eds. *Wolf and Man: Evolution in Parallel.* New York: Academic Press, 1978.

Haralson, Eric L. *Henry James and Queer Modernity.* Cambridge University Press, 2003.

Harrison, Lori B. "Bloodsucking Bloom: Vampirism as a Representation of Jewishness in *Ulysses*." *James Joyce Quarterly* 36 (1999), 781–97.

Havilland, Beverly. "Waste Makes Taste: Thorstein Veblen, Henry James, and the Sense of the Past." *International Journal of Politics, Culture, and Society* 7 (1994), 615–37.

Hayes, Kevin J., ed. *Henry James: The Contemporary Reviews.* Cambridge University Press, 1996.

Head, Dominic. *The Modernist Short Story: A Study of Theory and Practice.* Cambridge University Press, 1992.

Hendrickson, Robert. *More Cunning than Man: A Complete History of the Rat and its Role in Human Civilization.* New York: Kensington, 1983.

Herbert, Christopher. "Rat Worship and Taboo in Mayhew's London." *Representations* 23 (1988), 1–24.

Hervey, Mary F. S. *Holbein's "Ambassadors": The Picture and the Men; An Historical Study.* London: George Bell and Sons, 1900.

Hockney, David. *Secret Knowledge: Rediscovering the Lost Techniques of the Old Masters.* New York: Viking Studio, 2001.

Hodgson, Barbara. *The Rat: A Perverse Miscellany.* Berkeley, CA: Ten Speed Press, 1997.

Hofmannsthal, Hugo Von. *The Lord Chandos Letter and Other Writings.* Trans. Joel Rotenberg. New York: New York Review of Books, 2005.

Holland, Laurence B. *The Expense of Vision: Essays on the Craft of Henry James.* 1964. Baltimore, MD: Johns Hopkins University Press, 1982.

Holland, Peter, ed. *Shakespeare and Comedy. Shakespeare Survey* 56. Cambridge University Press, 2003.

Homer. *The Odyssey of Homer.* Trans. Richard Lattimore. New York: Harper and Row, 1967.

Horkheimer, Max, and Theodor W. Adorno. *Dialectic of Enlightenment.* 1947. Trans. John Cumming. New York: Continuum, 2002.

Hughes, Thomas P. *Networks of Power: Electrification in Western Society 1880– 1930.* Baltimore, MD, and London: Johns Hopkins University Press, 1983.

Hutchison, Hazel. "The Other Lambert Strether: Henry James's *The Ambassadors*, Balzac's *Louis Lambert*, and J. H. Lambert." *Nineteenth-Century Literature* 58 (2003), 230–58.

Huyssen, Andreas. *After the Great Divide: Modernism, Mass Culture, Postmodernism.* Bloomington: Indiana University Press, 1986.

Jacobus, Mary. "'The Third Stroke': Reading Woolf with Freud." In Rachel Bowlby, ed. *Virginia Woolf*, pp. 102–20.

The Poetics of Psychoanalysis: In the Wake of Klein. Oxford University Press, 2005.

James, Henry. *Roderick Hudson.* 1875. Ed. Geoffrey Moore. London: Penguin, 1986.

The American. 1877. Ed. James W. Tuttleton. New York: Norton, 1978.

The Portrait of a Lady. 1881. Ed. Geoffrey Moore. London: Penguin, 2003.

The Princess Casamassima. 1886. Harmondsworth: Penguin, 2006.

The Tragic Muse. 1890. In *Novels 1886–1890.* New York: Library of America, 1989.

What Maisie Knew. 1897. Ed. Adrian Poole. Oxford University Press, 2008.

The Awkward Age. 1899. Ed. Vivien Jones. Oxford University Press, 1999.

The Sacred Fount. 1901. Ed. John Lyon. London: Penguin, 1994.

The Wings of the Dove. 1902. Ed. Millicent Bell. London: Penguin, 2008.

The Ambassadors. 1903. Ed. S. P. Rosenbaum. 2nd edn. New York: Norton, 1994.

The Golden Bowl. 1904. Ed. Virginia Llewellyn Smith. Oxford University Press, 1983.

The Art of Fiction, and Other Essays. New York: Oxford Univ. Press, 1948.

Autobiography. 1913–17. Ed. Frederick W. Dupee. New York: Criterion Books, 1956.

Literary Criticism: French Writers; Other European Writers; The Prefaces to the New York Edition. New York: Library of America, 1984.

The Complete Notebooks. Ed. Leon Edel and Lyall H. Powers. Oxford University Press, 1987.

The Turn of the Screw: Authoritative Text, Contexts, Criticism. Ed. Deborah Esch and Jonathan Warren. New York: Norton, 1999.

The Complete Letters of Henry James, 1855–1872. Ed. Pierre A. Walker and Greg W. Zacharias. 2 vols. Lincoln, NE and London: University of Nebraska Press, 2006.

Jameson, Fredric. *A Singular Modernity: Essay on the Ontology of the Present.* London: Verso, 2002.

Jay, Martin. *Downcast Eyes: The Denigration of Vision in Twentieth-Century French Thought*. Berkeley, CA: University of California Press, 1993.

Johnson, Lawrence. *The Wolf Man's Burden*. Ithaca, NY: Cornell University Press, 2001.

Jones, Ernest. *Essays in Applied Psycho-Analysis*. 2 vols. London, Hogarth Press, 1951.

The Life and Work of Sigmund Freud. 3 vols. New York: Basic Books, 1953–57.

Josipovici, Gabriel, ed. *The Modern English Novel: The Reader, the Writer and the Work*. New York: Barnes and Noble, 1976.

Jottkandt, Sigi. *Acting Beautifully: Henry James and the Ethical Aesthetic*. Albany, NY: State University of New York Press, 2005.

Jouve, Nicole Ward. "Virginia Woolf and Psychoanalysis." In Sue Roe and Susan Sellers, eds. *The Cambridge Companion to Virginia Woolf*, pp. 245–72.

Joyce, James. *Dubliners*. 1914. Ed. Terence Brown. London: Penguin Books, 1992.

Draft of the "Proteus" episode of *Ulysses*. www.robotwisdom.com/jaj/ulysses/proteus0.html

A Portrait of the Artist as a Young Man. 1916. New York: Viking Press, 1964.

A Portrait of the Artist as a Young Man. 1916. Ed. Seamus Deane. Harmondsworth: Penguin, 2000.

Ulysses. 1922. Ed. Hans Walter Gabler. London: Bodley Head, 1986.

Ulysses. 1922. Ed. Jeri Johnson. Oxford University Press, 1993.

Finnegans Wake. 1939. London: Faber, 1964.

Stephen Hero. 1944. Ed. Theodore Spencer, John J. Slocum, and Herbert Cahoon. New York: New Directions, 1963.

Letters. Ed. Stuart Gilbert and Richard Ellmann. 3 vols. New York: Viking Press, 1957–66.

The Workshop of Dedalus: James Joyce and the Raw Materials for "A Portrait of the Artist as a Young Man." Ed. Robert Scholes and Richard M. Kain. Evanston, IL: Northwestern University Press, 1965.

Selected Letters of James Joyce. Edited by Richard Ellmann. New York: Viking Press, 1975.

James Joyce in Padua. Trans. Louis Berrone. New York: Random House, 1977.

Ulysses: *A Facsimile of Placards for Episodes 1–6*. Ed. Michael Groden. New York: Garland, 1978.

Poems and "Exiles." Ed. J. C. C. Mays. London: Penguin, 1992.

On Ibsen. Edited by Dennis Phillips. Los Angeles: Green Integer, 1999.

Kafka, Franz. *The Diaries of Franz Kafka, 1910–1923*. New York: Schocken Books, 1976.

Kanzer, Mark. Review of *The Wolf-Man by the Wolf-Man*, edited by Muriel Gardiner. *International Journal of Psycho-Analysis* 53 (1972), 419–22.

Kanzer, Mark, and Jules Glenn, eds. *Freud and His Patients*. New York: J. Aronson, 1980.

Kaplan, Fred. *Henry James: The Imagination of Genius; A Biography*. New York: Hodder and Stoughton, 1992.

Karnas, Todd. "Slavoj Žižek: Rat Man and Wolf-Man." *Symplokē* 10 (2002), 186–95.

Kaston, Carren. *Imagination and Desire in the Novels of Henry James.* New Brunswick, NJ: Rutgers University Press, 1984.

Kaufman, M. Ralph, *et al.*, eds. *Evolution of Psychoanalytic Concepts: Anorexia Nervosa: A Paradigm.* London: Hogarth Press, 1965.

Kellogg, John Harvey. *The Itinerary of a Breakfast: A Popular Account of the Travels of a Breakfast through the Food Tube and of the Ten Gates and Several Stations through Which It Passes, also of the Obstacles Which It Sometimes Meets.* Battle Creek, MI: Modern Medicine Publishing Company, 1918.

Kerrigan, John. *Revenge Tragedy: Aeschylus to Armageddon.* Oxford: Clarendon Press, 1996.

Kiberd, Declan. *Inventing Ireland.* 1996. Cambridge, MA: Harvard University Press, 1997.

Kilgour, Maggie. *From Communion to Cannibalism: An Anatomy of Metaphors of Incorporation.* Princeton University Press, 1990.

Kimball, Jean. *Joyce and the Early Freudians: A Synchronic Dialogue of Texts.* Gainesville, FL: University Press of Florida, 2003.

Kittler, Friedrich A. *Discourse Networks 1800/1900.* 1985. Trans. Michael Metteer and Chris Cullens. Stanford University Press, 1992.

Klein, Melanie. *The Psychoanalysis of Children.* 1932. Rev. edn. Trans. Alix Strachey. New York: Delacorte Press/S. Lawrence, 1975.

"Notes on Some Schizoid Mechanisms." *International Journal of Psychoanalysis* 27 (1946), 99–110.

Knowlson, James. *Damned to Fame: The Life of Samuel Beckett.* New York: Simon and Schuster, 1996.

Kristeva, Julia. *Powers of Horror: An Essay on Abjection.* Trans. Leon Roudiez. New York: Columbia, 1982.

Kuzniar, Alice A. *Melancholia's Dog.* Chicago: University of Chicago Press, 2006.

Lacan, Jacques. *The Four Fundamental Concepts of Psycho-Analysis.* 1973. Ed. Jacques-Alain Miller. Trans. Alan Sheridan. New York: Norton, 1998.

The Ethics of Psychoanalysis, 1959–1960. Translated by Dennis Porter. Seminar of Jacques Lacan 7. New York: Norton, 1992. Originally published as *L'Ethique de la psychanalyse, 1959–1960* (1986).

The Psychoses, 1955–1956. In *The Seminar of Jacques Lacan.* Vol. III. Ed. Jacques-Alain Miller. Trans. Russell Grigg. New York: Norton, 1997.

Laplanche, Jean. *Life and Death in Psychoanalysis.* 1970. Trans. Jeffrey Mehlman. Baltimore, MD: Johns Hopkins University Press, 1976.

Laplanche, Jean, and J.-B. Pontalis. *The Language of Psycho-Analysis.* 1967. Trans. Donald Nicholson-Smith. New York: W. W. Norton, 1973.

Leary, Lewis. *Motive and Method in the* Cantos *of Ezra Pound.* New York: Columbia University Press, 1954.

Leavis, F. R. *The Great Tradition.* New York University Press, 1963.

Leclaire, Serge. "A propos de l'episode psychotique que presente l'homme aux loups." *La Psychanalyse* 4 (1958), 83–110.

Ledger, Sally, and Scott McCracken, eds. *Cultural Politics at the* fin de siècle. Cambridge University Press, 1995.

Lee, Hermione. *Virginia Woolf.* London: Chatto and Windus, 1996.

Lemardeley-Cunci, Marie-Christine, Carle Bonafous-Murat, and André Topia. *L'inhumain.* Paris: Presses de la Sorbonne Nouvelle, 2004.

Leonard, Garry. *Reading "Dubliners" Again: A Lacanian Perspective.* Syracuse University Press, 1993.

Levi, Primo. *If This is a Man.* 1947/1958. Trans. Stuart Woolf. London: Vintage, 1996.

Levin, Harry. *The Gates of Horn: A Study of Five French Realists.* New York: Oxford University Press, 1963.

Levinas, Emmanuel. *Ethics and Infinity: Conversations with Philippe Nemo.* 1982. Trans. Richard A. Cohen. Pittsburgh: Duquesnes University Press, 1985.
    Collected Philosophical Papers. Trans. Alphonso Lingis. Dordrecht: Marinus Nijhoff Publishers, 1987.
    The Levinas Reader. Ed. Seán Hand. Oxford: Blackwell, 1989.

Levine, Jennifer Schiffer. "Originality and Repetition in *Finnegans Wake* and *Ulysses.*" *PMLA* 94 (1979), 106–20.

Lewin, Bertram D. "Letters Pertaining to Freud's 'History of an Infantile Neurosis.'" *Psychoanalytic Quarterly* 26 (1957), 449–60.

Lewis, Wyndham. *The Apes of God.* London: Nash and Grayson, 1930.

Lidman, Mark J. "Wild Men and Werewolves: An Investigation of the Iconography of Lycanthrophy." *Journal of Popular Culture* 10 (1976), 388–97.

Light, Alison. *Mrs. Woolf and the Servants: The Hidden Heart of Domestic Service.* London: Figtree, 2006.

Lodge, David. *Author, Author.* London: Secker and Warburg, 2004.

Lopez, Barry Holstun. *Of Wolves and Men.* New York: Scribner, 1978.

Lubin, Albert J. "The Influence of the Russian Orthodox Church on Freud's Wolf-Man: A Hypothesis (with an Epilogue Based on Visits with the Wolf Man)." *Psychoanalytic Forum* 2 (1967), 146–62.

Lund, Steven. *James Joyce: Letters, Manuscripts, and Photographs at Southern Illinois University.* Troy, NY: Whitston Publishing Company, 1983.

Lupton, Ellen, and J. Abbott Miller. *The Bathroom, the Kitchen and the Aesthetics of Waste: A Process of Elimination.* Cambridge, MA: MIT List Visual Arts Center, 1992.

Lyons, J. B. *James Joyce and Medicine.* Dublin: Dolmen Press, 1973.

Mahaffey, Vicki. *Reauthorizing Joyce.* Cambridge University Press, 1988.
    States of Desire: Wilde, Yeats, Joyce and the Irish Experiment. Oxford University Press, 1998.

Mahaffey, Vicki, ed. *Collaborative "Dubliners": Joyce in Dialogue.* Syracuse University Press, forthcoming.

Mahon, Peter. *Imagining Joyce and Derrida: Between "Finnegans Wake" and "Glas."* Toronto: University of Toronto Press, 2007.

Mahony, Patrick J. *Cries of the Wolf Man.* New York: International Universities Press, 1984.

Maitland, F. W. *Life and Letters of Leslie Stephen.* London: Duckworth, 1906.

Malcolm, Janet. *Psychoanalysis, the Impossible Profession.* New York: Knopf, 1981.
In the Freud Archives. New York: Knopf, 1984.

Manganiello, Dominic. *Joyce's Politics.* London: Routledge and Kegan Paul, 1980.

Mao, Douglas. *Solid Objects: Modernism and the Test of Production.* Princeton University Press, 1998.

Marcus, Laura. *Virginia Woolf.* 1997. Rev. edn. Tavistock: Northcote House, 2004.
"Oedipus Express: Trains, Trauma and Detective Fiction." *New Formations* 41 (2000), 173–88.

Marcus, Laura, ed. *"The Interpretation of Dreams": New Interdisciplinary Essays.* Manchester University Press, 1999.

Marrin, Albert. *Oh, Rats!: The Story of Rats and People.* New York: Dutton Children's Books, 2006.

Martin, Ann. *Red Riding Hood and the Wolf in Bed: Modernism's Fairy Tales.* Toronto: University of Toronto Press, 2006.

Martin, Augustine, ed. *James Joyce: The Artist and the Labyrinth.* London: Ryan Publishing, 1990.

Martin, J. "Paralysis Simony Gnomon and James Joyce: Conditions of the Representation of Desire in *Dubliners.*" *Cahiers victoriens et edouardiens* 14 (1981), 29–37.

Marx, Karl. *Capital: A Critique of Political Economy.* 1867. Vol. 1. Trans. Ben Fowkes. London: Penguin, 1976.

Masson, Jeffrey Moussaieff. Review of *Gesprache mit dem Wolfsmann: Eine Psychoanalyse und die Folgen,* by Karin Obholzer. *International Review of Psycho-Analysis* 9 (1982), 116–19.
The Assault on Truth: Freud's Suppression of the Seduction Theory. New York: Farrar, Straus and Giroux, 1984.

Mattelart, Armand. *Networking the World: 1794–2000.* Trans. Liz Carey-Libbrecht and James A. Cohen. Minneapolis: University of Minnesota Press, 2000.

Matthiessen, F. O. *Henry James, the Major Phase.* London: Oxford University Press, 1944.

May, Charles E., ed. *Short Story Theories.* Columbus: Ohio University Press, 1986.

Mayhew, Henry. *London Labour and the London Poor: A Cyclopaedia of the Condition and Earnings of Those That Will Work, Those That Cannot Work, and Those That Will not Work.* Vol. III, *The London Street-Folk.* London, 1851. Reprint, New York: A. M. Kelley, 1967.

MacCabe, Colin. *James Joyce and the Revolution of the Word*. 1978. Basingstoke, UK: Palgrave, 2003.

MacCabe, Colin, ed. *James Joyce: New Perspectives*. 1982. New York: Harvester Wheatsheaf, 1990.

McCormack, Peggy. *The Rule of Money: Gender, Class, and Exchange Economics in the Fiction of Henry James*. Ann Arbor, MI: UMI Research Press, 1990.

McCuskey, Brian. "Not at Home: Servants, Scholars, and the Uncanny." *PMLA* 121 (2006), 421–36.

McGann, Jerome. "Revision, Rewriting, Rereading; or 'An Error [Not] in *The Ambassadors*.'" *American Literature* 64:1 (1992), 95–110.

McHugh, Roland. *Annotations to "Finnegans Wake."* Baltimore, MD: Johns Hopkins University Press, 2006.

McWhirter, David, ed. *Henry James's New York Edition: The Construction of Authorship*. Stanford University Press, 1995.

Meisel, Perry. *The Absent Father: Virginia Woolf and Walter Pater*. New Haven, CT: Yale University Press, 1980.

The Literary Freud. London: Routledge, 2007.

Meissner, Collin. *Henry James and the Language of Experience*. Cambridge University Press, 1999.

Melchiori, Giorgio, ed. *Joyce in Rome: The Genesis of "Ulysses."* Rome: Bulzoni Editore, 1984.

Melville, Herman. *Tales, Poems, and Other Writings*. Ed. John Bryant. New York: Random House, 2002.

Menke, Richard. "'Framed and Wired': Teaching *In the Cage* at the Intersection of Literature and Media." *The Henry James Review* 25 (2004), 33–43.

Merleau-Ponty, Maurice. *The Visible and the Invisible*. 1964. Trans. Alphonso Lingis, ed. Claude Lefort. Evanston, IL: Northwestern University Press, 1968.

Miller, J. Hillis. *The Ethics of Reading: Kant, de Man, Eliot, Trollope, James, and Benjamin*. New York: Columbia University Press, 1987.

Literature as Conduct: Speech Acts in Henry James. New York: Fordham University Press, 2005.

Miller, Tyrus. *Late Modernism: Politics, Fiction, and the Arts Between the World Wars*. Berkeley, CA: University of California Press, 1999.

Mills, Charles W. *Blackness Visible*. Ithaca, NY: Cornell University Press, 1998.

Millot, Catherine. "On Epiphanies." In Bernard Benstock, ed. *James Joyce: The Augmented Ninth*, pp. 207–09.

Mirbeau, Octave. *The Torture Garden*. 1899. Trans. Michael Richardson. Sawtry, UK: Dedalus, 1995.

Moi, Toril, ed. *French Feminist Thought: A Reader*. Oxford: Blackwell, 1987.

Montagu, Ashley. *Touching: The Human Significance of the Skin*. New York: Columbia University Press, 1971.

Montrelay, Michèle. "Inquiry into Femininity." Trans. Rachel Bowlby. 1977. In Dana Breen, ed. *The Gender Conundrum*. London: Routledge, 1993, pp. 145–83.

Moon, Michael. *A Small Boy and Others: Imitation and Initiation in American Culture from Henry James to Andy Warhol.* Durham, NC: Duke University Press, 1998.

Moretti, Franco. *Signs Taken for Wonders.* Trans. Susan Fischer *et al.* 1983; London: Verso, 1988.

Modern Epic: The World-System from Goethe to García Márquez. 1994. Trans. Quintin Hoare. London: Verso, 1996.

Mosenthal, Salomon Hermann. *Leah, the Forsaken.* Trans. Augustin Daly from Mosenthal's *Deborah.* 1850. London and New York: Samuel French, n.d.

Mull, Donald L. *Henry James's "Sublime Economy": Money as Symbolic Center in the Fiction.* Middletown, CT: Wesleyan University Press, 1973.

Mullin, Bill, ed. *Revolutionary Tales: African American Women's Short Stories, from the First Story to the Present.* New York: Dell, 1995.

Mullin, Katherine. *James Joyce, Sexuality and Social Purity.* Cambridge University Press, 2003.

Myers, Robert Manson. *From Beowulf to Virginia Woolf: An Outstanding and Wholly Unauthorized History of English Literature.* 1951. Chicago: University of Illinois Press, 1984.

Naremore, James. *The World without a Self: Virginia Woolf and the Novel.* New Haven, CT: Yale University Press, 1973.

Nash, John. *James Joyce and the Act of Reception: Reading, Ireland, Modernism.* Cambridge University Press, 2006.

Nikolchina, Miglena. *Matricide in Language: Writing Theory in Kristeva and Woolf.* New York: Other Press, 2004.

Nordau, Max. *Degeneration.* London: Heinemann, 1913.

Norris, Margot. *Beasts of the Modern Imagination.* Baltimore, MD: Johns Hopkins University Press, 1985.

Joyce's Web: The Social Unraveling of Modernism. Austin: University of Texas Press, 1992.

Suspicious Readings of Joyce's "Dubliners." Philadelphia: University of Philadelphia Press, 2003.

Nye, David E. *Electrifying America: Social Meanings of a New Technology, 1880–1940.* Cambridge, MA: MIT Press, 1992.

Oates, Joyce Carol. *Haunted: Tales of the Grotesque.* New York: Dutton, 1994.

Obholzer, Karin. *The Wolf-Man: Conversations with Freud's Patient – Sixty Years Later.* 1980. Trans. Michael Shaw. New York: Continuum, 1982.

O'Brien, Joseph. *"Dear, Dirty Dublin": A City in Distress, 1899–1916.* Berkeley, CA: University of California Press, 1982.

Oppenheim, Janet. *The Other World: Spiritualism and Psychical Research in England, 1850–1914.* Cambridge University Press, 1985.

Orwell, George. *Nineteen Eighty-Four.* 1949. London: Penguin, 2000.

Otis, Laura. *Membranes: Metaphors of Invasion in Nineteenth-Century Literature, Science, and Politics.* Baltimore, MD: Johns Hopkins University Press, 1999.

Networking: Communicating with Bodies and Machines in the Nineteenth Century. Ann Arbor: University of Michigan Press, 2001.

Otten, Charlotte F., ed. *A Lycanthropy Reader: Werewolves in Western Culture.* Syracuse University Press, 1986.

Panichas, George E. "Vampires, Werewolves, and Economic Exploitation." *Social Theory and Practice* 7 (1981), 225–42.

Pater, Walter. *The Renaissance: Studies in Art and Poetry: The 1893 Text.* Ed. Donald Hill. Berkeley, CA: University of California Press, 1981.

Paulson, William R. *Enlightenment, Romanticism, and the Blind in France.* Princeton University Press, 1987.

Peebles, Malcolm W. H. *Evolution of the Gas Industry.* New York University Press, 1980.

Phillips, Adam. *On Flirtation.* Cambridge, MA: Harvard University Press, 1994.

Pick, Daniel. *Faces of Degeneration: A European Disorder, c. 1848–1918.* Cambridge University Press, 1989.

Pierce, David. *Reading Joyce.* Harlow, UK: Pearson Longman, 2008.

Plath, Sylvia. *The Collected Poems.* Ed. Ted Hughes. New York: Harper and Row, 1981.

Poole, Adrian. *Henry James.* New York: St. Martin's Press, 1991.

Poole, Roger. *The Unknown Virginia Woolf.* Brighton: Harvester, 1982.

Porter, Carolyn. *Seeing and Being: The Plight of the Participant Observer in Emerson, James, Adams, and Faulkner.* Middletown, CT: Wesleyan University Press, 1981.

Posnock, Ross. "Henry James, Veblen and Adorno: The Crisis of the Modern Self." *Journal of American Studies* 21 (1987), 31–54.

   The Trial of Curiosity: Henry James, William James, and the Challenge of Modernity. New York: Oxford University Press, 1991.

Potter, Beatrix. *The Roly-Poly Pudding* [*The Tale of Samuel Whiskers*]. New York: Frederick Warne and Co., 1908.

Pound, Ezra. *Selected Prose, 1909–1965.* Ed. William Cookson. New York: New Directions Publishing, 1973.

   The Cantos. London: Faber, 1975.

Przybylowicz, Donna. *Desire and Repression: The Dialectic of Self and Other in the Late Works of Henry James.* University of Alabama Press, 1986.

Putnam, James Jackson. *James Jackson Putnam and Psychoanalysis: Letters between Putnam and Sigmund Freud, Ernest Jones, William James, Sandor Ferenczi, and Morton Prince, 1877–1917.* Ed. Nathan G. Hale, Jr. Trans. Judith Bernays Heller. Cambridge, MA: Harvard University Press, 1971.

Pynchon, Thomas. *V.* 1961. New York: HarperCollins, 1999.

Rabaté, Jean-Michel. "Silence in *Dubliners*." In Colin McCabe, ed. *James Joyce: New Perspectives*, pp. 45–72.

   James Joyce: Authorised Reader. Baltimore, MD: Johns Hopkins University Press, 1991.

   Joyce Upon the Void: The Genesis of Doubt. Basingstoke, UK: Macmillan, 1991.

   Jacques Lacan: Psychoanalysis and the Subject of Literature. Basingstoke, UK: Palgrave, 2001.

"Watt/Sade: Beckett et l'inhumain à l'envers." In Marie-Christine Lemardeley-Cunci, Carle Bonafous-Murat, and André Topia. *L'inhumain*, pp. 71–83.

1913: The Cradle of Modernism. Malden, MA: Blackwell, 2007.

Rabelais, François. *The Histories of Gargantua and Pantagruel*. Trans. J. M. Cohen. London: Penguin, 1955.

Radden, Jennifer. *The Nature of Melancholy: From Aristotle to Kristeva*. Oxford University Press, 2000.

Rahv, Philip. "Attitudes Toward Henry James." In F. W. Dupee, ed. *The Question of Henry James*, pp. 273–80.

Raitt, Suzanne. *Virginia Woolf's "To the Lighthouse."* New York: St. Martin's Press, 1990.

Vita and Virginia: The Work and Friendship of V. Sackville-West and Virginia Woolf. Oxford: Clarendon Press, 1993.

Rawlings, Peter, ed. *Palgrave Advances in Henry James Studies*. New York: Palgrave Macmillan, 2007.

Reynolds, Joshua. *Discourses on Art*. 1769–90. Ed. Robert Wark. San Marino, CA: Huntingdon Library, 1959.

Rickels, Laurence A. "Kafka and Freud on the Telephone." *Modern Austrian Literature* 22 (1989), 211–25.

The Vampire Lectures. Minneapolis: University of Minnesota Press, 1999.

Ritvo, Harriet. *The Animal Estate: The English and Other Creatures in the Victorian Age*. Cambridge, MA: Harvard University Press, 1987.

Rivkin, Julie. *False Positions: The Representational Logics of Henry James's Fiction*. Stanford University Press, 1996.

Rodwell, James. *The Rat! And Its Cruel Cost to the Nation*. London: Reynell and Weight, 1850.

Roe, Sue, and Susan Sellers, eds. *The Cambridge Companion to Virginia Woolf*. Cambridge University Press, 2000.

Rohman, Carrie. *Stalking the Subject: Modernism and the Animal*. New York: Columbia University Press, 2009.

Ronell, Avital. *The Telephone Book: Technology – Schizophrenia – Electric Speech*. Lincoln, NE: University of Nebraska Press, 1989.

Rose, Jacqueline. "Virginia Woolf and the Death of Modernism." *Raritan* 18.2 (1998), 1–18.

Rowe, John Carlos. *The Other Henry James*. Durham, NC: Duke University Press, 1998.

Royle, Nicholas. *Telepathy and Literature: Essays on the Reading Mind*. Oxford: Blackwell, 1991.

The Uncanny. Manchester and New York: Manchester University Press/Routledge, 2003.

Royle, Nicholas, ed. *Deconstructions: A User's Guide*. Houndmills, UK: Palgrave, 2000.

Rudnytsky, Peter L. *The Psychoanalytic Vocation: Rank, Winnicott, and the Legacy of Freud*. New Haven, CT: Yale University Press, 1991.

Rupprecht, Caroline. *Subject to Delusions: Narcissism, Modernism, Gender*. Evanston, IL: Northwestern University Press, 2006.

Ryan, Catherine. "Leopold Bloom's Fine Eats: A Good Square Meal." *James Joyce Quarterly* 25 (1988), 378–83.

Ryan, Simon "Franz Kafka's *Die Verwandlung*: Transformation, Metaphor, and the Perils of Assimilation." *Seminar* 4 (2007), 1–18.

Sacks, Oliver. *An Anthropologist on Mars*. New York: Knopf, 1995.

Sade, Marquis de. *The Marquis de Sade: The 120 Days of Sodom and Other Writings*. Trans. Austryn Wainhouse and Richard Seaver. New York: Grove Press, 1966.

Sadovnikov, D. N., comp. *Riddles of the Russian People: A Collection of Riddles, Parables, and Puzzles*. 1986. Trans. Ann C. Bigelow. Ann Arbor: Ardis, 1986.

Salmon, Richard. *Henry James and the Culture of Publicity*. Cambridge University Press, 1997.

Sax, Boria. *Animals in the Third Reich: Pets, Scapegoats, and the Holocaust*. New York: Continuum, 2000.

Schivelbusch, Wolfgang. *Disenchanted Night: The Industrialization of Light in the Nineteenth Century*. Berkeley, CA: University of California Press, 1995.

Schleifer, Ronald. *Modernism and Time: The Logic of Abundance in Literature, Science, and Culture, 1880–1930*. Cambridge University Press, 2000.

Schneider, Daniel J. *The Crystal Cage: Adventures of the Imagination in the Fiction of Henry James*. Lawrence: Regents Press of Kansas, 1978.

Schnitzler, Arthur. *Night Games and Other Stories and Novellas*. Trans. Margret Schaefer. Chicago: Ivan R. Dee, 2002.

Schreber, Daniel Paul. *Memoirs of My Nervous Illness*. Trans. and ed. Ida Macalpine and Richard A. Hunter. London: W. Dawson, 1955.

Sconce, Jeffrey. *Haunted Media: Electronic Presence from Telegraphy to Television*. Durham, NC: Duke University Press, 2000.

Sedgwick, Eve Kosofsky. *Between Men: English Literature and Male Homosocial Desire*. New York: Columbia University Press, 1985.

Epistemology of the Closet. Berkeley, CA: University of California Press, 1990.

Segal, Naomi. *André Gide: Pederasty and Pedagogy*. Oxford: Clarendon Press, 1993.

Seltzer, Mark. *Henry James and the Art of Power*. Ithaca, NY: Cornell University Press, 1984.

Bodies and Machines. New York: Routledge, 1992.

Senn, Fritz. "Gnomon Inverted." In Rosa Maria Bosinelli Bollettieri and Harold Mosher, eds. *ReJoycing: New Readings of* Dubliners, pp. 249–57.

Sheehan, James J., and Morton Sosna, eds. *The Boundaries of Humanity: Humans, Animals, Machines*. Berkeley, CA: University of California Press, 1991.

Shell, Marc. "The Family Pet." *Representations* 15 (1986), 121–53.

Shengold, Leonard. "More on Rats and Rat People." In Mark Kanzer and Jules Glenn eds. *Freud and his Patients*, pp. 180–202.

Sheridan, Alan. *André Gide: A Life in the Present*. London: Penguin, 1998.

Silverman, Kaja. "Too Early/Too Late: Subjectivity and the Primal Scene in Henry James." *Novel* 21 (1988) 147–73.

Simmel, Georg. *Georg Simmel: On Women, Sexuality, and Love.* Trans. Guy Oakes. New Haven, CT: Yale University Press, 1984.

   Simmel on Culture: Selected Writings. Ed. David Frisby and Mike Featherstone. London: Sage Publications, 1997.

Singh, J. A. L., and Robert M. Zingg. *Wolf-Children and Feral Man.* New York: Harper, 1942.

Skal, David J. *Hollywood Gothic: The Tangled Web of "Dracula" from Novel to Stage to Screen.* New York: Faber, 2004.

Skubal, Susanne. *Word of Mouth: Food and Fiction after Freud.* New York: Routledge, 2002.

Small, Nathaniel. "The Ineluctable Modality of the Triangle: Shaping Desire in Joyce." Unpublished paper, Northwestern University, 2006.

Smith, Joseph H., and Humphrey Morris, eds. *Telling Facts: History and Narration in Psychoanalysis.* Baltimore, MD: Johns Hopkins University Press, 1992.

Smith, Stephen. *Underground London: Travels Beneath the City Streets.* London: Little, Brown, 2004.

Spillius, Elizabeth Bott, ed. *Melanie Klein Today: Developments in Theory and Practice.* 2 vols. London: Routledge, 1988.

Spoo, Robert. "'Una Piccola Nuvoletta': Ferrero's *Young Europe* and Joyce's Mature *Dubliners* Stories." *James Joyce Quarterly* 24:4 (1987), 401–11.

Squier, Susan Merrill. *Virginia Woolf and London: The Sexual Politics of the City.* Chapel Hill and London: University of North Carolina Press, 1985.

Stafford, Barbara Maria. *Body Criticism: Imaging the Unseen in Enlightenment Art and Medicine.* Cambridge, MA: MIT Press, 1991.

Stallybrass, Peter, and Allon White. *The Politics and Poetics of Transgression.* Ithaca, NY: Cornell University Press, 1986.

Starobinski, Jean. "The Inside and the Outside." *Hudson Review* 28 (1975), 333–51.

Starobinski, Jean, and John A. Gallucci. "The Body's Moment." *Yale French Studies* 64 (1983), 273–305.

Staten, Henry. "The Decomposing Form of Joyce's *Ulysses.*" *PMLA* 112 (1997), 380–92.

Stein, Gertrude. *Look at Me Now and Here I Am.* Ed. Patricia Meyerowitz. Harmondsworth: Penguin, 1984.

Stevenson, Simon. "The Anorthoscopic Short Story." *Oxford Literary Review* 26 (2004), 63–78.

Stoker, Bram. *Dracula.* Ed. Maud Ellmann. 1986. Oxford University Press, 1998.

Stone, Allucquère Rosanne. *The War of Desire and Technology at the Close of the Mechanical Age.* Cambridge, MA: MIT Press, 1995.

Strathern, Andrew. "Why is Shame on the Skin?" *Ethnology* 14 (1975), 347–56.

Strathern, Marilyn. "The Self in Self-Decoration." *Oceania* 49 (1979), 241–57.

Sullivan, Robert. *Rats: Observations on the History and Habitat of the City's Most Unwanted Inhabitants.* New York: Bloomsbury, 2004.

Sussman, Henry. *Franz Kafka: Geometrician of Metaphor*. Madison, WI: Coda Press, 1979.

 The Hegelian Aftermath: Readings in Hegel, Kierkegaard, Freud, Proust, and James. Baltimore, MD: Johns Hopkins University Press, 1982.

Syrotinski, Michael, and Ian Maclachlan, eds. *Sensual Reading: New Approaches to Reading in its Relations to the Senses*. Lewisburg, PA: Bucknell University Press, 2001.

Tanner, Tony. *Adultery in the Novel: Contract and Transgression*. Baltimore, MD: Johns Hopkins University Press, 1979.

Taylor, Andrew. *Henry James and the Father Question*. Cambridge University Press, 2002.

Taylor, Mark C. *The Moment of Complexity: Emerging Network Culture*. Chicago: University of Chicago Press, 2001.

Terr, Lenore C. "Who's Afraid in Virginia Woolf? Clues to Early Sexual Abuse in Literature." *The Psychoanalytic Study of the Child* 45 (1990), 533–46.

Thayer, William. "The New Story-Tellers and the Doom of Realism." 1894. In Eugene Current-García and Walter R. Patrick, eds. *Realism and Romanticism in Fiction: An Approach to the Novel*, pp. 150–59.

Thurschwell, Pamela. *Literature, Technology and Magical Thinking, 1880–1920*. Cambridge University Press, 2001.

Thurston, Luke. "Writing the Symptom: Lacan's Joycean Knot." 1997. PhD thesis, University of Kent.

 James Joyce and the Problem of Psychoanalysis. Cambridge University Press, 2004.

Thurston, Luke, ed. *Re-Inventing the Symptom: Essays on the Final Lacan*. New York: Other Press, 2002.

Tintner, Adeline R. *Henry James and the Lust of the Eyes: Thirteen Artists in His Work*. Baton Rouge, LA: Louisiana State University Press, 1993.

Tobey, Ronald C. *Technology as Freedom: The New Deal and the Electrical Modernization of the American Home*. Berkeley, CA: University of California Press, 1997.

Tóibín, Colm. *The Master: A Novel*. New York: Scribner, 2004.

Tolman, Edward Chase. "Cognitive Maps in Rats and Men." 1948. In *Collected Papers in Psychology*. Berkeley, CA: University of California Press, 1951.

Torgovnick, Marianna. *The Visual Arts, Pictorialism, and the Novel: James, Lawrence, and Woolf*. Princeton University Press, 1985.

Tougaw, Jason Daniel. *Strange Cases: The Medical Case History and the British Novel*. New York: Routledge, 2006.

Trask, Michael. "Getting Into It with James: Substitution and Erotic Reversal in *The Awkward Age*." *American Literature* 69 (1997), 105–38.

Trotter, David. "e-Modernism: Telephony in British Fiction 1925–1940." *Critical Quarterly* 51:1 (2009), 1–32.

Tucker, Lindsey. *Stephen and Bloom at Life's Feast: Alimentary Symbolism and the Creative Process in James Joyce's "Ulysses."* Columbus: Ohio State University Press, 1984.

Turner, Terence. "The Social Skin." In Jeremy Cherfas and Roger Lewin, eds. *Not Work Alone: A Cross-Cultural View of Activities Superfluous to Survival*, pp. 112–40.

Valente, Joseph. *James Joyce and the Problem of Justice: Negotiating Sexual and Colonial Difference*. Cambridge University Press, 1995.

"A Child is Being Eaten: Mourning, Transvestism, and the Incorporation of the Daughter in *Ulysses*." *James Joyce Quarterly* 34 (1996/1997), 21–64.

Dracula's Crypt: Bram Stoker, Irishness, and the Question of Blood. Urbana: University of Illinois Press, 2002.

Valéry, Paul. *L'idée fixe, ou Deux hommes à la mer*. 1932. In *Oeuvres*. Pleiade edition. Vol. 11. Ed. Jean Hytier. Paris: Gallimard, 1960.

Vanderham, Paul. *James Joyce and Censorship: The Trials of Ulysses*. New York University Press, 1998.

Veblen, Thorstein. *The Theory of the Leisure Class*. 1899. New York: Penguin Books, 1979.

Vitz, Paul C. *Sigmund Freud's Christian Unconscious*. New York: Guilford Press, 1988.

Wagner, Tamara S., and Narin Hassan, eds. *Consuming Culture in the Long Nineteenth Century: Narratives of Consumption, 1700–1900*. Lanham, MD: Lexington Books, 2007.

Warne, Frank Julian. *The Immigrant Invasion*. New York: Dodd, Mead and Company, 1913.

Warner, John M. "'In View of Other Matters': The Religious Dimension of *The Ambassadors*." *Essays in Literature* 4 (1977), 78–94.

Watson, John B. "Kinaesthetic and Organic Sensations; Their Role in the Reactions of the White Rat." *Psychological Review* 8:33 (1907), 1–100.

Watt, Ian. "The First Paragraph of *The Ambassadors*: An Explication. " *Essays in Criticism* 10 (1960), 250–74.

Webster, John. *The White Devil; The Duchess of Malfi; The Devil's Law-Case; A Cure for a Cuckold*. Ed. René Weis. New York: Oxford University Press, 1996.

Weir, David. "Gnomon is an Island: Euclid and Bruno in Joyce's Narrative Practice." *James Joyce Quarterly* 29 (1991), 343–60.

Anarchy and Culture: The Aesthetic Politics of Modernism. Amherst, MA: University of Massachusetts Press, 1997.

Weizsäcker, Victor V. "Dreams in So-Called Endogenic *Magersucht* (Anorexia)." In M. Ralph Kaufman *et al.*, eds. *Evolution of Psychoanalytic Concepts: Anorexia Nervosa: A Paradigm*, London: Hogarth Press, 1964, pp. 181–97.

West, Rebecca. *Henry James*. New York: Henry Holt and Co., 1916.

Wharton, Edith. *The Writing of Fiction*. London: Charles Scribner's Sons, 1925.

Whitman, Walt. *Leaves of Grass*. 1891–92. In *Complete Poetry and Collected Prose*. Ed. Justin Kaplan. New York: Library of America, 1982.

Wicke, Jennifer. *Advertising Fictions: Literature, Advertisement and Social Reading*. New York: Columbia University Press, 1988.

"Henry James's Second Wave." *The Henry James Review* 10:2 (1989), 146–51.

"Vampiric Typewriting: *Dracula* and its Media." *English Literary History* 59 (1992), 467–93.

Wilde, Oscar. *The Complete Works of Oscar Wilde.* London: Collins, 1966.

Williams, Patricia J. *Seeing a Color-Blind Future: The Paradox of Race.* New York: Noonday Press, 1998.

Williams, Trevor L. "No cheer for the 'gratefully oppressed' in Joyce's *Dubliners.*" *Style* 25:30 (1991), 416–39.

Wilson, Elizabeth A. *Psychosomatic: Feminism and the Neurological Body.* Durham, NC: Duke University Press, 2004.

Winer, Robert. "Echoes of the Wolf Men: Reverberations of Psychic Reality." In Joseph H. Smith and Humphrey Morris, *Telling Facts: History and Narration in Psychoanalysis.* Baltimore, MD: Johns Hopkins University Press, 1992, pp. 140–59.

Wolf Man [Sergius Pankejeff]. "Letters Pertaining to Freud's History of an Infantile Neurosis." *Psychoanalytic Quarterly* 26 (1957), 449–60.

Woolf, Leonard. *Beginning Again: An Autobiography of the Years 1911–1918.* London: Hogarth Press, 1964.

Downhill All the Way: An Autobiography of the Years 1919–1939. London: Hogarth Press, 1967.

The Journey Not the Arrival Matters: An Autobiography of the Years 1939–1969. London: Hogarth Press, 1969.

In Savage Times: Leonard Woolf on Peace and War, Containing Four Pamphlets. New York: Garland, 1973.

Woolf, Virginia. *The Voyage Out.* 1915. Ed. Lorna Sage. Oxford University Press, 2002.

Jacob's Room. 1922. Ed. Suzanne Raitt. New York: W. W. Norton, 2007.

To the Lighthouse. 1927. Ed. David Bradshaw. Oxford University Press, 2008.

A Room of One's Own. 1929. Ed. Susan Gubar. Orlando, FL: Harcourt Inc., 2005.

The Waves. 1931. Ed. Kate Flint. London: Penguin, 1992.

Flush, a Biography. 1933. Ed. Kate Flint. Oxford University Press, 1998.

Between the Acts. 1941. Ed. Stella McNichol. Notes and Introduction by Gillian Beer. 1992; London: Penguin, 2000.

Between the Acts. 1941. Ed. Susan Dick and Mary Millar. Oxford : Blackwell, 2002.

A Haunted House and Other Stories. London: Hogarth Press, 1943.

Moments of Being/Virginia Woolf. Ed. Jean Schulkind. 1976. Rev. edn. Hermione Lee. London: Pimlico, 2002.

The Letters of Virginia Woolf 1888–1941. Ed. Nigel Nicholson and Joanne Trautmann. 6 vols. London: Hogarth Press, 1975–80.

The Essays of Virginia Woolf. Edited by Andrew McNeillie. 4 vols. London: Hogarth Press, 1986–94.

Wurzer, Wilhelm S., ed. *Panorama: Philosophies of the Visible.* London: Continuum, 1992.

Yeazell, Ruth Bernard. *Language and Knowledge in the Late Novels of Henry James*. Chicago: University of Chicago Press, 1976.

Yoder, Edwin M., Jr. *Lions at Lamb House: Freud's "Lost" Analysis of Henry James*. New York: Europa Editions, 2007.

Ziolkowski, Theodore. *Varieties of Literary Thematics*. Princeton University Press, 1983.

Žižek, Slavoj, ed. *Jacques Lacan: Critical Evaluations in Cultural Theory*. 4 vols. London: Routledge, 2003.

Zinsser, Hans. *Rats, Lice, and History*. London: George Routledge and Sons, 1935.

Zola, Emile. *Germinal*. 1885. Trans. Leonard Tancock. London: Everyman, 1991.

Zwerdling, Alex. *Virginia Woolf and the Real World*. Berkeley, CA: University of California Press, 1986.

Index